# *Historical* ATLAS *of* TEXAS METHODISM

WILLIAM C. HARDT & JOHN WESLEY HARDT

MAPS BY JOHN WESLEY SAUER

*Published in conjunction with the*
*Texas United Methodist Historical Society*

🏠 CrossHouse

*Dedicated to future generations*
*who will continue to be inspired by Wesleyan spiritual traditions.*

Published by
CROSSHOUSE PUBLISHING
PO Box 461592
Garland, Texas 75046-1592
www.crosshousepublishing.com
1-877-212-0933

Printed in the United States of America
by Lightning Source, LaVergne, TN
Cover design by Dennis Davidson


ISBN 978-1-934749-07-4
Library of Congress Control Number: 2007938969

TO ORDER ADDITIONAL COPIES, SEE PAGE 255

# INTRODUCTION

The book you are now holding may have the appearance of a reference book, but we must admit that it is far more. In the interest of full disclosure we must declare that both authors have been shaped by the Texas Methodist experience. Some of the forces that molded us are obvious. For a great deal of our lives the basic question of where we lived was determined by a Methodist conference appointment. Our higher education was obtained at Methodist colleges and universities. Our closest friends have been our church friends. Our summer recreation was very often at a Methodist encampment. Our outlook on social and political issues has been shaped by church teaching on those subjects. This work is thus not strictly a reference book. It is at least in part an attempt for us to understand how our world—the world of Texas Methodism—was created.

Our first recorded Texas Methodist ancestor was Milton Stringfield. His name is listed in the oldest Texas Quarterly Conference minutes extant.

Those minutes show that he was licensed as an exhorter at that Quarterly Conference of the Nacogdoches Circuit at McMahan's Campground on September 8, 1838, at which Robert Alexander presided. His great-granddaughter, Ida Wilson Hardt, was our mother and grandmother. Some years later, on Christmas Eve, 1861, Hamilton G. Horton, a young Methodist preacher appointed to the Victoria Circuit stopped at Weesatche in Goliad County for the night. The Methodist family with whom he had intended to spend the night had moved further west, but the Henry Christian Hardt family took him in. The next morning Horton offered to lead the family in Christmas devotions. That experience led to the conversion of the family. One of his sons, Henry George Hardt, married Fanny Weimers. The Weimers Oak, under whose branches a Methodist circuit rider organized a German Methodist church, still stands in Medina County. Daily prayers, Bible reading, and faithful church attendance led to four of Henry George Hardt's sons accepting God's call to enter the Methodist ministry. A daughter became a Methodist missionary. One of those sons, Wesley from the German branch of Texas Methodism, married Ida from the English branch and thus brought together two of the historic currents running through Texas Methodist history. The senior author's childhood was spent in a succession of small country churches. Some were sawmill towns. Others depended upon cotton. The junior author's childhood did not involve so many relocations, but the one that occurred at the impressionable age of twelve, from a Piney Woods county seat town to a coastal refining and industrial city was memorable. A knowledge of geography depends upon knowing differences between places, and the childhood experiences of both authors provided by the Methodist itinerant system produced a great motivation for learning about place and asking the basic geographic question, "Why are things where they are?"

In 2000 the life situation of both authors changed in such a way that a joint project on Texas Methodist history seemed obvious to both. The junior author retired after a career of high-school teaching in which his great passion was teaching about Texas history. He had published numerous educational materials on the subject and was widely known as a lecturer and workshop leader on the subject. His retirement included moving from the city of Houston to Austin County. As he became involved in local history interests, he realized that within a ten-mile radius of his residence were the sites of the 1834 and 1835 Caney Creek Camp Meetings, Robert Alexander's grave, John Wesley Kenney's grave, David Ayres's intended Methodist town of Center Hill, and points on William Medford's 1834 circuit. He now began to use his knowledge of Texas history to focus on the early Methodist experience in Texas.

At the same time the senior author completed twelve years as Bishop in Residence at Perkins School of Theology at SMU. He took the title of Bishop in Residence Emeritus and received a very warm letter from Dr. Valerie Hotchkiss, who was then Director of Bridwell Library at Perkins. Her letter included her invitation to occupy a carrel in Bridwell and be available as a resource consultant. After accepting her invitation and frequent conversations with Page Thomas, Director of the Center for Methodist Studies at Bridwell, the senior author's name was listed among the Bridwell Staff as a Consultant for the Center of Methodist Studies in the *Perkins Journal*. Both authors began using the resources at Bridwell and became enthusiastic about a work intended for publication. When this interest was shared with Dr. Hotchkiss and Page Thomas, they both added their encouragement, and opened the resources of Bridwell Library for the research which such a volume would demand. The support and encouragement of the entire Bridwell staff became a primary source of inspiration and support for pursing this objective. Other Bridwell staff members including Elizabeth Perry and Wanda Smith provided invaluable help in locating materials.

We are also grateful for the assistance of Carol Roszell at the Eunice and James West Library at Texas Wesleyan University in Fort Worth, Kathryn Stallard of the A. Frank Smith, Jr. Library at Southwestern University, and Faulk Landrum and Jim Crawford at the Texas Conference Archives at Lon Morris College. Dr. Robert Sledge provided useful comments. The Reverend Timothy Greenawalt was generous with his time and his insights into Free Methodist Church history. Cathy Fortner of the Marston

Memorial Historical Center of the Free Methodist Church in Indianapolis, Indiana, was most helpful in providing documents related to that denomination's Texas history.

We are also deeply grateful to John Wesley Sauer who produced all the maps in this work. Mr. Sauer had a successful career as an energy company executive and in his retirement turned to ranching and local history interests. His maps constitute an important contribution to the field of Texas Methodist history.

The collaborative effort has been a wonderful experience for us both, personally and intellectually. The appreciation we already had for Texas Methodism has only deepened as we learned about the many branches of Texas Methodism. Our personal and family history is in the United Methodist tradition. One of the inspiring outcomes of our research is an increased appreciation of the other Wesleyan denominations with whom we feel a spiritual kinship. We have also grown closer to members of the Texas United Methodist Historical Society and numerous local church historians.

# TABLE OF CONTENTS

# CHAPTER 1

# BRANCHES OF THE VINE

The *World Methodist Council Handbook of Information: 2002-2006* lists twenty denominations with churches in the United States in its "Statistics of World Methodism." All twenty claim some historic relationship to the Wesleyan movement. Approximately one-half of the denominations listed in the "Statistics" have some presence in Texas and are represented in this work. There are other denominations such as the **Methodist Protestant Church** and **Evangelical United Brethren** which no longer exist but continue in the United Methodist Church. The chart on the following page is a visual representation of the relationship among the various Methodist bodies, past and present, that have had churches in Texas.

Methodism, as a separate denomination, began at Baltimore in December 1784, with the Christmas Conference. That conference changed the Wesleyan movement of the Protestant Episcopal Church (also known as the Anglican Church or Church of England) into a denomination. The church formed by that conference was the **Methodist Episcopal Church (MEC).** Soon after the formation of the MEC, parallel organizations, the **Evangelical Association (EA)** and the **United Brethren In Christ (UBC)**, arose among German speaking evangelicals in the United States. The stream of Methodism was also broadened by the creation of the **African Methodist Episcopal Church (AME)** and the **African Methodist Episcopal Church, Zion (AMEZ)**, by African-American Methodists who withdrew in protest of their second-class treatment by white Methodists. In 1830 the **Methodist Protestant Church (MP)** was created by reformers who wished to increase the role of the laity in church governance. In 1844 the MEC was divided over the question of slavery. Most southern churches withdrew from the MEC and re-organized themselves as the **Methodist Episcopal Church, South (MECS)** in 1846. In 1843 a group of abolitionist Methodists formed the **Wesleyan Church of America**. That church is now known as the **Wesleyan Church**.

Both the MEC and the MECS experienced divisions in the years immediately preceding the Civil War. The **Free Methodist Church (FM)** was formed from the

# Branches of the Vine

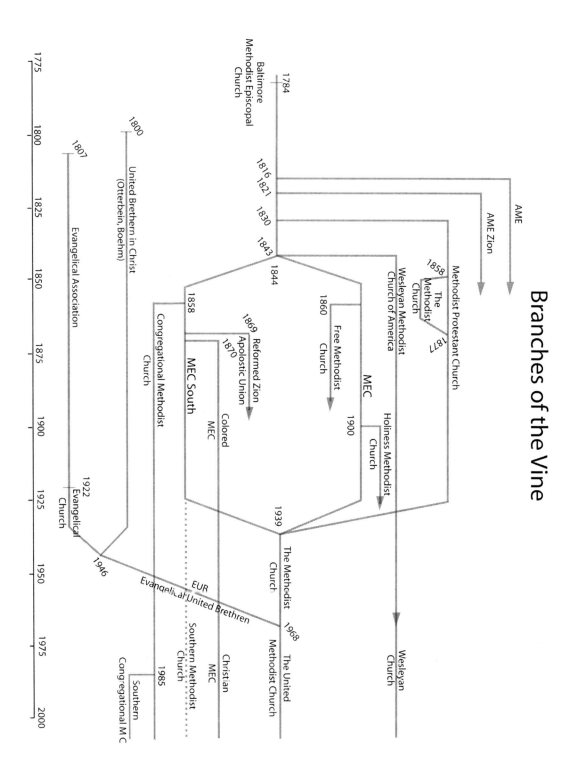

MEC by Methodists who objected to formalism in worship, pew rent, and slavery. The issue that prompted the formation of the **Congregational Methodist Church (CM)** in 1852 from the MECS was lay representation.

The MECS suffered a huge decline in membership immediately after the Civil War as tens of thousands of African-American members who were now free to organize their own religious lives left the denomination that was so closely associated with slavery. The MECS, appalled at the idea of southern African-Americans affiliating with the "northern" MEC, AME, and AMEZ denominations, sponsored the creation of the **Colored Methodist Episcopal Church (CME)**. That denomination later changed its name to the **Christian Methodist Episcopal Church.**

The Holiness Movement of the late 19th and early 20th centuries also gave rise to new denominations. One of them, the **Church of the Nazarene,** holds membership in the World Methodist Council.

Immediately following the Civil War at least a few Methodists began calling for reunion of the MEC and MECS. Their main argument was that the reason for the schism, slavery, no longer existed. The fact that the northern and southern churches had maintained the same doctrine and polity from 1844 to 1866 gave advocates of reunion hope. It took, however, decades for sectional reconciliation to advance to the point that joint committees could meet in the expectation that their recommendations for union would be accepted. One important consequence of the long delay was that Methodist Protestants joined the discussions about union. Eventually a plan of union was hammered out that was acceptable to most MEC, MECS, and MP annual conferences. In 1939 those three denominations met in Kansas City to create the **Methodist Church (MC)**.

Disputes between liberals and conservatives in the 20th century resulted in the creation of several conservative Methodist denominations. The **Southern Methodist Church** was created in 1940 to continue the traditions of the MECS after 1939. A group of conservatives led by Rev. John Henry Hamblen, formerly of Abilene's First Methodist Church, wished to maintain Biblical infallibility. They organized the **Evangelical Methodist Church** in 1946. Mergers of that denomination with the **Evangel Church, Inc**. and the **People's Methodist Church** occurred in 1960 and 1962 respectively. The **Southern Congregational Methodist Church** was organized in 1985 by members of the Congregational Methodist Church who felt that congregational autonomy was weakened by a succession of *Discipline* revisions.

The union of 1939 was a forecast of mergers to follow. In 1946 the Evangelical Association and the United Brethren In Christ merged to form the **Evangelical United Brethren** or **EUB**. In 1968 the Methodist Church and EUB churches merged to become the **United Methodist Church** or **UMC**.

In neither 1939 nor 1968 did the merging denominations have to make doctrinal concessions as the price of unification. Church organization and polity questions dominated the negotiations leading to mergers.

Historians should exercise particular care when writing Methodist history to specify which branch of Methodism is under consideration. Very strictly speaking, the term "The Methodist Church" should be reserved for the period from 1939 to 1968 for one particular denomination. The following chart is intended as guide to help with such specificity. The abbreviations are those which will be used in this atlas.

| DENOMINATION | ABBR. | YEARS IN EXISTENCE | TEXAS NOTES | DISPOSITION |
|---|---|---|---|---|
| Methodist Episcopal Church | MEC | 1784-1939 | Missionary activity during Mexican and Republic Period. Created Texas Annual Conference in 1840. Retreated during Civil War but returned afterwards. | United with MECS and MP churches to form Methodist Church in 1939. |
| Methodist Protestant Church | MP | 1830-1939 | At least one MP preacher known to be in Texas by 1834. Texas included in Mississippi Conference in 1841. | United with MEC and MECS churches to form Methodist Church in 1939. |
| Methodist Episcopal Church, South | MECS | 1846-1939 | Created in 1846 as result of dispute at 1844 General Conference over slavery. Was the branch of Methodism with largest Texas membership throughout its existence. | United with MEC and MP to form the Methodist Church in 1939. |
| Methodist Church | MC | 1939-1968 | Created by merger of MEC, MECS, and MP churches. | United with EUB church in 1968 to become the United Methodist Church. |
| United Methodist Church | UMC | 1968-present | Created by merger of MC and EUB churches. | |
| African Methodist Episcopal Church | AME | 1816-present | Excluded from Texas until after the Civil War, then missionaries established the denomination in Texas. | |
| African Methodist Episcopal, Zion Church | AMEZ | 1821-present | Excluded from Texas until after the Civil War, then missionaries established the denomination in Texas. | |
| Free Methodist Church | FM | 1860-present | First Texas appointment was in 1878. | |
| Colored Methodist Episcopal Church | CME | 1870-1954 | African-American denomination sponsored by MECS, Texas Conference one of original conferences. | Name changed to Christian Methodist Episcopal Church in 1954. |
| Christian Methodist Episcopal Church | CME | 1954-present | See above. | |
| Evangelical Association | EA | 1803-1946 | Visit by Bishop Escher to San Antonio in 1879 resulted in several churches. | Merged with United Brethren in Christ to become EUB. |
| United Brethren in Christ | UBC | 1800-1946 | North Texas Conference established in 1908 but most of its churches were in OK and NM. | Merged with Evangelical Association to become EUB. |
| Evangelical United Brethren | EUB | 1946-1968 | Denomination formed by merger of EA and UBC. | United with MC in 1968 to form UMC. |

| DENOMINATION | ABBR. | YEARS IN EXISTENCE | TEXAS NOTES | DISPOSITION |
|---|---|---|---|---|
| Congregational Methodist Church | CMC | 1852-present | Split from MECS over lay representation. | Reported 39 churches in Texas in 2007. Head-quarters are in Florence, MS. |
| Southern Methodist Church | SMC | 1940-present | Formed to continue the traditions of the MECS. | Reported 2 churches in Texas in 2007. Headquarters are in Orangeburg, SC. |
| Evangelical Methodist Church | EMC | 1946-present | First General Superintendent was John Henry Hamblen, formerly of First Methodist Church, Abilene. | Reported 11 churches in Texas 2007. Conference headquarters are in Fort Worth. |
| Southern Congregational Methodist Church | SCMC | 1985-present | Formed from the Congregational Methodist Church by members who felt congregational autonomy was being eroded. | Reported 3 churches in Texas 2007. Headquarters are in Alma, GA. |
| Wesleyan Methodist Church | WMC | 1843-present | Founded by Orange Scott and other anti-slavery activists as Wesleyan Methodist Connection, then Wesleyan Methodist Church of America. Adopted current name after merger with Pilgrim Holiness Church in 1968. | Reported 10 churches in Texas 2007. |

*References:*

congregationalmethodist.net

www.emchurch.org/history.htm

www.scmchurch.com

www.umc.org

Copeland, Kennard Bill, *History of the Methodist Protestant Church in Texas, Commerce,* n.d.

Fowler, Wilton Jr., *A History of the Congregational Methodist Church,* M.A. Thesis, Stephen F. Austin State College, 1957.

*World Methodist Council: Handbook of Information 2002-2006.* Published by the World Methodist Council, Biltmore Press, 2002.

CHAPTER 2

# FIRST STEPS

Methodism's arrival in Texas owes a large debt to the revivals which swept the Cumberland River Valley of the Tennessee-Kentucky border from about 1798 to 1810. Although the origin of these revivals was Scotch-Irish Presbyterianism, Methodists quickly appropriated the camp-meeting revival as their own. Emigrants from the Cumberland Basin pressing westward to Missouri, Arkansas, and Texas included Methodist preachers and lay members. Those emigrant groups, often linked by family and church relationships, became the first identifiable Methodists in Texas.

The first preacher for whom records exist was Rev. William Stevenson, a former resident of Smith County, Tennessee, who immigrated to Bellevue, Missouri, in 1809. As was customary for the period, Stevenson did not devote full time to preaching. He farmed and participated in the civic life of his community, losing an election for a seat in the General Assembly of the Missouri Territory to his neighbor and friend, Stephen F. Austin.

William Stevenson's brother, James moved to southwestern Arkansas, just north of the great bend of the Red River. In 1814 James persuaded William to accompany him to Arkansas and preach in that region. William Stevenson returned the next year (1815) and extended his preaching to settlements south of the Red River at Pecan Point in present day Red River County, Texas.

The Red River and its Texas tributaries, the Sulfur River and Cypress Bayou, had attracted the attention of traders, speculators, and farmers. Since it was part of the Mississippi River's drainage, it was by geography part of the Louisiana Purchase, and therefore United States territory. The prospects of trading with Native Americans induced Americans to push past the "great raft" or mass of logs on the Red River and establish commercial outposts on the Red River. Pecan Point was such an outpost.

Stevenson's home in Missouri was in the bounds of the Tennessee Conference which embraced not only Tennessee, but also Indiana, Illinois, Kentucky, Missouri, Mississippi, and Louisiana. In 1816 a Missouri Conference was organized which also included Arkansas, Missouri, and Illinois. Stevenson was appointed to Hot Springs,

# William Stevenson
## First Recorded
## Methodist Preacher
## In Texas

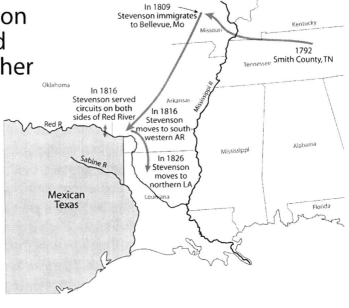

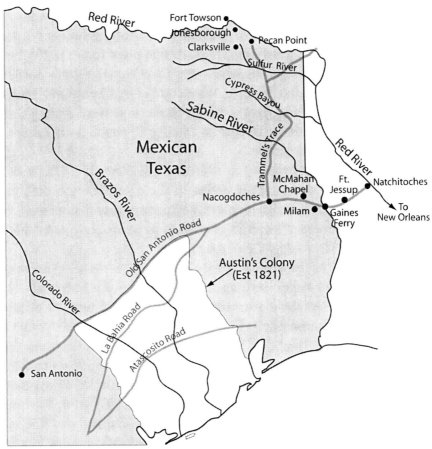

Arkansas. He moved to southwestern Arkansas in 1816 and served circuits which embraced charges on both sides of the Red River. He also persuaded a substantial number of his Missouri Methodist neighbors to immigrate to Arkansas with him. Some of them later immigrated to Texas. In 1816, another Methodist family from Smith County Tennessee immigrated to Pecan Point. That was the Claiborne Wright family. Their home became a preaching point. Later the Wright's nephew, Littleton Fowler, also from Smith County, Tennessee, would volunteer for missionary service in Texas.

By 1818 Methodist work in the Red River region had expanded to the point that a circuit was organized. The Missouri Conference appointments for that year list Pecan Point, the first time a Texas place name appears in a list of appointments. Other Methodist preaching points included Jonesboro and Sulfur Fork. The Adams-Onis Treaty of 1819 between the United States and Spain placed the settlements south of the Red River under nominal Spanish jurisdiction. Such transfer of sovereignty appears to have little or no impact on continuing immigration from the United States. General Manuel de Mier y Terán, head of the 1828 Mexican border inspection, complained about illegal immigrants from the United States coming to northeastern Texas. The establishment of Fort Towson by the U.S. Army in 1824 just north of the Red River in present day Oklahoma actually increased the possibilities of trade.

William Stevenson, as both presiding elder and missionary, proved effective in planting Methodism in northeast Texas. At one point in the 1820s, he had five circuits. He also supervised preachers who were to evangelize both northeastern and other regions of Texas. Thomas Tennant, Washington Orr, Green Orr, Henry Stephenson, and William Stevenson's son, James Porter Stevenson were among the most prominent Methodist preachers along the Red and Sulfur Rivers in northeastern Texas from 1818 through the 1820s and 1830s.

William Stevenson moved to northern Louisiana in 1826, soon after Rev. Jesse Hale arrived in Arkansas. Hale enforced the disciplinary prohibitions against slave owners holding offices in Methodism. The controversy that resulted was a contributing factor in both Stevenson's and Stephenson's move to Louisiana which at that time was a district in the Mississippi Conference.

In the meantime, Stephen F. Austin, whom Stevenson had known in both Missouri and Arkansas, had begun settling colonists under the terms of his first empresario contract with the Mexican government. A substantial number of those first colonists came from the Arkansas/Red River settlements in which Methodist circuits had been established. Among the "Old Three Hundred" to move from the region of Arkansas served by Stevenson were the Rabb, Gilleland, Ingram, Kuykendall, Crownover, and Gates families. When these families arrived in Austin's Colony, they tended to claim their land grants fairly near each other in present day Austin, Washington, and Fayette Counties. Henry Stephenson came to Austin's Colony in 1824, and, according to Homer Thrall, preached secretly at seven homes. Much later in a letter to the *Texas Christian Advocate* (February 16, 1860) Lydia McHenry wrote about her June 1834, conversations with Stephenson in which he related that his main purpose in coming to Austin's Colony was collecting a debt. He also visited with Stephen F. Austin about the possibility of missionary efforts in the colonies, but Austin said, "one Methodist preacher would do more mischief than a dozen horse-thieves." In that same letter, McHenry characterized Stephenson as a "very timid man." In any case, Methodists respected Austin's wishes and made little or no effort to organize churches. Henry Stephenson made at least two more trips to the Austin Colony. Informal religious services, including both sermons and funerals, did occur, especially after the arrival of local preachers William Medford (1832) and John Wesley Kenney (1833). When Stephenson visited the colony in 1834, he found the political situation changed enough (and Stephen F. Austin could not object because he was in a Mexican prison) so that the Methodists of the region could hold a camp meeting. That story is told in a later chapter.

In the meantime, though, the focus of Methodist activity in Texas retreated to another border region. William Stevenson, James Porter Stevenson, and Henry Stephenson were now living in Louisiana. The gateway to Texas from Louisiana was the Nachitoches to Nacogdoches Road which crossed the Sabine at Gaines Ferry. The road constituted the easternmost extension of the Old San Antonio Road.

All the settlers crossing the Sabine at Gaines Ferry did not press on to Austin's Colony. Some settled immediately west of the Sabine in present day Sabine and San Augustine Counties. A camp meeting was held at Milam in Sabine County in 1832, and in 1833 James Porter Stevenson, serving the Sabine Circuit of the Mississippi Conference was assigned to preach in Texas. Stevenson presided over a three-day meeting at Samuel McMahan's home near Milam in 1833. The participants at that meeting demanded a more formal organization, so Stevenson organized them into a "religious society." Calling it a church would have invited opposition from the Mexican authorities. The next year (1834) Henry Stephenson was appointed to the Texas Circuit, again in the Mississippi Conference. After Texas independence in 1836, the society reorganized itself into a church. The continued existence of that church, McMahan's Chapel, gives it the title of the oldest Methodist church in Texas.

*References:*

Jackson, Jack, ed., *Texas by Terán: The Diary Kept by General Manuel Mier y Terán on his 1828 Inspection of Texas,* Austin, University of Texas Press, 2000.

Vernon, Walter, *Methodism moves across North Texas,* Historical Society of the North Texas Conference, 1967.

Vernon, Walter, *William Stevenson: Riding Preacher, Dallas,* Southern Methodist University Press, 1964.

Conkin, Paul, *"What Caldwell's Boys Did in the Cumberland," Border States On Line,* Georgetown College, Georgetown, Kentucky.

*New Handbook of Texas*—entries on William Stevenson, James Porter Stevenson, Henry Stevenson, *Texas Christian Advocate,* Feb. 15, 1860.

Phelan, Macum, *A History of Early Methodism in Texas*, Nashville.Cokesbury Press, 1924.

Thrall, Homer, *History of Methodism in Texas*, Houston, Cushing Publishers, 1872.

Cantrell, Gregg, *Stephen F. Austin, Empresario,* Yale University Press, 1999.

Frizzell, Isabell, *Bellville: The Founders and Their Legacy,* New Ulm Enterprise, New Ulm, 1992.

CHAPTER 3

# ESTABLISHING METHODISM IN AUSTIN'S COLONY

The most successful of the empresarios authorized to promote colonization of Mexican Texas was Stephen F. Austin. The generous land grants available in Austin's Colony lured a stream of immigrants from the United States. A Methodist presence developed in the northern part of Austin's original colony during the last years of Mexican rule. Several of Austin's early colonists had been active lay persons, class leaders, lay preachers, or even conference members before they immigrated to Texas. A typical Methodist preacher's career in the first half of the 19th century in the trans-Appalachian frontier was that a young man in his late teens or early twenties would become a preacher and itinerate for no more than ten years. There was great pressure on these young men not to marry. Francis Asbury both set the example by remaining single himself and also admonished preachers not to marry. At any rate, the low pay and constant travelling made family life difficult. After several years of being a travelling preacher, a man often married and then had to settle down to support a family. Men faced with such a life situation would often "locate". That is, they would not accept an appointment to be a travelling preacher but would become "local preachers." Because he had been travelling, the preacher had not spent his prime working years in establishing a farm. Austin's Colony, with its cheap land, was an attractive option for men facing such circumstances. A good example is the career of John Wesley Kenney who was born in western Pennsylvania in 1799 to a mother who had been converted by John Wesley himself on one of his trips to Ireland. Kenney was admitted to the Ohio Conference in 1818. He married Maria McHenry in 1824 and located in 1828. He immigrated to Texas in 1833 and began farming near William Medford, who had also been a member of the Ohio Conference (1818-1824), and Benjamin Babbitt of the Missouri Conference.

The region on either side of La Bahia Road from the Brazos to the Colorado Rivers (Washington to LaGrange) became the core area from which Texas Methodism grew.

# Core of Texas Methodism

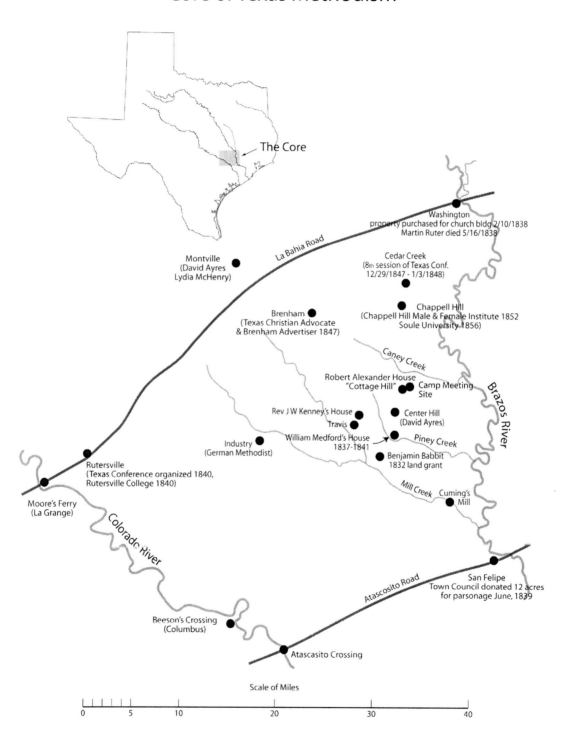

The Core

Washington
property purchased for church bldg 2/10/1838
Martin Ruter died 5/16/1838

La Bahia Road

Montville
(David Ayres
Lydia McHenry)

Cedar Creek
(8th session of Texas Conf.
12/29/1847 - 1/3/1848)

Chappell Hill
(Chappell Hill Male & Female Institute 1852
Soule University 1856)

Brenham
(Texas Christian Advocate
& Brenham Advertiser 1847)

Caney Creek

Brazos River

Robert Alexander House
"Cottage Hill"

Camp Meeting
Site

Rev J W Kenney's House

Travis

Center Hill
(David Ayres)

William Medford's House
1837-1841

Piney Creek

Industry
(German Methodist)

Benjamin Babbit
1832 land grant

Rutersville
(Texas Conference organized 1840,
Rutersville College 1840)

Mill Creek

Cuming's
Mill

Moore's Ferry
(La Grange)

Colorado River

San Felipe
Town Council donated 12 acres
for parsonage June, 1839

Atascosito Road

Beeson's Crossing
(Columbus)

Atascasito Crossing

Scale of Miles

0    5    10         20            30            40

The presence of Reverends Kenney, Medford, and Babbitt, along with strong lay members such as Lydia McHenry (Kenney's sister-in-law), Thomas Bell, Horatio Chriesman, and David Ayres made the region a hotbed of Methodist activity. From September 3-5, 1834, the Rev. Henry Stephenson joined Kenney, Medford, and Babbitt in leading a camp meeting on a tributary of Caney Creek near Kenney's residence. Preachers arriving in Texas from the United States almost always came to the core. Methodist schools were established at Rutersville and Chappell Hill. The *Texas Christian Advocate and Brenham Advertiser* was founded at Brenham. The camp meeting tradition, begun at the Caney Creek site in 1834, continued into the twentieth century on or near the same site. In 1835, when revolutionary turmoil was beginning, another camp meeting was held near the location of the 1834 meeting. An outcome of that meeting was the organization of a quarterly conference. Medford and Kenney presented their ordination papers, and David Ayres was instructed to correspond with the Missionary Board of the M. E. Church requesting missionaries.

The core area provided a base from which missionary efforts could be extended to settlements in both the Brazos and Colorado River valleys. The Republic of Texas authorized a postal system with the routes radiating from San Felipe. Methodist activity followed these same routes to Bastrop, Victoria, Matagorda, etc. The concentration of Methodist activity in the region made Rutersville a logical choice for the organization of the Texas Conference of the Methodist Episcopal Church in 1840.

*References:*

Cartwright, Olive Hotchkiss, "Records of the Early Families Austin County, Texas" 1962-1963, Bellville Historical Society Archives, Bellville, Texas.

*Journal of the Texas Conference 1865.*

Finley, James Bradley *Sketches of Western Methodism,* Methodist Book Concern, Cincinnati, 1854.

Thrall, Homer S., *History of Methodism in Texas,* E. H. Cushing, Publisher, Houston, 1872.

Lee, Mrs. A. J., "Rev. J. W. Kenney," *The Texas Methodist Historical Quarterly,* vol 1, #1, July, 1909.

Beggs, S. R., *Pages from the Early History of the West and North West,* Methodist Book Concern, Cincinnati, 1866.

Bangs, Nathan, *A History of the Methodist Episcopal Church, vol iv. From the year 1829 to 1840,* New York, published by T. Mason and G. Lane for the Methodist Episcopal Church, 1839.

CHAPTER 4

# A LOUD AND URGENT CALL

As delegates to General Conference of the MEC assembled in Cincinnati in May, 1836, news from the Texian victory at San Jacinto was making its way to the northern states. Although many of the rebels had recently immigrated to Texas from the United States and were bound to the United States by birth, kinship, and culture, support for the Texian cause was by no means universal in the United States. Volunteer troops from southern states rushed to Texas, but many northerners looked upon the rebellion as a land grab by slaveholders.

Northern opinion, as judged by newspaper editorials, became more sympathetic to the Texians after news of the Alamo and Goliad massacres became known. When news of the victory at San Jacinto became known, many Protestant Americans interpreted the event as a triumph of freedom over Roman Catholic tyranny.

The appeals for missionaries from the quarterly conference organized at the Caney Creek camp meeting and from William Barret Travis had been circulated among Methodists in the United States. Rev. Nathan Bangs, D.D., Secretary of the Board of Missions, described the situation in Mexican Texas

> *Among those who removed to Texas, there were several members of our own Church, some of whom were local preachers, and with a view to preserve their piety, they assembled together for mutual edification and comfort, sending in the meantime a loud and urgent call to their brethren in the United States for help*

Delegates to General Conference responded to the news of San Jacinto with a proposal to send missionaries to Texas. Reverend Martin Ruter, president of Allegheny College, who had been a delegate to the 1836 General Conference, volunteered for the Texas Mission. Fifty-one years old at the time, Ruter had been serving in the ministry for thirty-five years. He had served churches, been a delegate to seven general confer-

1837
First Appointed Missionaries to Texas
Martin Ruter, Littleton Fowler, Robert Alexander

PA
MD
WV
OH
Martin Ruter

Meadville, Pa
Ruter leaves
in July

New Albany, IN
home of
Martin Ruter's brother Calvin
& David Ayres' brother Silas

Martin Ruter & David Ayres
leave in November

NC
SC
GA
Florida Territory

MI
IN
IN
TN
Tuscumbia, Al

Wisconsin Ter
IL
Martin Ruter & David Ayres

Iowa
Territory
MO
AR

Littleton Fowler
Memphis, TN
Little Rock
Rodney, MS
Natchez, MS
Robert Alexander

Clarksville
home to Fowler's
Aunt & 2 brothers
Gaines
Ferry

Republic
of Texas

OK
AR
LA

Red River
Sulfur River
Clarksville
Cypress Bayou
Sabine River

Martin Ruter
Littleton Fowler
Robert Alexander

Gaines
Ferry
McMahan
Chapel
San
Augustine
Milam

Nacogdoches

Republic
of Texas

Washington
Camp Meeting Site
Houston
J W
Kenney's
Center Hill
(David Ayres)
Brazos River

ences and helped found three Methodist educational institutions. In addition, he had established the Methodist Book Concern in Cincinnati. One indication of his prominence was the fact that at the 1836 General Conference he chaired two committees, the Book Concern and Education Committees. The General Conference, however, was not the body to organize a mission effort. The Board of Missions, in consultation with the bishops, thought it prudent to wait until the success of the Texas Revolution was assured before sending missionaries. In April, 1837, one year after San Jacinto, Martin Ruter was named to head a mission to Texas. Two younger preachers, Robert Alexander of the Mississippi Conference, and Littleton Fowler of the Tennessee Conference, were also appointed to the mission.

Alexander arrived in Texas first, crossing Louisiana from Natchez, Mississippi, to Gaines Ferry on the Sabine. He preached at a camp meeting at McMahan's and organized the San Augustine Circuit on September 16, 1837. He then traveled to John Wesley Kenney's and the Caney Creek camp meeting site. He met Fowler at Kenney's on November 12, 1837.

Martin Ruter, acting as head of the mission, wrote to Fowler on July 5, 1837, and suggested they meet in Natchez, Mississippi, and travel the rest of the way to Texas together. The letter indicates that Ruter had already been researching conditions in Texas. For example, he cautions Fowler to avoid San Augustine. "The town of San Augustine is said to have many rough and wicked people loitering in it night and day. Instead of tarrying there, some are in the habit of stopping near it, but not in it." Fowler did not follow Ruter's suggestion. Instead, Fowler traveled from Memphis through Little Rock to northeast Texas to visit his mother's family, the Wrights, near Clarksville. He preached at Clarksville and Nacogdoches, and he, too, made his way to Kenney's. Fowler went to Houston to begin lobbying the Congress of the Republic of Texas to grant a charter for a Methodist university. Alexander retraced his steps to Gaines Ferry on his way back to Natchez to attend the Mississippi Annual Conference. It was at Gaines Ferry on November 21, 1837, that he met Martin Ruter and David Ayres who had come by boat down the Ohio and Mississippi Rivers to Rodney, Mississippi, and then overland through Louisiana.

Ayres and Ruter had waited in New Albany, Indiana, for cooler weather and diminished yellow fever danger. Martin Ruter's brother, Calvin, was presiding elder of the New Albany District in the Indiana Conference. Another brother, Alonson Ruter, also resided in New Albany. Ruter intended for his family to stay there through the winter, and in the spring he planned to return to bring them to Texas. David Ayres also had family in New Albany. His brother Silas was engaged in a mercantile business in that river port city across the Ohio River from Louisville, Kentucky. Silas Ayres, and his mercantile partners, David Heddin and Silas Day, invested in several of Ayres' land development ventures in Texas. For two years they even held a mortgage on Center Hill, Ayres' most ambitious promotion of all. It appears that Ayres was combining church business and his own business on the trip to accompany Martin Ruter to Texas.

Ruter and Ayres made their way through San Augustine, Nacogdoches, Washington, and back to Center Hill, David Ayres' home about three miles south of the Caney Creek camp meeting site. In mid-December Ruter met Fowler in Houston and joined him in his lobbying efforts. He returned to Center Hill, in January, but unfortunately died in May 1838. He was buried at Washington on the Brazos, but later reinterred in Navasota. Fowler became a major force in Texas Methodism, serving as presiding elder and delegate to General Conference. He died at age 43 in 1846 and is buried at McMahan's Chapel. Of the three missionaries who responded to the "loud and urgent call" Robert Alexander cast the longest shadow. He lived until 1881 and served faithfully as preacher, presiding elder, General Conference delegate, and member of several important educational committees. He was buried at Chappell Hill, but was later reburied at Brenham.

*References:*

Ruter to Fowler, July 5, 1837, Archives, Center for Methodist Studies at Bridwell Library, Perkins School of Theology, Southern Methodist University, Fowler Papers.

Woolworth, Laura Fowler, *Littleton Fowler, Saint of the Saddlebags*, Shreveport, 1936.

Deed Records of Austin County, Texas, January 1, 1841, mortgage on Lott League and Labor, plus 2009 acres in adjacent Stanley Survey, and 1000 acres in Stephenson Survey. Mortgage released Dec. 29, 1842.

Cody, C. C. "Rev. Martin Ruter," A. M., D. D., *Texas Methodist Historical Quarterly*, vol. 1, no. 1., July, 1909.

Phelan, Macum, *A History of Early Methodism in Texas: 1817-1866*, Cokesbury Press, Nashville, 1924.

Bangs, Nathan, *A History of the Methodist Episcopal Church, vol iv. From the year 1829 to 1840, New York,* published by T. Mason and G. Lane for the Methodist Episcopal Church, 1839.

CHAPTER 5

# A REPRESENTATIVE CIRCUIT OF THE REPUBLIC OF TEXAS: JESSE HORD'S "RIDE AND PREACH, AND PREACH AND RIDE"

After the death of Martin Ruter, the superintendency of the Texas Mission fell upon the shoulders of Littleton Fowler. In addition to his other duties, Fowler made several trips to the United States to recruit more missionaries for Texas. While he was in Huntsville, Alabama, attending the Tennessee Annual Conference of 1838, he met Jesse Hord who had previously volunteered for the Texas Mission and been appointed by Bishop Hedding to that work. Isaac L. G. Strickland and Samuel A. Williams also volunteered for Texas at that annual conference.

Hord and Strickland journeyed overland, arriving in Texas at Gaines Ferry on November 29, 1838. On December 10, at San Augustine, Fowler, in his capacity as superintendent, assigned the three new recruits to their respective circuits: Williams to the San Augustine Circuit, Strickland to the Montgomery Circuit, and Hord to the Houston Circuit. Hord later referred to the San Augustine event as "what we choose to call the first Texas Conference." In actuality it was a division of the Texas Mission by its superintendent. (Although not named superintendent, Robert Alexander was the *de facto* superintendent of the western charges, and the northeastern appointments were supplied from Arkansas.) Hord's circuit embraced that part of Texas to the south and southwest of Houston and provides a valuable insight into the difficulties posed by distance and poor roads. Hord died in Goliad in January 1886, but in the months immediately prior to his death, he wrote a series of reminiscences about his first year in Texas for the *Texas Christian Advocate*. The following account of that year is based on those articles.

Hord arrived in Houston on Dec. 23, 1838, and introduced himself to William Y. Allen, the Presbyterian minister, and also to Congress then in session. Almost immedi-

# Jesse Hord's Circuit
## Dec 1838 - 1839

Area shown below.

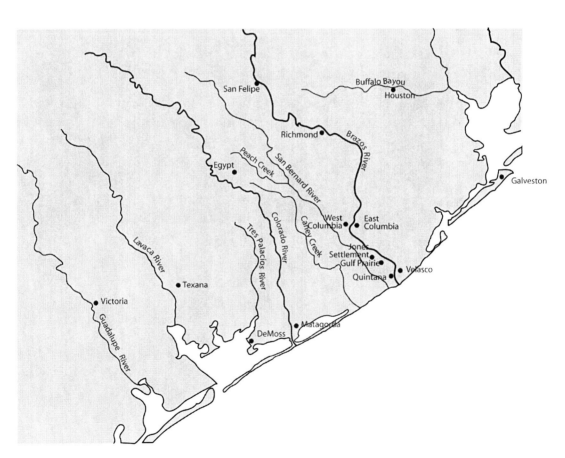

ately Hord set off for Richmond where he preached on Dec. 26. His circuit embraced much of the present day Harris, Galveston, Brazoria, Matagorda, Jackson, Fort Bend, Wharton, and Waller Counties.

The sheer distance involved in meeting all his preaching appointments would have been difficult enough, but the difficulties were compounded by a cold, wet February. Both the Brazos and Colorado Rivers flowed through his circuit, but crossing those streams was relatively easy since ferries existed. Far more difficult were the secondary streams, including the East and West Bernard Rivers, Peach Creek, Caney Creek, the Lavaca River, and countless smaller bodies of water. Adding to the rigor of travel was a jumble of timber in the bottom lands, felled by a February ice storm.

Hord persevered and met his preaching appointments which numbered about twenty. Those preaching places ranged from settlements of three or four families to towns such as Houston, Richmond, Egypt, and Matagorda. Macum Phelan later called him "the great pathfinder of the coast country." Hord described his own time on the circuit as "ride and preach, and preach and ride."

*References:*
Phelan, Macum, *A History of Early Methodism in Texas: 1817-1866.* Cokesbury Press, 1924.
Hord, Jesse, "Notes of Travel in Texas" *The Texas Christian Advocate,* Nov. 8, 1884-Nov. 14, 1885.

# CHAPTER 6

# ORGANIZING
# THE TEXAS CONFERENCE

Missionaries from the United States continued to travel to the Republic of Texas after Martin Ruter's death in May, 1838. Littleton Fowler recruited Samuel A. Williams from the Tennessee Conference and Joseph Sneed from the Mississippi Conference. Abel Stevens, later to become a famous Methodist historian, came from the Baltimore Conference. The Mississippi Conference of December 1838 listed a Texas Mission District with the following appointments:

> Littleton Fowler, P.E.
> Abel Stevens, Galveston and Houston
> Samuel A. Williams, Nacogdoches
> Robert Alexander, Washington
> Isaac L. G. Strickland, Washington
> Jesse Hord, Montgomery,
> Joseph Sneed, Brazoria

A year later the Texas Mission District of the Mississippi Annual Conference was divided into two new districts, East and West. The new names that appeared in the appointments were Daniel Carl, Francis Wilson (Ohio Conference), Henderson Palmer (licensed by Fowler), Moses Spear (Arkansas), Robert Crawford, Chauncey Richardson (President of the Rutersville College), John Haynie (a local preacher since 1811), Robert Hill, Edward Fontaine (Mississippi), T. O. Summers (Baltimore Conference), and J. Lewis. Strickland had died. Stevens had returned to the north.

Although the Texas Mission was growing rapidly, the relationship to the Mississippi Annual Conference was a source of continuing difficulties. Before December 1838 the missionaries to Texas were supported by the Board of Missions in New York City and were under appointment of Bishop Elijah Hedding. At the

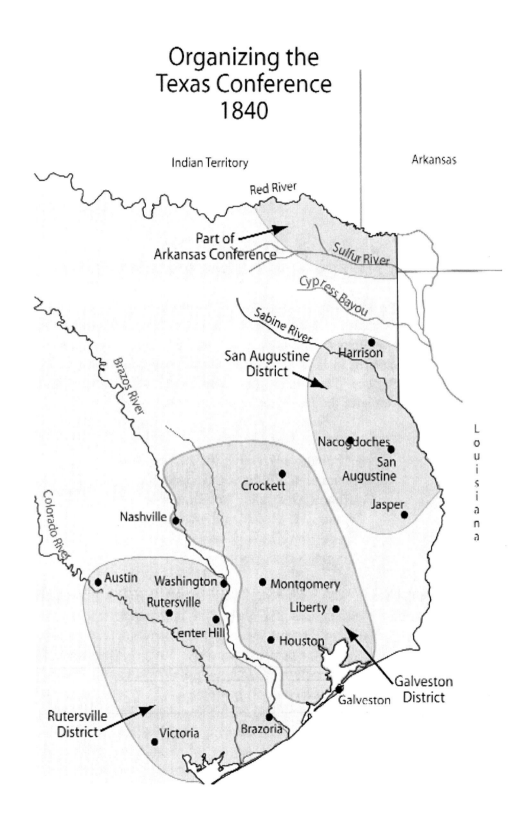

# Organizing the Texas Conference 1840

Indian Territory

Arkansas

Red River

Part of Arkansas Conference

Sulfur River

Cypress Bayou

Sabine River

San Augustine District

Harrison

Brazos River

Nacogdoches

San Augustine

Crockett

Jasper

Nashville

Colorado River

Austin

Washington

Montgomery

Rutersville

Liberty

Center Hill

Houston

Louisiana

Galveston District

Rutersville District

Victoria

Brazoria

Galveston

Mississippi Annual Conference, meeting in Grenada in December 1838 the missionaries were placed in the Texas Mission District of that Conference and under the appointment of the bishop presiding over that conference. In 1838 that bishop was Bishop Thomas A. Morris. There were problems with such a relationship. One problem was financial. Should the funds raised by the Board of Missions be directed through the Mississippi Conference or remitted directly to the Texas Mission?

Even thornier was the problem of personnel as exemplified by the case of Lewellyn Campbell. Rev. Campbell, of the Kentucky Conference, volunteered for Texas and was in Houston by June 1838. The following fall, when the Texas work was attached to the Mississippi Annual Conference, Bishop Morris appointed Campbell to New Orleans. Campbell had strong ties to the Texas Mission. It was he who performed the marriage ceremony for Littleton Fowler and Missouri Porter in June 1838. Campbell later married Sybil Ruter, daughter of the late Martin Ruter. Campbell's appointment to New Orleans was a blow. Writing to Fowler from the Mississippi Annual Conference he said, "I assure you that I have never received an appoint(ment) with as much reluctance in my life . . .." (Campbell to Fowler, Dec. 12, 1838, Bridwell Library, Perkins School of Theology, SMU, Archives, Box 8A)

Morris tried to justify his taking Campbell out of Texas in a June 11, 1839, letter to Littleton Fowler.

> *Respecting Brother Campbell's being detained one year from Texas to supply New Orleans, it was a case of necessity entered into with great reluctance by him and by me. It was very natural for you to doubt the policy of this, but we who carry such a load of responsibility have to keep an eye on every part of the work. Tho Texas is an important field, and one for which we feel deeply interested, New Orleans, the great commercial depot of the Mississippi Valley with its 100,000 inhabitants, is no less so, and it is not near so well supplied with laborers as Texas is, having but two preachers, while you, with fewer people, have seven . . ..*
>
> (Morris to Fowler, June 11, 1839)
>
> reprinted in L. Fowler Woolworth, *Littleton Fowler: Saint of the Saddlebags*, 1936

The "one year" mentioned in the letter stretched on. He served twenty-two years in the Mississippi Annual Conference and was never appointed to a Texas charge.

David Ayres, after visiting the Board of Missions in New York, reported that the Campbell incident prevented Martin Ruter's brother, Calvin, from volunteering for Texas. (Ayres to Fowler, Nov. 22, 1839, Bridwell Library, Perkins School of Theology, SMU, Archives, Box 8B.) The relationship with Mississippi also irked Abel Stevens, another early volunteer for Texas. After less than a year in Texas, Stevens returned to New England. He, too, wrote Fowler and criticized the Mississippi connection:

*I have used my influence to induce them to reinforce us by additional laborers, but our unfortunate connection with the Mississippi Conference interferes with everything. It is owing to this that all applications are referred to the Bishop at that conference and the Cor[responding] Sec[retary] at New York has thrown all the trouble on his boards . . . and suppose they should by letter apply to the Bishop at Mississippi Conference how is he to judge at that distance of their suitableness for the place?*

(Stevens to Fowler, Sept. 18, 1839 Providence, R.I.)

Bridwell Library, Perkins School of Theology, SMU, Archives, Box 8B

From Campbell's point of view the threat that volunteers for the Texas Mission could not be assured of a Texas appointment hindered the effort. Stevens criticized the arrangement because a volunteer from one of the northern conferences could not apply for Texas work directly to his own bishop or to the Board of Missions. In either case preachers who wanted to volunteer for Texas would be thwarted.

On the other hand, Texas was gaining population so rapidly that it was reasonable to believe that the Texas dependency upon Mississippi would be brief. In the same letter that Bishop Morris tried to justify his sending Campbell to New Orleans instead of Texas, he wrote "But be of good cheer. The day is not far distant when Texas will be able to sustain itself as a Conference, and save all these inconveniences."

The complaints about being a mission district in the Mississippi Conference overlooked the fact that there were few acceptable alternatives. Directing the missionaries from the Board of Missions in New York would leave the missionaries in their home conferences and therefore subject to even greater division. Only General Conference could create a new conference. That of 1836 was too early. A Texas Conference would have to wait until the General Conference of 1840 in any case. Measures in the interim would be considered temporary expedients. A more logical arrangement might have been to attach the Texas missionaries to the Arkansas Conference since northeastern Texas appointments were already supplied by the Arkansas Conference. A problem with attaching Texas to the Arkansas Conference was that the Arkansas Conference had just been created by the General Conference of 1836 and was in its organizing period.

The 1840 General Conference met in Baltimore in May and acted favorably on a petition presented by Benjamin Drake of the Mississippi Conference to create a Texas Annual Conference. Bishop Beverly Waugh, also of Baltimore, was instructed to organize that conference. After landing in Galveston, Waugh made his way to Rutersville, Bastrop, and Austin where he observed the Congress of the Republic of Texas in session. He retraced his path to Rutersville, site of the newly founded Rutersville College by December 25, 1840. The significance of the date to Bishop Waugh was not that it was Christmas but that the Methodist Episcopal Church had been founded on that date in 1784. He wrote, "We organized in the name of our Lord Jesus Christ, nothing daunted at the fewness of our number, remembering . . . the first annual conference of the Methodist Episcopal Church which convened on Christmas Day, fifty-six years ago . . .." Bishop Beverly Waugh to *Christian Advocate and Journal*, Jan.2, 1841, reprinted in *Texas Methodist Historical Quarterly*, vol II, #1, July, 1910.

The General Conference, when creating the Texas Conference, had specifically ordered that the charges in Northeast Texas, along the Sulfur and Red Rivers, stay in the Arkansas Conference. The first appointments in the Texas Conference were grouped into three districts as follows:

San Augustine – Littleton Fowler, P.E.
    San Augustine – Francis Wilson
    Nacogdoches – to be supplied
    Harrison – Nathan Shook
    Jasper – Henderson Palmer

Galveston – Samuel A. Williams, P. E
    Galveston and Houston – Thos. O. Summers
    Brazoria – Abner P. Manley
    Montgomery – Richard Owen, Jas. H. Collard
    Liberty – to be supplied
    Crockett – Daniel Carl
    Nashville – Robert Crawford

Rutersville – Robert Alexander, P. E.
    Austin – John Haynie
    Washington – Jesse Hord
    Centre Hill – Robert H. Hill
    Matagorda – Daniel V. N. Sullivan
    Victoria – Joseph P. Sneed
    President, Rutersville College – Chauncey Richardson

*References:*

Letters used by permission of Archives, Center for Methodist Studies at Bridwell Library, Perkins School of Theology, Southern Methodist University.

*Journal of the Mississippi Annual Conference of the MECS*, 1860.

Thrall, Homer S., *A History of Texas Methodism*, E. H. Cushing Publisher, Houston, 1872.

CHAPTER 7

# BISHOP MORRIS'
# EPISCOPAL VISIT

"I shall preach in the most populous towns of this republic until the roads become good, and then expect to labor in the country." So wrote Rev. Daniel Baker to his wife after being in Texas for almost two months on February 25, 1840.

When the Presbyterian missionary Daniel Baker finally traveled into the countryside of Texas, he found that Methodist preachers had preceded him. Methodist preachers submitted to a life of itinerancy that included coping with even the most severe elements. Presiding elders also spent most of their time travelling, and election to the epscopacy only increased the number of miles traveled per year. Neither the circuit rider, the presiding elder, nor the bishop had the luxury of waiting in cities for the roads to improve. Annual conferences in Texas, as in the other southern states usually met in the winter when roads were at their worst. As bad as they were in Texas, they were likely to be even worse in the northern states. Those conferences had their conferences in the spring.

The second session of the Texas Conference convened in San Augustine in December 1841. Bishop Thomas Asbury Morris presided. He and his son brought three preachers (John Clark, J. W. Whipple, and Orceneth Fisher) from Illinois to transfer to the Texas Conference. They came by wagon, buggy, and horse from St. Louis to Texas. New blood was needed because, as Morris said, the first preachers were "nearly worn out." After presiding over the conference, he could have returned home, but instead Bishop Morris went on a grand swing through much of the Methodist work in Texas. Many of the people with whom he stayed constitute a roster of early Methodist leaders in Texas. Here is his itinerary:

Dec. 17, 1841...........enters Texas at Gaines Ferry from Nachitoches

Dec. 18........................Milam to San Augustine

Dec. 19-29................in San Augustine conducting the second session of the Texas Annual Conference

Dec. 30........................to Melrose

Dec. 31........................to Nacogdoches

Jan. 1-3, 1842...........to Douglass stayed at M'Knight's

Jan, 4...........................into Houston County, stayed at M'Lean's

Jan. 5............................to Crockett

Jan. 6............................past a new Methodist campground to Stephen White's house on the east side of the Trinity a few miles down from Cincinnati

Jan. 7............................crossed Trinity, camped a few miles east of Huntsville

Jan. 8............................through Huntsville to William Robinson's

Jan. 9-10....................preached at Robinson's

Jan. 11.........................crossed the San Jacinto, stayed at Porter's on the road to Washington

Jan. 12.........................to King's

Jan. 13.........................to Washington, visited Martin Ruter's grave, stayed at Sheriff Lynch's

Jan. 14-16.................through Independence to Dr. Hoxey's preached at the Academy

Jan. 17.........................to Chrisman's (Horatio Chriesman)

Jan. 18.........................to Kerr's

Jan. 19-23.................Rutersville

Jan. 24-25.................to Middleton Hill's on Colorado, Gage's School House, Wiley Hill's, McGee

Jan. 26.........................Bastrop to Haynie's

Jan. 27-30.................Austin City, stayed at Judge Webb's

Jan. 31-Feb. 3..........return to Rutersville

Feb. 4............................departs for Houston accompanied by Robert Alexander, stayed with Colonel Thomas

Feb. 5-6......................preaches at Center Hill (David Ayres)

Feb. 7............................to San Felipe, D. H. Matthews

Feb. 8............................arrives in Houston, stays at Miss Morgan's Boarding House

Feb. 9............................steamboat *Patrick Henry* to Galveston to secure passage to New Orleans.

Morris calculated that he traveled 700 miles in Texas. The trip was conducted during the worst season for travel. Roads were muddy. He was expected to preach every Sunday. Accommodations were uncertain and of uneven quality, but the general tone of his letters is cheerful.

The hosts with whom Bishop Morris stayed who can be identified are as follows:

**Robinson, William** (1785-1878). Colonial official at San Felipe and participant in conventions leading to formation of Texas government.

**Webb, James** (1792-1856). Appointed U.S. District Judge for Florida by President John Q. Adams, immigrated to Texas, 1838, secretary of treasury and attorney general in Lamar administration. State senator 1841-1844, secretary of state (1849-1851), Judge of 14th Judicial District (Corpus Christi) 1854-1856), Webb County named for him.

**Hoxey, Asa** (1800-1863). Physician, planter, signer of the Texas Declaration of Independence, promoted settlement at Independence and Washington on the Brazos. Benefactor of Baylor University at Independence.

**Chriesman, Horatio** (1797-1878). Surveyor for S. F. Austin, captain in colonial militia, town of Chriesman in Burleson County named for him.

**Kerr, Hugh**. Immigrated to eastern Washington County from Tennessee to Texas in 1831 Son was Alfred Benjamin Fontaine Kerr (b. 1823) admitted to Texas Conference 1847,

**Haynie, John** (1786-1860). Ordained deacon in Holston Conference in 1815 by Francis Asbury, immigrated to Texas 1839, chaplain of the Texas House of Representatives, as member of Mississippi Conference organized the Austin Circuit. Bishop Morris received him into full connection at 1841 conference and reappointed him to Austin Circuit. Haynie Chapel in southeast Travis County named for him.

**Thomas, Nathan** (1809-1881). Colonel in Tennessee militia, immigrated to Texas in 1837, represented Austin County in 5th Congress, (1840-41).

**McKnight, F.** Was postmaster of Douglass 1849. McKnight Congregational Church and cemetery still in operation between Cushing and Sacul.

**Ayres, David** (1793-1881). Immigrant to Texas in 1832, distributed Bibles, secretary of unofficial quarterly conference in 1835, founded a school, and a town (Center Hill), later publisher of *Texas Christian Advocate*.

Two years later, Bishop James Osgood Andrew presided over the 1843 Texas Annual Conference in. It was held at Robinson's in southwestern Walker County. Andrew came to Galveston by boat from New Orleans and then traveled overland, crossing the San Jacinto River with great difficulty. After conducting the conference, he detoured westward into Grimes County to avoid the San Jacinto on his travel back

# Bishop Morris
## Episcopal Visit
### Dec 17, 1841 February 9, 1842

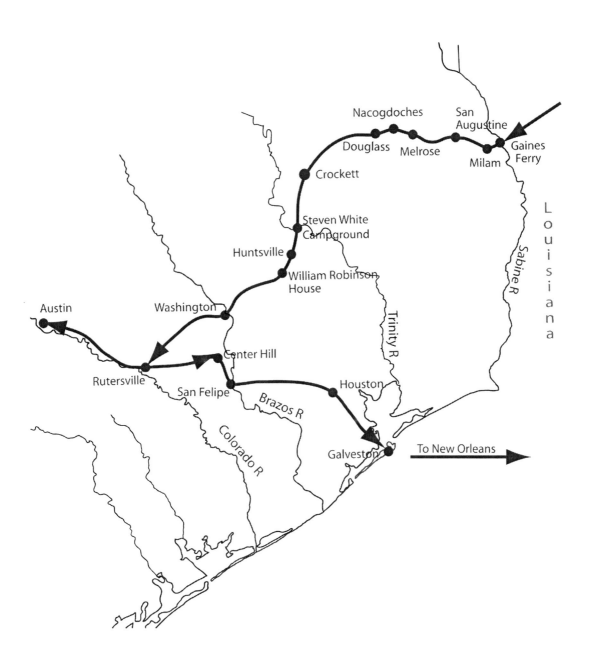

to Galveston. In 1849 He entered Texas at Harrison County and conducted the East Texas Annual Conference at Henderson. He then traveled to La Grange to conduct the Texas Conference and left Texas by boat from Galveston.

*References:*

*Miscellany: Consisting of Essays, Biographical Sketches, and notes of Travel by Rev. T. A. Morris, D.D., one of the bishops of the Methodist Episcopal Church,* Cincinnati, 1. Swormstedt & A. Poe, for the Methodist Episcopal Church at the Western Book Concern, 1854.

*New Handbook of Texas*

Baker, William, T*he Life and Labor of the Reverend Daniel Baker, D.D., prepared by his son, Reverend William Baker*, Austin, 1858.

CHAPTER 8

# FROM ONE CONFERENCE TO TWO

The 1844 General Conference of the MEC, meeting in New York City, is best remembered for the slavery controversy which resulted in the creation of the MECS. The Texas Conference was represented at General Conference by Littleton Fowler and John Clark. Delegates were faced with two specific issues. Rev. Francis Harding of the Baltimore Conference had married a woman who owned slaves. The Baltimore Conference ordered him to emancipate the slaves. He did not do so and appealed his case to the General Conference. Even more prominent was the case of Bishop James O. Andrew who was also married to a woman who owned slaves. Northern delegates introduced a motion to suspend Bishop Andrew from his episcopal duties "as long as this impediment remains."

The Texas delegation mirrored the division in the larger church. Fowler voted with the South. Clark voted with the North and did not return to Texas after the vote. He transferred to the Troy (NY) Annual Conference that same year. After losing the General Conference vote, southern delegates began making plans for a new organization, the Methodist Episcopal Church, South. That body was brought into being by a 1845 convention at Louisville, Ky., and then a General Conference at Petersburg, Va. in 1846.

Although the North-South division dominated business at the 1844 General Conference, delegates also approved an East-West division of Texas. The last few months of the Republic of Texas would have an Eastern Texas Annual Conference and a Western Texas Conference. The boundary between those conferences was the Trinity River. The churches in northeastern Texas that had been served by appointments from the Arkansas Conference would now be part of the Eastern Texas Conference. Littleton Fowler introduced a resolution at General Conference that the first session of the Eastern Texas Conference should be held jointly with the Western Texas Conference. Such a joint session was held in San Augustine in January 1845 with newly-elected Bishop Edmund Janes presiding. Appointments for the two conferences are given

# From One Conference to Two 1844

Texas Conference    East Texas Conference

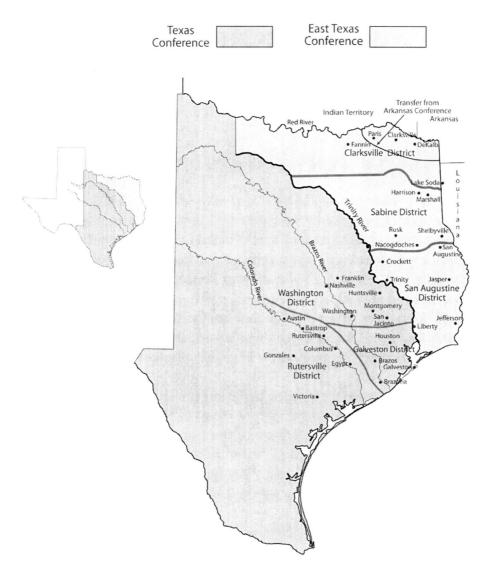

below. For the next two years, 1844-1845, the conferences were known as the Eastern Texas and Western Texas Conferences, but both were renamed at the first General Conference of the MECS. The Eastern Texas Conference became the East Texas Conference, and the Western Texas Conference became the Texas Conference.

## EASTERN TEXAS CONFERENCE

San Augustine District – Francis Wilson, P. E.
    San Augustine – J. W. Fields, J. T. P. Irvine
    Jasper – Jacob Crawford, H. Z. Adams
    Jefferson – James W. Baldridge
    Liberty – L. S. Friend
    Trinity – Isaac Tabor
    Crockett – M. H. Jones, Wm. K. Wilson
    Wesley College – L. Janes, N. W. Burks

Sabine District – Littleton Fowler, P. E.
    Nacogdoches – John C. Woolam, Silas Camp
    Rusk – Henderson Palmer, Wm. Craig
    Shelbyville – Orin Hatch
    Marshall – S. A. Williams, F. M. Stovall
    Harrison – TBS

Clarksville District – Daniel Payne, P. E.
    Clarksville – N. Shook
    DeKalb – E. P. Chisholm
    Paris – Jeff Shook, Andrew Davis
    Fannin – Daniel Shook
    Lake Soda – P. W. Hobbs, Robert Crawford

## WESTERN TEXAS CONFERENCE

Galveston District – Robert Alexander, P. E.
    Galveston – I. M. Williams
    Houston – J. W. Whipple
    Brazoria – D. N. V. Sullivan, W. S. Hamilton
    Brazos – James M. Wesson
    San Jacinto – W. G. Booker

Washington District – Mordecai Yell, P. E.
    Washington – R. B. Wells, L. D. Bragg
    Montgomery – James G. Johnson
    Huntsville – Wm. C. Lewis

Franklin – James H. Collard
Nashville – Pleasant M. Yell

Rutersville District – Chauncey Richardson, P. E.
Rutersville – Homer Thrall
Bastrop – John S. Williams
Columbus – Robert Guthrie
Egypt – Daniel Carl, Jesse Hord
Victoria – David L. Bell
Gonzales – John W. DeVilbiss
Rutersville College – Chauncey Richardson, President, Homer
Thrall, Professor

Neither of the divisions of 1844 was permanent. The North-South split ended in 1939 with the unification of the MEC, MECS, and MP churches. The East-West division ended in 1902 when the Texas Conference (minus the Austin District) and the East Texas Conference were reunited and retained the name "Texas Conference."

*References:*

Nail, Olin, et al., ed. *Texas Methodist Centennial Yearbook*, 1934.

Phelan, Macum, *History of Early Methodism in Texas :1817-1866*, Nashville, Cokesbury Press, 1924.

Thrall, Homer S. *History of Methodism in Texas*, E. H. Cushing, Publisher, Houston, 1872.

Vernon, Walter, et al., *The Methodist Excitement in Texas: A History*, The Texas United Methodist Historical Society, Dallas, 1984.

West, C. A., ed., *Texas Conference Methodism on the March:1814-1960*, Nashville, Parthenon Press, 1960.

MEC General Conference *Journal*, 1844.

Texas Annual Conference, *Journal*, 1845, 1845.

East Texas Annual Conference, *Journal*, 1845.

# CHAPTER 9

# FROM TWO CONFERENCES TO FIVE

From 1844 until 1858 Texas contained two annual conferences of the MECS, the Texas (named Western Texas for one year, 1845) and East Texas (named Eastern Texas from 1845-1857). The Trinity River was the boundary between the two. The General Conferences immediately preceding and following the Civil War recognized the increasing population of the state by creating three new conferences.

Robert Alexander, a delegate to the 1858 General Conference held in Nashville, Tennessee, introduced a resolution to divide the Texas Conference and create a new conference, the Rio Grande Mission Conference. The boundaries were as follows:

> *All that part of the state of Texas lying west and southwest of a line beginning at the mouth of the Guadalupe River, thence up said river to where it is crossed by the road from San Antonio to Fredericksburg, thence on said road to Fort Mason, thence due north to the Colorado River, thence up said river to the big spring, thence north to the state line.*

The Rio Grande Mission Conference was organized into three districts. Two districts, San Antonio and Goliad, were English. The third was a German district, seated sometimes at Fredericksburg and sometimes at New Braunfels. Appointments for 1861 included the following:

> San Antonio District
> > San Antonio Station
> > Medina Circuit
> > Pleasanton Mission
> > Cibolo Mission
> > Sutherland Springs Ct.
> > Sandies Ct.

Guadalupe Colored Mission
Kerrsville (sic) Ct.
Uvalde Mission
Eagle Pass and Fort Clark Mission

Goliad District
Goliad Ct.
Corpus Christi Station
Clinton Mission
Kemper Mission
St. Mary's Mission
Nueces Bay Mission
Helena Mission
Engleside and Padre Island
Oakville Mission
Browsville (sic) and Rio Grande City

New Braunfels District (German)
New Braunfels Mission
Fredericksburg Mission
New Fountain Mission
Yorktown and Goliad Mission
San Antonio Mission
Llano Mission

The outbreak of the Civil War soon after the creation of the Rio Grande Mission Conference created considerable disruption for a territory so far removed from the major theaters of operation of the war. The withdrawal of Union troops from the frontier forts, antagonism toward some Germans by Confederate loyalists, the Confederate cotton exports through Mexico, and military engagements along the coast and Rio Grande all had their impact upon Methodists in the region. The removal of the Union forts left farms and roads vulnerable to Indian raids. The cotton exports were vital to the Confederate war effort. Those factors combined to insure that many church members were able to remain at home during the war as part of a home guard or engaged in the cotton trade. The Rio Grande Conference (no longer a mission conference) actually reported an increase in membership during the Civil War years. The Texas Conference, on the other hand, reported considerable losses as shown in the following chart:

| | YEAR 1861 | | YEAR 1865 | |
|---|---|---|---|---|
| Conference | White members | Colored members | White members | Colored members |
| Rio Grande (Mission) | 1,357 | 180 | 1,474 | 298 |
| Texas Conference | 13,547 | 1,673 | 7,430 | 2,191 |

# Rio Grande Mission Conference

## established 1858

*all of that part of the state of Texas
lying west and southwest of a line beginning
at the mouth of the Guadalupe River,
thence up said river to where it is crossed by the road
from San Antonio to Fredericksburg,*

*thence up said road to Fort Mason,*

*thence due north to the Colorado River,*

*thence up said river to the big spring,*

*thence north to the state line*

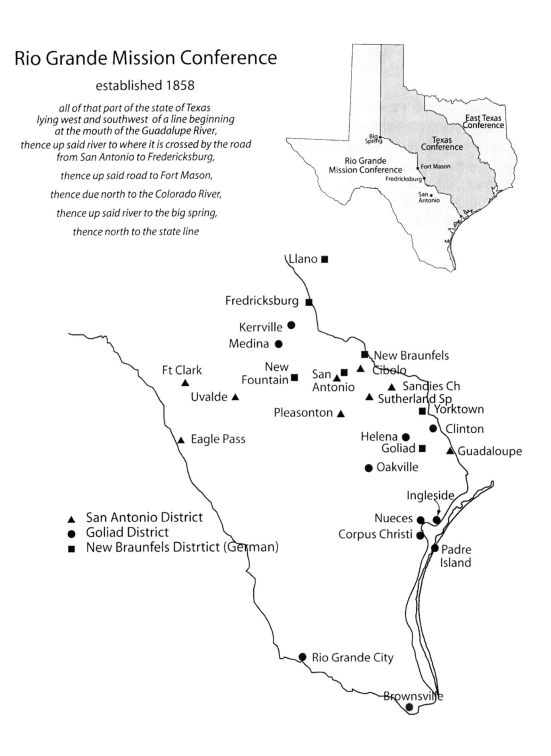

Llano ■

Fredricksburg ■

Kerrville ●
Medina ●

New Braunfels ■
Cibolo

Ft Clark ▲

New Fountain ■
San Antonio ▲

Sandies Ch ▲

Uvalde ▲

Sutherland Sp ▲
Yorktown ■

Pleasonton ▲

Clinton ●

Eagle Pass ▲

Helena ●
Goliad ■
Guadaloupe ▲

Oakville ●

Ingleside

Nueces ●
Corpus Christi

Padre Island

▲  San Antonio District
●  Goliad District
■  New Braunfels Distrtict (German)

Rio Grande City ●

Brownsville

Big Spring
East Texas Conference
Texas Conference
Rio Grande Mission Conference
Fort Mason
Fredricksburg
San Antonio

The Rio Grande Conference thus increased 235 members during the Civil War while the Texas Conference decreased by 5,599 members.

One significant wartime disruption did occur. MECS bishops were not able to travel to Texas to conduct annual conference. Six of the first seven sessions of the Rio Grande Conference were conducted in the absence of a bishop. Conference stalwarts including Jesse Boring, John W. DeVilbiss and R. H. Belvin presided over those sessions.

As part of the reorganization of the conferences in 1866, the Rio Grande Conference was renamed the West Texas Conference and its territory was increased by shifting its northeastern boundary away from the Guadalupe. Victoria, Halletsville, and Gonzales were among the charges that were shifted from the Texas Conference to the West Texas Conference. The conference was renamed again at the 1939 unification to become the Southwest Texas Annual Conference.

The MECS General Conference scheduled for 1862 was not held because of the Civil War. The 1866 General Conference, meeting in New Orleans, therefore had more than the usual amount of work to consider. That general conference, held in New Orleans elected the first MECS bishop to be elected while serving a Texas appointment. Enoch Marvin, a Missouri Methodist preacher, was serving the Methodist church at Marshall Texas at the conclusion of the Civil War. Although he was not a delegate to the 1866 General Conference, he was elected while en route from Marshall.

General Conference also took actions to accommodate Texas' growing population. The northern halves of both the Texas Conference and the East Texas Conference were broken off to form new annual conferences.

The resolution dividing the Texas Conference came from that very conference. Delegates voted to divide the Texas Conference to "commence at the south-east corner of Leon county on the Trinity River; thence west along the south line of Leon, Robinson (sic), and Milam, to the eastern corner of Travis county; thence along the south line of Williamson county to its south-west corner; thence by a direct line to the mouth of the Perdenales (sic); thence up that stream until it intersects the boundary line of the Rio Grande Conference. Your committee recommend that their request be granted, and the new Conference be known as the North-west Texas Conference."

The Trinity Conference, organized in 1867, was formed from the northern counties of the East Texas Conference. Its boundaries, as described in the *Discipline* were as follows:

> . . . *bounded on the north by the Red River; on the east by the Western state lines of Arkansas and Louisiana; on the south commencing at the Louisiana State line in Caddo Lake; thence up said lake to the mouth of Little Cypress River; up said river to Taylor's bridge; thence in a direct line to Fort Crawford; thence in a direct line*

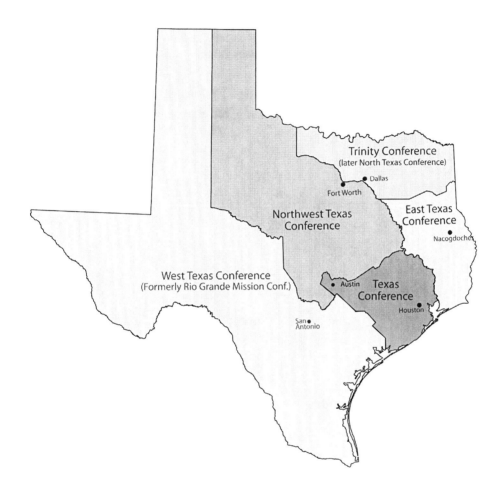

Trinity Conference
(later North Texas Conference)

• Dallas

Fort Worth

Northwest Texas
Conference

East Texas
Conference

Nacogdoches

West Texas Conference
(Formerly Rio Grande Mission Conf.)

• Austin

Texas
Conference

Houston

San
Antonio

49

*to Fredonia\*, on Sabine River; thence following said river to Belzora\*\*; thence by a direct line to the south-east corner of Van Zant (sic) county, including the Canton and Garden Valley Circuits; thence along the southern boundaries of Van Zant (sic) and Kaufman counties to Trinity River; and on the west by Trinity River and West Fork to its source, and by a direct line from that source to Red River.*

*Fredonia – on south bank of Sabine in Gregg County
**Belzora – a ferry crossing on the Sabine in northern Smith County

The Trinity Conference became the North Texas Conference in 1874. In 1894 its easternmost counties were transferred to the Texas Conference, and it has continued through both the 1939 and 1968 mergers.

*References:*

*MECS Discipline,* 1858.

*Rio Grande Mission Conference Journal,* 1861, 1865.

*Texas Conference Journal,* 1865.

Nail, Olin W., *"A History of the West Texas Conference" in Nail, ed. Texas Methodist Centennial Yearbook,* 1934.

Godbold, Albea, and Ness, John H., "Table of United Methodist Church Annual Conferences 1796-2001," General Commission on Archives and History at www.gcah.org.

Hardt, John Wesley, *Forward in Faith: The Ministry and Mission of Marvin United Methodist Church 1848-1998,* Austin, Nortex Press, 1999.

*MECS General Conference Journal Minutes, 1866, 1870.*

*New Handbook of Texas*

CHAPTER 10

# THE MEC ON THE EVE
# OF THE CIVIL WAR

The events of 1844-1846 that resulted in the creation of the Methodist Episcopal Church South by churches that withdrew from the Methodist Episcopal Church produced considerable rancor in Texas. The Texas Conference sent two delegates to the 1844 General Conference in New York, Littleton Fowler, one of the original missionaries who had come in 1837, and John Clark who had transferred from the Illinois Conference in 1841. As the General Conference debated and voted on a series of proposals relating to slavery and the church, Fowler supported the southern side and Clark the northern.

The General Conference failed to find a compromise, and most southern delegates resolved to form a new denomination. Clark never returned to Texas. He had taken his family with him to New York. At the conclusion of the General Conference he transferred to the Troy Conference. When news of his siding with northern delegates reached Texas, there was a firestorm of criticism. The Washington and Montgomery Circuits were particularly vehement in their denunciation of this "Judas". The Washington Circuit pastor, Robert B. Wells, took a prominent role in printing denunciations. Clark responded with letters in defense of his position, but the mood in Texas would not allow calm debate on the subject.

Both the Texas and East Texas Conferences became charter members of the new MECS when it was organized in 1846. The MEC disappeared from Texas.

That disappearance was brief. Migration of farmers from Upper South and border states to Texas continued during the 1840s and 1850s. Some of those immigrants to Texas were MEC members so that by 1852 when the General Conference of MEC reconstituted the Arkansas Conference, one of the districts in that conference was the Texas Mission. Churches in the Texas Mission were concentrated in Denton, Grayson, and Fannin Counties. By 1855 the Texas Mission reported 142 members, 21 probationers, and 4 local preachers. Presiding Elder Anthony Bewley had five appointments in his district.

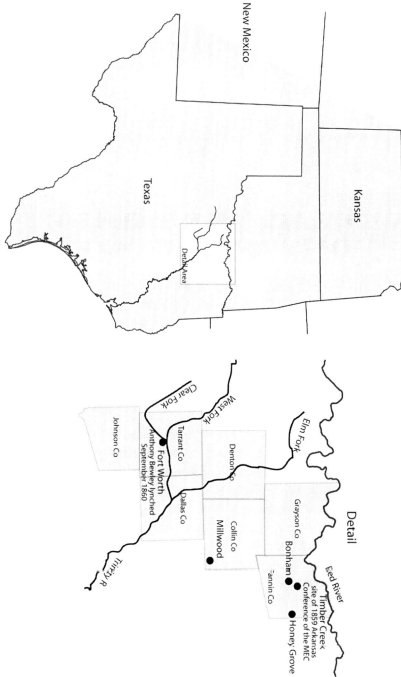

MEC Kansas Conference 1860

New Mexico

Texas

Kansas

Detail Area

**Detail**

Johnson Co

Clear Fork

West Fork

Tarrant Co

Fort Worth
Anthony Bewley lynched
September 1860

Dallas Co

Trinity R.

Denton Co

Elm Fork

Collin Co
Millwood

Grayson Co

Bonham

Fannin Co

Honey Grove

Red River

Timber Creek
site of 1859 Arkansas
Conference of the MEC

In March 1859 the Arkansas Conference of the MEC held its annual conference at Timber Creek near Bonham in Fannin County. By 1859 there had already been years of open warfare in southeastern Kansas and adjacent areas of Missouri between pro and antislavery forces. Holding a meeting of an antislavery body, the Arkansas Conference of the MEC, in a slave state produced a violent reaction. Newspaper editorials denounced the meeting. An armed mob from Bonham interrupted the Conference and presented a list of demands including the withdrawal of the MEC preachers from Texas.

Bishop Edmund Janes, the presiding officer of the conference, continued the Texas District and made five appointments even in the face of such a threat of violence. One year later, however, at the 1860 annual conference held in Franklin County, Arkansas, the Texas District was dissolved. Even though the district was dissolved, there were still two men, Anthony Bewley and T. M. Willet, who were appointed "Missionary to Texas." When the General Conference of the MEC met in 1860, it took the Texas Mission away from the Missouri-Arkansas Conference and added it and New Mexico Territory east of the Rockies to the Kansas Conference. It is hard to imagine a more foolish action. Kansas by 1860 had already become "Bleeding Kansas," and both religious and civic life were thoroughly radicalized.

Bewley recognized that continuing to preach around his home in Johnson County was too dangerous, but he proposed to travel to the German Hill Country settlements and preach there. The MEC had a significant presence in the German areas in Iowa, New York, Pennsylvania, St. Louis, and Cincinnati, Ohio, among other places. Perhaps the Hill Country Germans of Texas would also be receptive.

Bewley never got a chance to preach in the German settlements. In September, 1860 a fraudulent letter incriminating Bewley in plans for an incendiary terrorist campaign across Texas was widely reprinted in Texas newspapers. A committee in Fort Worth raised money for a reward for capturing Bewley. A mob pursued him and kidnapped him near Springfield, Missouri. He was returned to Fort Worth and lynched.

The nation soon turned its attention to its larger national crisis, but the Bewley murder was instrumental in shaping MEC attitudes toward Texans.

*References:*

Shettles, E. L., "The Disturbance in Texas," *The Texas Methodist Historical Quarterly*, vol. II. #3, January, 1911.

M. E. C. *Discipline*, 1852, 1856, 1860.

General Minutes of the Conferences of the MEC, 1852 through 1861.

*Ladies Repository*, vol. 20, issue 1, January 1860 and vol. 20 issue 12, December 1860.

Leftwich, W. M., *Martyrdom in Missouri: A History of Religious Proscription, Seizure of Churches, and the Persecution of Ministers of the Gospel, in the State of Missouri During the Late Civil War*, S. W. Book and Publishing Co. St. Louis, 1870.

Elliott, Charles, *A History of the M. E. Church in the South-West from 1844 to 1864 Comprising the Martyrdom of Bewley and Others; Persecutions of the M. E. Church and its Reorganization, etc.* Poe and Hitchcock, Cincinnati, 1868.

CHAPTER 11

# 1880s
# REDRAWING OF CONFERENCE BOUNDARIES

The Texas Annual Conference brought a petition to the 1866 General Conference of the MECS. It asked that its territory be divided and its northwestern portion be organized into a new conference to be named the North-west Texas Conference. The Texas Annual Conference even suggested the boundary. It was to "commence at the south-east corner of Leon county (*sic*) on the Trinity River; thence west along the south line of Leon, Robinson (*sic*, should be Robertson), and Milam, to the eastern corner of Travis county, thence along the south line of Williamson county . . .."

The General Conference of 1866 granted the Texas Annual Conference petition, and Bishop Enoch Marvin organized the Northwest Texas Annual Conference at Waxahachie on September 26, 1866. By proposing the boundary that it did, the Texas Conference was voluntarily relinquishing an area that was among the most rapidly growing areas in the state, the Blackland Prairie south of the Trinity River. The fertile soils of Hill, Ellis, McLennan, Bell, and Williamson Counties had certainly attracted farmers before the Civil War since the "black waxy", as it was called, ranked among the most fertile soils in the world. That pre-Civil War settlement was only a prelude to the rush of population into the region after the Civil War as the grassland was converted to cotton farms.

The line suggested by the Texas Annual Conference had retained Travis County, and therefore Austin, the state capital, within its own boundaries. The action, however, left Travis County as an awkward western projection, squeezed between the West Texas and Northwest Texas Conferences. It was not until 1902 that the boundary was rationalized by the cession of the Austin District to the West Texas (later Southwest Texas) Annual Conference. The boundary between the Northwest Texas and Texas Annual Conferences proved to be source of contention as settlement and transportation patterns changed. In 1877, just eleven years after suggesting the boundary, the Texas

# 1880s Redrawing

Conference tried to redraw it. The Texas Conference petitioned the Northwest Texas Conference to cede some of its territory. The petition was referred to committee and rejected in the following resolution:

*First – Our conference is full and we have no foot of ground to spare*

*Second – Our boundary lines are remarkably well regulated whereas the change proposed would break up the compact form of our conference*

*Third – Our western prairie preachers have no affinity with nor adaptation to the peculiar class of population within the territory of the Texas Conference*

*Second* (sic) *– We* sincerily (sic) *believe that the relief our mother conference prays for can be more effectually and with better results to our Texas Methodists by giving off a portion of her territory to West Texas and then obliterating the line between the Texas and East Texas Conference.*

In its rejection of the Texas Conference petition, the Northwest Texas Conference had suggested precisely what would occur twenty-five years later.

The Texas Conference did not take "no" for an answer. It memorialized the General Conference of 1878 to transfer Leon, Robinson (sic), Milam, and Williamson Counties from the Northwest Texas Conference to the Texas Conference. The General Conference rejected the memorial. The General Conference usually granted boundary changes only when all conferences involved in the change agreed.

The Texas Conference persisted in its efforts, and finally in 1881 the Northwest Texas Conference agreed to return Leon, Freestone, Robertson, Milam, Falls, and the southern portion of Limestone Counties to the Texas Conference. That agreement was ratified by the General Conference of 1882.

Changing transportation patterns help explain why the NWT Conference was willing to agree to the retrocession. By the 1880s Texas had two emerging railroad systems. The first was concentrated in the northern Blackland Prairie. Dallas became the main focus. This system tied Texas to the rest of the United States through St. Louis, Kansas City, and Chicago. It also extended rail lines farther west and northwest, and southwest into that portion of the Blackland Prairie between Dallas and San Antonio. This system, centered on Dallas, served the booming cities of the Northwest Texas Annual Conference: Fort Worth, Corsicana, Waco, Waxahachie, Temple, Hillsboro, etc.

The other system was focused on Houston and Galveston Bay. The Houston city motto, "Where Seventeen Railroads Meet the Sea" expressed much of its economic life before the petroleum discoveries of the early 20th century. A web of rails stretched into Texas farmland to transport cotton to the ports of Houston and Galveston. The Houston and Texas Central and Gulf Coast and Santa Fe Rail lines tied most of the population in the six counties being ceded more closely to the Texas Conference than to the Northwest Texas Conference.

At the same time the expansion of rail lines such as the Texas and Pacific and the Fort Worth and Denver City was creating new opportunities for the Northwest Texas Annual Conference. New towns were being established by the railroads. Railroad executives recognized the value of churches in the towns being established in attracting more population and therefore facilitated the acquisition of lots upon which churches could be built. The NWT Conference was responsible for a vast area now being settled. It could easily return six eastern counties to the Texas Conference.

*References:*

*Journal of the General Conference of the MECS, 1866, 1878, 1882.*

*Journal of the Northwest Texas Annual Conference, 1877, 1881.*

CHAPTER 12

# 1894 BOUNDARY CHANGES

The December 7, 1893, *Texas Christian Advocate* contained a hint of impending changes in annual-conference boundaries in Texas when it opined, "The North Texas, like the Northwest Texas Conference, is too big. The Committee on Boundaries at the Next General Conference will have to relieve us in some way." Not only did the General Conference provide such relief, in doing so it changed a longstanding pattern of using rivers and rail lines as conference boundaries. All of the Texas boundary changes of 1894 conformed to county lines rather than rivers and rails.

A growing imbalance among the Texas annual conferences was evident. At the close of the 1880s the annual conferences reported the following memberships:

| | |
|---|---|
| West Texas Conference | 11,648 |
| Texas Conference | 14,614 |
| North West Texas Conference | 39,243 |
| East Texas Conference | 20,699 |
| North Texas Conference | 37,405 |

*(General Minutes of the Annual Conferences of the Methodist Episcopal Church, South, 1889)*

Population increases within the boundaries of the North Texas and North West Texas Annual Conferences were due mainly to the establishment of cotton farms in the Blackland Prairie. By 1890 both conferences were crisscrossed by numerous rail lines which provided easy transport of the "white gold." The agricultural and transportation changes also spurred urban growth, most notably at Dallas, but also at many other county seat towns such as Sherman, Paris, Sulphur Springs, Hillsboro, Waxahachie, Denton, and Decatur. As early as 1889 the East Texas Conference voted to petition General Conference to remedy the growing imbalance. The East Texas Conference passed the following resolution that year:

*Whereas there has been great increase in the population of the state in the past few years, and the center of population has moved very much to the west where it was when the present Conference lines were established, Therefore, be it resolved that the General Conference be requested to so rearrange the boundary lines of the Conference within our State that they may better conform to the present requirements of the work and best interest of our church and State.*

Delegates to the 1894 General Conference of the MECS which met in Memphis, Tennessee, were amenable to the prospect of redrawing conference boundary lines to achieve the "relief" needed by the conferences in question. The only dispute was where the new line should be drawn. Two competing resolutions were debated in the Committee on Boundaries, chaired by John Tigert. (Tigert was to be elected bishop at the General Conference of 1906 and died in November of that same year.)

W. L Clifton of the North Texas Conference proposed that his conference cede to the East Texas Conference those churches in Bowie, Cass, Marion, and Morris Counties and portions of Titus, Camp, Wood, and Van Zandt Counties by using both the Cotton Belt and Texas and Pacific Railway as new conference boundaries between the East Texas and North Texas Conferences. The Committee on Boundaries rejected the Clifton resolution and instead voted favorably for a resolution from the East Texas Conference. That resolution called for the transfer of Bowie, Cass, Marion, Titus, Morris, Camp, Upshur, Wood, Rains, and the portion of Van Zandt County not already in the East Texas Conference. The East Texas Conference received all the Jefferson District, plus several churches in the Paris and Sulphur Springs Districts. Wills Point, Mt. Pleasant, Atlanta, Linden, DeKalb, Texarkana, Winnsboro, Pittsburg, Jefferson, and others for a total of 23 charges, 58 local preachers, 18 travelling preachers, and 7.808 members changed their conference affiliation.

There were at least two important factors underlying the drawing of the new boundary between North Texas and East Texas Conferences. The boundary made sense because it separated the Piney Woods from the Blackland Prairies. In effect, the North Texas Conference shed its forested portion and became a "prairie" conference. Although farmers did clear forests and plant cotton in the Piney Woods, the yields from those sandy soils could not match those of the Blackland Prairie. In a nutshell, the fertile soils of the Blackland Prairie could support greater population densities and generate more wealth. Unequal population and wealth contributed to cultural differences between the regions so the cession of the nine plus counties was a reasonable action for the General Conference. The other important factor was the use of county boundaries rather than rail lines for conference boundaries. Rivers and rail lines had both been employed by prior conferences. The problem with both rivers and transport lines is that they bring people together rather than divide them. In other words, both features make poor boundaries because they do not separate. County lines in late 19th

# 1894 Boundary Changes

### Before

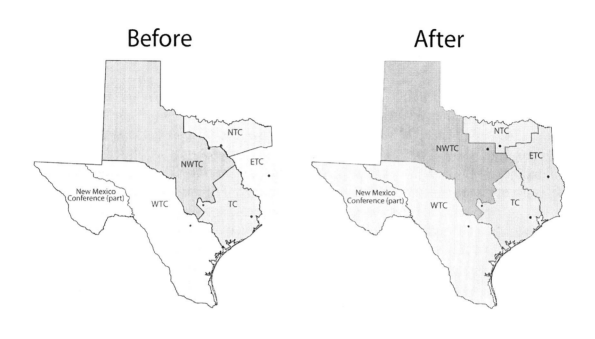

### After

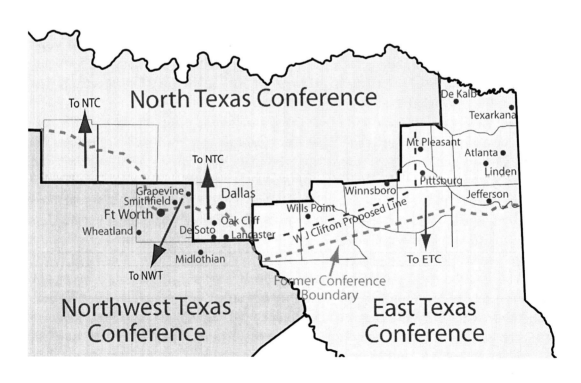

century Texas were far preferable. The largest urban place, and therefore the center of religious activity, in most counties was the county seat. (Bowie County was an important exception since Texarkana was the largest city, but not the county seat.) The county seat was almost always near the center of the county making conference and circuit organization simpler. For example, had the Clifton resolution prevailed, Mount Pleasant, on the Cotton Belt RR would be on the conference boundary and assigned to the North Texas Conference. A Mount Pleasant Circuit that embraced charges on the east side of Mount Pleasant would fall into the bounds of the East Texas Conference.

The use of counties rather than rivers was also employed to redraw the boundary between the North Texas and Northwest Texas Conferences. The Trinity River had been a conference boundary since 1844. The 1894 General Conference made boundaries in the Dallas/Fort Worth area conform to county lines rather than the river. Charges south of the Trinity in Dallas County had been part of the North West Texas Conference. Charges north of the Trinity in Tarrant County had been part of the North Texas Conference. The General Conference put all of Tarrant County into the North West Texas Conference and all of Dallas County, as well as Jack and Wise Counties into the North Texas Conference.

North Texas Conference received charges in Oak Cliff, Lancaster, Midlothian, West Dallas, and Wheatland. North West Texas received Grapevine, Smithfield, and North Fort Worth.

The population disparities that prompted the changes of 1894 actually increased in the decades following. The North Texas Conference continued its explosive growth but retained the boundaries drawn by the General Conference of 1894. The Northwest Texas Conference also continued to grow and in 16 years was split to create another annual conference.

References:

Minutes of the General Conference of the Methodist Episcopal Church, South, 1894.

Texas Christian Advocate 12/7/1893, 5/17/1894, 5/24/1894, 12/20/1894.

Minutes of the East Texas Conference of the MECS, 1889, 1894.

Nail, Olin, ed., Texas Methodist Centennial Yearbook, 1934.

General Minutes of the Annual Conferences of the MECS, 1889.

CHAPTER 13

# NEW MEXICO CONFERENCE

The boundaries of the New Mexico Conference of the UMC are based mainly on those presented by resolution at the 1890 General Conference of the MECS. The General Conference *Minutes* reported the adoption of the following

> *Resolved, That the Conference concurs in the memorials from the Denver and North-west Texas Conferences, that a new Conference be formed, to be known as the New Mexico Conference, which shall include all of that part of the Territory of New Mexico south of the 36th parallel of latitude, and all of that part of the state of Texas west of the Pecos River . . ..*

(footnote: For point of reference, Espanola, site of McCurdy School is located
at 35.991 degrees north latitude. The Denver Conference would retain
Chama, Taos, Raton, etc, but not Santa Fe or Albuquerque.)

The New Mexico Conference shared some territory with the Mexican Border Mission Conference whose boundaries in 1890 included the Mexican states of Tamaulipas, Nuevo Leon, Chihuahua, Coahuila, Durango, Sonora, Sinaloa, Baja California and *all Mexican population within the southern border of the United States of America* (emphasis added).

The New Mexico Conference in 1890 was mainly still an optimistic prospect not far removed from a mission. The MEC, the MECS, and the EA all faced challenges in New Mexico. Most of those challenges were the result of the cultural heritage that made most of New Mexico quite unlike other mission fields. One of those challenges was the north-south division. The population in northern New Mexico was majority Hispano-Native American Roman Catholic. The region boasted communities already well established before the arrival of the Puritans in Massachusetts in the 1620s. Their self-identification tended to be Spanish rather than Mexican, a distinction often lost on Methodist missionaries. During most of the Mexican period of their history they were

# New Mexico Annual Conference 2006

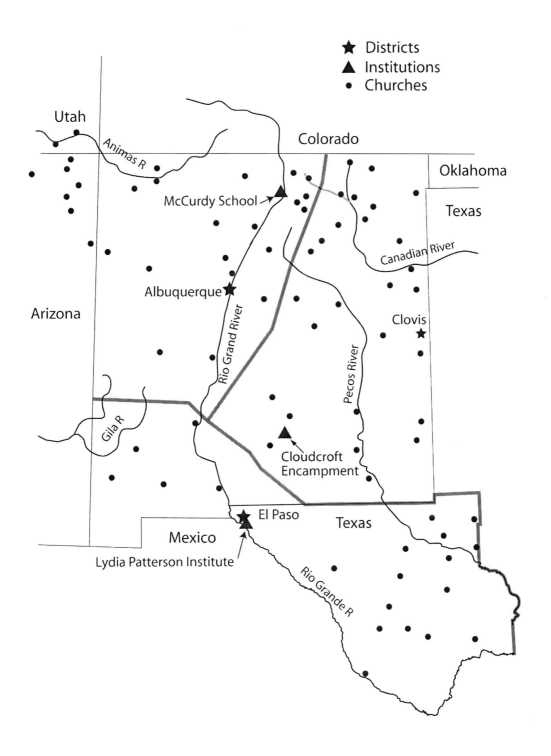

★ Districts
▲ Institutions
• Churches

Utah

Colorado

Animas R

Oklahoma

Texas

McCurdy School

Canadian River

Arizona

Albuquerque

Rio Grand River

Clovis

Pecos River

Gila R

Cloudcroft
Encampment

El Paso

Mexico

Texas

Lydia Patterson Institute

Rio Grande R

far removed from the ecclesiastical centers of Mexico, and neglect of religious matters was common. It is ironic, therefore, that the transfer of northern New Mexico to the United States via the Treaty of Guadalupe Hidalgo (1848) spurred a revival of Roman Catholicism in New Mexico. That was accomplished under the leadership of the legendary French priest Jean Baptiste Lamy who served in Santa Fe from 1851 to 1888. Protestant missionaries in northern New Mexico thus faced a reinvigorated Roman Catholicism.

The southern portion of New Mexico was several hundred miles and worlds apart from the northern part. Its development was also influenced by the cession of 1848. Only a few months after the Treaty of Guadalupe Hidalgo was signed, gold was discovered in California. Gold seekers from the eastern United States had a choice of several routes to California, one of which went through El Paso, Texas, and southern New Mexico. The stream of travelers stimulated the growth of commercial centers and a military post, Fort Bliss (founded 1854). The population of those new towns tended to be from the American South and amenable to organization by the MECS.

Both the MEC and the MECS made a few feeble efforts to send preachers to the region in the 1850s. In 1858 the Trans Pecos fell into the bounds of the Rio Grande Mission Conference upon its creation. In 1859 Bishop Pierce appointed John Harper to El Paso. Harper served only one year. The 1861 Journal of the Rio Grande Mission Conference listed Eagle Pass/Fort Clark, over four hundred miles to the east of El Paso, as the westernmost appointment. Even that appointment was "to be supplied."

The turmoil of the Civil War and the low population densities of New Mexico and western Texas precluded establishing circuits through the 1860s and 1870s.

The development that finally led to Methodist evangelization of the Trans Pecos region of Texas and much of New Mexico was railroad construction in the 1880s. The Southern Pacific and Texas Pacific which shared track between Sierra Blanca and El Paso solidified El Paso's role as one of the most important transportation nodes in North America. The addition of the Atchison, Topeka, and Santa Fe and the Fort Worth and Denver City railroad also in the 1880s spurred the organization of towns and churches in northeastern New Mexico. Soon after the railroads were completed, communities grew up to serve ranching, irrigated farming, and mining communities. It is little coincidence that the New Mexico Conference was created immediately after the completion of these railroads. As S. W. Thornton, Superintendent of the MEC New Mexico English Mission reported in 1888, "It was only with the building of the Atchinson, Topeka, & Santa Fe Railway in 1879-80 that these centres (sic) of population sprang up, and our mission work among English speaking people properly dates from that time."

A few examples of disciplinary boundaries before and after the coming of the railroads illustrates the scarcity of population before and the possibilities for church organization afterward. Even with the development of farming, ranching, and mining towns populated mainly by southern Protestants, New Mexico was still solidly Roman

# New Mexico & Trans-Pecos
# Railroad Development

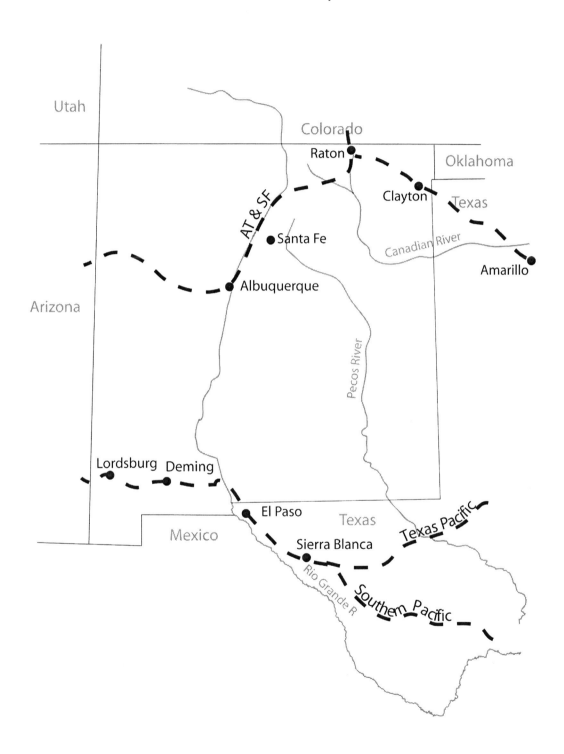

| MECS | 1854 | • California Conference boundaries: California plus New Mexico west of the Rocky Mountains.<br>• Kansas Mission Conference: Kansas plus New Mexico east of the Rocky Mountains. |
|------|------|---|
| MEC | 1860 | • California Conference boundaries: California, the Sandwich Islands (Hawaii), Utah Territory, New Mexico Territory west of the Rocky Mountains.<br>• Kansas Conference : Kansas, Texas, New Mexico east of the Rocky Mountains. |
| MECS | 1886 | • Denver Conference boundaries: Colorado and New Mexico. |
| MEC | 1892 | • New Mexico (English speaking): New Mexico plus El Paso County, Texas.<br>• New Mexico (Spanish speaking): New Mexico, El Paso County, Arizona, Colorado, Chihuahua, Sonora.<br>• Navajo Indian Mission: northeastern Arizona, northwestern New Mexico. |

Catholic. The *Census of Religious Bodies, 1906* reported the following statistics for New Mexico:

> MEC – 3,513 members in 62 churches
> MECS – 2,882 members in 48 churches
> CME – 165 members in 5 churches
> Roman Catholic – 121,558 members in 330 churches

An examination of such statistics reveals one motivation behind the cession of the Trans Pecos region of Texas by the West Texas Conference in 1890. There were too few Methodists in New Mexico Territory to make a viable conference. The addition of the westernmost portion of Texas was necessary for that purpose. El Paso added the most members and had strong historic, cultural, and economic ties with southern New Mexico, Arizona, Chihuahua, and Sonora. The eastern boundary of the conference was later shifted away from the Pecos River to include "oil patch" cities such as Odessa, Monahans, Crane, and Kermit.

*References:*

Hoyt, A. F., "Methodism in New Mexico," *The Gospel in All Lands*, Feb. 1888.

Thornton, S. W.,"Missions Among the English Speaking People of New Mexico," *The Gospel in All Lands*, Feb. 1888.

Harwood, Thom., "New Mexico Spanish Methodist Episcopal Mission," *The Gospel in All Lands*, Feb. 1888.

Walker, Charles Summerfield, Jr., *Southern Methodism on the Last Frontier: The Beginnings of the Southern Methodist Church in the Region Now Embraced by the New Mexico Conference of the Methodist Church 1855-1890*, Bac. Div. Thesis, Southern Methodist University, 1944.

Walker, Randi Jones, "Protestantism in Modern New Mexico," in *Religion in Modern New Mexico*, Ferenc M. Szasz and Richard W. Etulain, ed., University of New Mexico Press, 1997.

*Census of Religious Bodies, 1906.*

CHAPTER 14

# 1900s REDRAWING CONFERENCE BOUNDARIES OF THE MECS

The annual conference boundaries of the United Methodist Church in the 21st century are basically those drawn by the MECS in the first decade of the 20th century. By 1910 the state had been crisscrossed by rail, making all parts the state open to settlement. Urban development in Houston, Dallas, Fort Worth, and San Antonio pointed the way to their future status as regional hubs of commercial activity. Most importantly, population growth in the western part of Texas had produced tensions in the relationships among the conferences of the MECS. The Northwest Texas Annual Conference, created in 1866, embraced both the portions of western Texas being rapidly populated by railroad land promotions and most of the Blackland Prairie, the most populous region of Texas according to the U.S. census of 1900. The North Texas Conference also contained Blackland Prairie Counties, Dallas, Collin, Grayson, and Fannin, the counties which benefited the most from rail connections to the rest of the United States, and gave the North Texas Conference a rapidly expanding population. The Texas and East Texas Conferences, while not declining in absolute membership, were losing ground relative to the explosive growth of the Northwest and North Texas Annual Conferences. A readjustment in the boundary between the Texas and Northwest Annual Conferences had already taken place with the cession of Leon, Falls, Robertson, Milam, Freestone, and part of Limestone to the Texas Conference, but the population imbalance continued.

The arena in which the tensions were aired and finally resolved was the Committee on Boundaries of the General Conference. Petitions from the Texas annual conferences, districts, and even local churches provided much of that committee's agenda in each MECS General Conference from 1866 to 1910. Texas was not without influence in the General Conference. Texas stalwarts such as Robert Alexander (1874) and John H. McLean (1906) chaired the Committee on Boundaries, and the various Texas conferences put some of their most able delegates on that committee.

Although there were several minor adjustments in almost every General Conference, two major boundary reorganizations produced the current boundaries, those of the General Conferences of 1902 and 1910.

## 1902

In 1902 the Texas and East Texas Conferences were combined into a new conference that kept the name Texas Conference. The Austin District of the Texas Conference was moved to the West Texas Conference. Travis County had been an awkward westward projection of the Texas Conference, squeezed between the West Texas and Northwest Texas Conferences. By transferring the Austin District to the West Texas Conference and rationalizing its western boundary, it was giving up some of its oldest churches. Fayette, Colorado, Bastrop, and parts of Matagorda, Wharton, and Austin Counties all became part of the West Texas Conference. Even Rutersville, the site of the founding of the Texas Conference in 1840, was no longer within the boundaries of the Texas Conference.

If the Texas Conference gave up one historic site in 1902, it may be said that it gained another. Its merger with the East Texas Conference meant that McMahan's Chapel would now be within its boundaries.

In addition to receiving Travis County from the Texas Conference, the West Texas Conference also received Mills, Lampasas, Burnet, and part of Williamson Counties from the Northwest Texas Annual Conference. The Northwest Texas Annual Conference continued as the largest Annual Conference in Texas. Its membership of 66,876 in 1900 exceeded the combined membership of the Texas and East Texas Conferences (55,329).

## 1910

The adjustments of 1902 had dealt with the issue of membership imbalance among the conferences by reducing the number of conferences wholly within Texas from five to four. That solution proved to last through only two quadrennia. The basic problem from 1902 to 1910 was that the Northwest Texas Annual Conference was too large. It extended from the densely populated Blackland Prairie counties of Williamson, Bell, McLennan, etc. all the way across the Cross Timbers, Lower Plains, and High Plains to the New Mexico border. In 1900 five of the largest ten churches in Texas Methodism were in the Northwest Texas Annual Conference (Corsicana, Waco, Weatherford, Waxahachie, and Georgetown). As the ranches of western Texas were being converted to farms, population was increasing rapidly in both the Lower Plains and the High Plains. Methodist churches were being organized in the towns that served the farmers of the plains, and a movement to separate the sprawling Northwest Texas Annual Conference gained momentum.

At the 1908 Northwest Texas Conference held in Waco, November 11-17, the issue was defined by competing resolutions. One was offered by Hiram Boaz. He recognized

# 1900s Redrawing Conference Boundaries

## 1902

1. The Texas and East Texas Conferences were combined into a new conference named the Texas Conference.

2. The Austin District of the Texas Conference was moved to the West Texas Conference.

3. The West Texas Conference received territory from the Northwest Texas Conference.

## 1910

The Central Texas Conference was created from the eastern 1/3 of the Northwest Texas Conference.

The new Central Texas Conference had a majority of the membership, and the Northwest Texas Conference had a majority of the area.

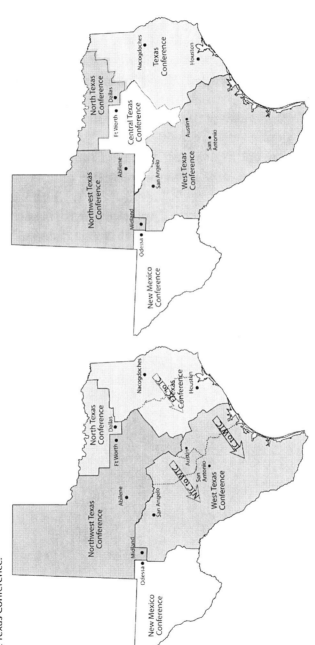

the need to adjust the boundaries, but wished such adjustment to be limited to redrawing the boundary between the West Texas and Northwest Texas Conferences. Horace Bishop offered a substitute motion to appoint a committee to split the Northwest Texas Conference "into two strong conferences." The Bishop motion prevailed over the Boaz motion by a vote of 162 to 107. The committee was appointed with John M. Barcus, a prominent advocate of division, as chair, and Boaz as secretary.

The Committee on Division met at Cleburne on March 24, 1909 and unanimously approved a recommendation to divide the conference along a Young-Stephens-Eastland-Brown County line to the Colorado River. The 1909 Annual Conference meeting in Stamford approved the committee report and petitioned General Conference to enact it.

The General Conference of 1910 acted favorably on the Northwest Texas Annual Conference memorial by creating the Central Texas Annual Conference from the eastern third of the old Northwest Annual Conference. The new Central Texas Conference retained a majority of the membership, and the old conference retained a majority of the area.

The creation of the Central Texas Conference in 1910 was the last major redrawing of conference boundary lines in Texas for at least a century. Those lines, with only a few very minor adjustments, were to last through the mergers of 1939 and 1968, population growth, urbanization, and suburbanization of Texas.

*References:*

*Minutes of the General Conference of the Methodist Episcopal Church South, 1866, 1870, 1874, 1878, 1882, 1886, 1890, 1894, 1898, 1902, 1906, 1910.*

*Journal of the Northwest Texas Annual Conference, 1908, 1909.*

Vernon et al., *The Methodist Excitement in Texas.*

Arbingast et al., *Atlas of Texas*, Bureau of Business Research, University of Texas at Austin, 1973.

# CHAPTER 15

# MP EXPANSION AND CONTRACTION OF ANNUAL CONFERENCES IN TEXAS

The Methodist Protestant Church began as a reform movement in the Methodist Episcopal Church of the 1820s. The same democratic spirit that was reshaping American political life was also affecting church governance. The main expressions of the new spirit in civic life, sometimes referred to as "Jacksonian Democracy", included an expansion of the franchise to include most adult white men and mass political campaigning. Reformers with a democratic bent in the Methodist Episcopal Church focussed on two issues, curbing the episcopal power of appointment and lay representation at annual and general conferences. After failing in their efforts to influence the 1824 General Conference on these subjects, reformers met in Baltimore on November 15 and 16, 1826, to organize an effort to elect delegates friendly to their cause to the 1828 General Conference. One action of the meeting was an effort to increase the distribution of the reformers' periodical, "The Mutual Right of Ministers and Members of the Methodist Episcopal Church", published in Baltimore.

The leadership of the MEC reacted to the reform movement by first suspending and then expelling several of the pastors and laymen leading the reform effort. Expulsions occurred in Maryland, Tennessee, Virginia, Pennsylvania, Ohio, and North Carolina. When the General Conference of 1828 provided no relief to the reformers, they called a general convention for November 1828 to meet at Baltimore. Methodists attending that convention agreed to sever ties to the MEC and form a new church, tentatively named the Associated Methodist Churches. A committee was appointed to prepare a *Discipline* to present to a general conference to be held two year hence.

One hundred fourteen delegates from fourteen annual conferences met in Baltimore on Nov. 2, 1830, adopted the *Discipline* and formed the Methodist Protestant Church. Much of the MP *Discipline* would be familiar to MEC members. There was little change in doctrine. MP polity, though, was radically different. There

71

were no bishops or presiding elders. Annual conferences were retained, but they were presided over by elected presidents who concurrently served churches. Even the president of the annual conference did not have the power of appointment. Preachers were stationed by a "Committee on Stationing" at annual conference. Another provision of the *Discipline* provided for lay delegates to be elected to both annual and general conferences.

## Methodist Protestants in Texas

Dissident members of the MEC began organizing themselves into "societies" in anticipation of the 1830 establishment of the MP Church. One such was the Tennessee Conference, organized in 1829, which sent preachers to Arkansas as early as 1832. One such preacher, William Eliot, moved to Texas in 1837. William P. Smith, who was identified as a local MP preacher and physician, was at the 1835 Caney Creek camp meeting and later was in attendance at Martin Ruter's death in Washington.

In 1839 Revs. R. P. Rucker and J. McClver were sent by the Tennessee Conference to Texas. Two years later the Mississippi Conference was organized with boundaries to include that state plus Louisiana and Texas. Also in 1841 Henry M.A. Cassidy was appointed missionary to the Republic of Texas. Cassidy organized churches in Harris, Washington, Montgomery, and Leon Counties which were affiliated with the Mississippi Conference. In 1846 Louisiana and Texas separated from Mississippi and became the Louisiana Conference.

Cassidy, now living in Leon County, heard about MP preachers from the Tennessee Conference who had moved to northeastern Texas. In 1847 he went to meet with them and obtained consensus that they should attempt to form their own conference. Cassidy then obtained permission from the Louisiana Conference for the creation of a Texas Conference.

The organizing conference was held in Bowie County in 1848. That conference defined its boundaries optimistically as the Sabine River on the east, the Red River on the north, the Gulf of Mexico on the south, and the Pacific Ocean on the west. There were fewer than 120 MP members in all of Texas when the conference was organized. Growth did occur. The reports to the General Conference of 1854 show that the Texas Conference had about 550 members organized into eight circuits.

Other branches of Methodism in the 19th century tended to organize new conferences when population growth justified such a move. The Texas Conference of the MP Church was faced with a different problem. There were three distinct clusters of churches: in the northeast as a result of the missionary activities from Tennessee and Arkansas; between the Trinity and Brazos Rivers around Leon and Robertson Counties; and in the Colorado River Valley. MP circuits tended to be even longer than MEC and MECS circuits, often requiring two hundred miles of travel to complete one round. In the MEC and MECS bishops and presiding elders traveled even more miles than did circuit riders. By doing so they strengthened the bonds that kept the organization together. By rejecting such offices, the MP had to rely on the preachers themselves. The MPs were fiercely democratic, but democracy in the 19th century depended upon face-to-face meetings to conduct business. The long distances between the three clusters of Texas MP churches constituted a huge burden on the preachers who were already in the saddle for months on end. One solution would be to split the territory into smaller conferences.

At its 12th Annual Conference meeting in Leon County in November 1860, the eleven preachers attending the Texas Annual Conference agreed that the Texas Conference be divided into three. The Colorado Conference would be Texas west of the Brazos. The McCaine Conference would include charges between the Trinity and Brazos Rivers, and Texas east of the Trinity would constitute the Texas Conference. The total MP membership in Texas in 1860 was probably less than 600.

The Civil War hampered MP activity in Texas, as it did other denominations, but the Reconstruction era immigration to Texas boosted the MP membership. By the middle of the 1870s, the denomination numbered about 3,500 members. Further conference creation occurred as a result of a dispute in the McCaine Conference in 1878. One faction carried the democratic principles of Methodist Protestantism to the point that they came to believe that churches should have the right to call their preachers. The other faction wished to continue the work of the stationing committees at annual conference. The dispute was resolved by dividing the McCaine Conference. The northern half became the Central Texas Conference and retained stationing committees. The southern half retained the former name and allowed local churches to call their own pastors. The division was brief as the two conferences reunited in 1888 as the Central Texas Conference.

In 1892 the Northwest Texas Mission Conference was organized. Although the new conference hypothetically extended all the way to New Mexico, all the churches were in the Fort Worth vicinity. A similar effort was made through the creation of the Southwest Texas Mission Conference, organized in 1893. That mission eventually had circuits at San Saba, Leakey, Lone Grove, San Angelo, Pontotoc, Noxville, Fredonia, Block House, Cottonwood, and Missionary.

Significant developments occurred for the MP church in the period from 1890-1915. Methodist Protestants had traditionally concentrated their efforts on small, rural churches. The rural population of Texas continued to grow, both on farms and in the new sawmill towns being built in East Texas. In 1906 the various conferences reported their membership:

> Texas Conference – 21 charges
>
> Colorado-Texas (colored) Conference – 12 charges
>
> Northwest Texas Conference – 11 charges
>
> Central Texas Conference – 20 charges
>
> Southwest Texas Mission Conference – 8 charges

# Methodist Protestant Preachers
## 1884

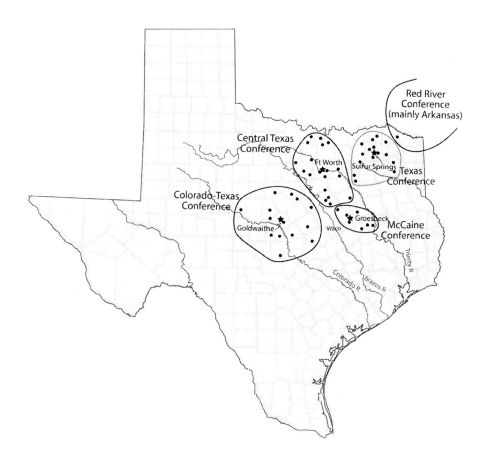

The MP church recognized that growth required expansion into urban areas. It also needed a better educated clergy to preach in the cities. During the period 1890-1915, the MP church attempted to solve both problems. In 1895 it created a college, Westminster, in Collin County near McKinney. When the Presbyterians moved Trinity College from Tehuacana to Waxahachie in 1902, the facilities at Tehaucana were offered to the Methodist Protestants. Westminster College then relocated to Tehuacana in Limestone County. That college was one of the assets the Methodist Protestant Church brought to the 1939 union. Westminster continued as a junior college affiliated with Southwestern University until 1950 when it closed.

Methodist Protestants also directed more efforts to Texas towns. Eventually churches were established in towns such as Paris, Corsicana, Dallas, Greenville, Mount Vernon, Cooper, and Teague.

By the early twentieth century the expansion of the railroads in Texas had effectively ended the main reason for having several conferences in Texas. In a series of consolidations (1912, 1916, and 1929) the five European-American annual conferences in Texas were reduced from five to one. That one conference, the Texas Conference, existed until 1939 and the union of the MP, MEC, and MECS churches.

The map on the opposite page shows the location of Methodist Protestant preachers in 1884.

The Methodist Protestant Church also formed a mission to African-Americans in 1878. The Mission grew so that in ten years it was able to report eight preachers serving 484 members in eleven churches. Eventually the African-American Mission was able to achieve conference status. It was called the Colorado District Conference. The *Constitution and Discipline* (1936) set its boundary as all of Texas west of the Brazos River. Most of its membership was in Hays and Caldwell Counties.

*References:*

Copeland, Kennard Bill, *History of the Methodist Protestant Church in Texas, Commerce Journal,* Commerce, N. D.

Bassett, Ancel H., *A Concise History of the Methodist Protestant Church with Biographical Sketches of Several Leading Ministers of the Denomination and also a Sketch of the Author's Life,* Pittsburgh, 1887.

*The Methodist Protestant Church, The Methodist Protestant Yearbook for 1884, no. III.*

*Minutes of the 49th Annual Conference of the Methodist Protestant Church Colorado/Texas District (colored), 1927.*

# Chapter 16

# THE SOUTHERN CONFERENCE OF THE MEC

The work of the MEC in post-Civil War Texas had striking parallels with that of the Republican Party during the same era. The task for both organizations was to create institutions in regions from which they had previously been excluded. They also had to contend with considerable animosity on the part of white southerners because both party and church were closely linked with abolition of slavery and the triumph of the Union forces in the Civil War. Both the Republican Party and the MEC placed the newly freed African-American at the center of their agenda for Texas. In each institution there was conflict between idealists and realists. Idealists saw the concern for African-Americans as the very embodiment the institution's purpose. Realists recognized that a vigorous struggle for racial equality would result in perpetual minority status. Both political party and church in Texas rested upon a solidly African-American base, but also courted other groups that were not part of the dominant Anglo southern culture.

As one reads the minutes of the various conferences of the MEC, one forms an impression that the denomination always had difficulty with how to organize its work among white southerners in general and white Texans in particular. When the General Conferences of 1872 and 1876 allowed conferences to organize along racial and ethnic lines, the delegates were solving one problem and creating several others. On the one hand, organization of African-American churches into all black conferences was a pragmatic accommodation to southern racism. On the other hand, it deeply distressed some northern Methodists who wanted full equality for African-Americans.

Texas presented a special case for the MEC. The ethnic diversity of Texas was unique among southern states. No other ex-Confederate state had such large numbers of Spanish, Swedish, and German speakers. Finding the best way to organize churches among these linguistic minorities AND English speaking white Texans provided formidable challenges to the MEC. Several conferences, some independent and some

## MEC English Speaking
## White Conferences, 1912

## MEC on Eve of Merger
## 1938-1939
## Southern Conference

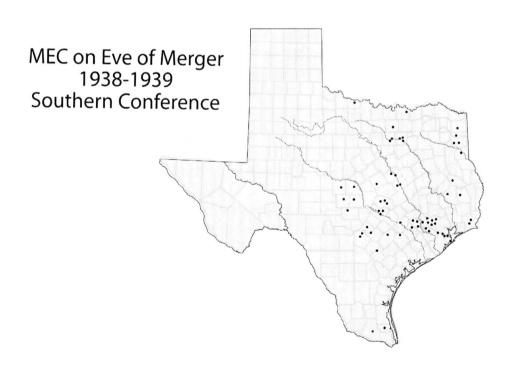

mission, were tried. Combining Texas charges with the neighboring states of Louisiana, Oklahoma, and New Mexico, and with Mexico were all part of the effort. While the African-American conferences (the Texas and West Texas) enjoyed the greatest territorial stability and longevity of any annual conferences in any branch of Texas Methodism, the white conferences of the MEC seemed to be always looking for a new and better way to organize.

The Texas Conference of the MEC was organized in January 1867. Except for the three German pastors in attendance, the pastors were African-American. The Texas Conference existed until 1874 as a biracial institution. Delegates to the 1872 General Conference of the MEC voted to allow the Texas Conference to divide along racial lines. That move was accomplished in 1874 with the creation of two African-American conferences (the Texas and West Texas), and the Southern German conference, After the 1876 General Conference the MEC added the Austin Conference for English speaking whites. Eventually (1912) a Swedish Mission Conference was added. While the German, African-American, and Swedish conferences are considered in other chapters, the work among English speaking whites by the MEC is considered below.

Although most of Texas was included in the Austin Conference in 1877, the designation was little more than lines on a map. For the first ten years of its existence the Austin Conference pursued three emphases, all of which avoided the traditional white Anglo southerner. The first was starting churches in principal cities. The appointments for 1887 show churches in Austin, San Antonio, Waco, Dallas, Fort Worth, and Houston. These growing cities were attracting migrants from the north and provided a constituency for the MEC. A second theme was serving the Swedish Methodists in a "Scandinavian District." This district later evolved into its own mission conference. The third thrust involved planting churches in the Panhandle. The names of Tascosa, Mobeetie, Childress, Clarendon, and Epworth (Hale County) all appear in the appointments for 1887. Church development actually preceded the construction of the Fort Worth and Denver Railroad through the Panhandle.

The eastern counties of Texas were allied with Louisiana through most of closing decades of the 19th and beginning of the 20th centuries. The conference was named Gulf Mission 1895-96, Gulf Mission Conference 1896-1926, and then Southern Conference 1926-1939.

The real boom of MEC work among English speaking whites in Texas waited until railroad land development promotions encouraged northern migration to the coastal plains. The Gulf Coastal Plains of Texas and Louisiana had been largely unsettled until the 1890s. Settlers avoided the region as unhealthy and too poorly drained for farming. Much of the unoccupied land was awarded to railroad corporations as payment for laying track. The railroads then had an incentive to settle those lands.

The result was that the coastal plains of both Texas and Louisiana were criss-crossed by rail lines in the period between 1890 and 1915. Railroad corporations often platted new towns along the rails and then surveyed their extensive holdings into small farms. They marketed their real estate mainly to Midwestern farmers who were being displaced by the increasing mechanization of grain farming. Railroads offered free excursions to Texas and Louisiana to Midwestern farmers idle during the winter months. A typical excursion would include a visit to a demonstration fruit or vegetable farm and a sales pitch. Life on a 10 to 20 acre citrus or berry farm in a semi-tropical climate seemed much more attractive than continuing to try to squeeze a living out of an Iowa grain farm. The result was an influx of northerners to a great arc around the western Gulf of Mexico from approximately Lafayette, Louisiana, to Brownsville, Texas. Place names preserve some of the land development history. Missouri City in Fort Bend County, two Iowa Colonies (one in Brazoria and one in Matagorda Counties), Ohio Colony, and Illinois Colony also in Matagorda County often indicate links to the source of origin of the settlers.

The MEC seemed at times to be part of the sales force for the real estate developers. The *Journal* of the 1896 Gulf Mission of the MEC sought to dispel the lingering doubts about the geography. "An error prevails among some of our church officials that ought be corrected. The territory now occupied by the Gulf Mission is not a waste, marshy and unhealthy section, but is composed of vast table-lands. From the Gulf north there is a strip of perhaps twenty miles of low land…. All the remaining territory is fine table-land, well watered, well settled—emphatically a summer land of fruits and flowers. Sixty thousand northern people are within the bounds of the Mission and others coming." S. J. Manning, District Superintendent of the Rio Grande Valley District of the Gulf Annual Conference mixed images from the Old Testament book of Joshua and 20th century Valley chambers of commerce when he wrote, "I am glad to bring greetings from the Magic Valley, the home of the grape fruit, and a land that flows with milk and honey. By the help of the Lord, we will possess this land." Other MEC journals of the Texas conferences contained advertisements from real estate agents.

MECS preachers were often aware of the immigrants and of their Methodist background. Rev. E. L Shettles of the Texas Conference of the MECS was appointed to Eagle Lake in 1897. The immigrant community of Rock Island was near. Shettles later wrote, "Rock Island was a new town on the Aransas Pass Railroad about 15 miles southwest of Eagle Lake and was settled mostly by people from Iowa, Kansas, and Nebraska, brought there by a townsite company with high hopes, expectations and with a little money that was soon spent. We did our best to encourage them and keep them . . .. It so happened that most of them were Methodist, with a few Baptists."

Many of the MEC churches in Texas were served by pastors who transferred from conferences in the north. The disciplinary question "Who have been received by transfer, and from what Conference?" revealed transfers from eight conferences: Western Swedish, Oklahoma, Northern New York, Northwest Nebraska, Illinois, New England, Missouri, and Wisconsin. On the other hand, it is obvious from District Superintendent reports in the minutes that retention of qualified pastors was a problem.

Carl Urbantke complained that some of the transferring pastors were tuberculosis patients coming south for a cure. There are reports of appointed pastors refusing to serve, of preachers leaving after only two weeks, of pastors returning to the north because their wives refused to live in Texas, and of able preachers going over to the MECS. One such incident occurred at the MEC South Houston church in 1910,

> Upon the strong recommendation of a worthy brother, and request of the representatives of the church, G.F. Clark, a supernumerary of the Northern Minnesota Conference, was appointed to the charge. He began well, captured the people and led in the building of a much needed church which in a few months he left uncompleted and, financially in a serious condition, to preach for the Southern Methodists for whom he had shown a preference and who promised him more money for his services.
>
> (D.T. Summerville, District Superintendent of the Fort Worth District,
> Minutes of the Austin Annual Conference, 1910)

In 1927 the Swedish and German Conferences were merged into the English speaking white conferences. Texas then contained three white conferences which existed until Union with the MECS and MP in 1939: the Southern which also included Louisiana, the Oklahoma, and the New Mexico Conferences.

As Union grew closer, so did anxieties on the part of some of the MEC preachers in Texas. One member of the Southern Conference, Rev. H. C. Leonard, was Associate Superintendent of Department of Church Extension of the Board of Home Missions and Church Extension. That Board's office was in Philadelphia so Rev. Leonard's perspective was that of a southern MEC (not Southern) preacher working in the north and possessing numerous denominational contacts. He wrote his colleague, Rev. H. M. Hopkins of Waco in April 1938

> It has been a surprise to some of our good friends up this way to discover that there are a lot of people down in the South who do not love the Methodist Episcopal people . . .. I heard Frank Smith, now the Bishop, say one time that his Presiding Elder, Caspar Wright, back in 1920 and 1923 had only three reasons against the merger under discussion in that day. They were-1. You could not trust the Yankee before the war. 2. You could not trust the Yankee during the war. 3. You could not trust the Yankee after the war. . . But believe me Brother Hopkins, the presence of us boys as members of some of those Texas conferences is not going to be very pleasing to a good many of those Southern Methodist Preachers . . ..

Such anxieties proved to be relatively unfounded. Hostility to former MEC preachers by former MECS preachers and congregations proved milder in Texas than in states such as Oklahoma and Missouri where the MEC and MECS were more equal. Texas had few MEC preachers by comparison, and they were divided among all six of the MC conferences after the merger rather than being concentrated in one conference. The merger played out differently in different communities. The merger of Norhill (MEC) and Woodland Heights (MECS) in Houston to create St. Mark's Methodist Church was accomplished in 1938 and became a widely-recognized model for other mergers. There were also cases of former MEC and MECS churches choosing not to merge after 1939. St. John's (former MEC) and First (former MECS) continued to serve in Georgetown in very close proximity.

The Texas Conference assimilated about 30 MEC churches, including three in Houston, the largest city of the conference. The former German speaking congregations of Harris, Waller, and Fort Bend Counties constituted another group. Other MEC churches were in the "new" towns of the Coastal Plains such as LaPorte, Texas City, Pearland, and Port Arthur. A fourth cluster of churches to enter the Texas Conference was in Panola, Harrison, Marion, and Cass Counties. The presence of MEC churches in the Piney Woods was mainly the result of the commercial timber industry. After the northern forests of Minnesota and Michigan had been cut, timber companies turned their attention to the South. The MEC followed the workers to the mill towns. These charges had been attached more closely to Louisiana than to Texas and were in the Lake Charles District upon merger.

The Southwest Texas Conference received former German and Swedish churches and two churches in the Rio Grande Valley. The Central Texas Conference received the Swedish churches in Williamson County, German churches in the Waco area and urban churches in Fort Worth and Waco.

The North Texas Conference boundaries contained three churches in Dallas, and one each in Denton, Denison, and Wichita Falls. The Northwest Texas Conference had two small churches in Dalhart and Follet that had previously been associated with the Oklahoma Conference. The MEC work in El Paso was related to the New Mexico Conference.

*References:*

*Journal of the 4th Annual Session of the Gulf Mission of the MEC, 1896.*

*H. C. Leonard to H. M. Hopkins, November 23, 1936,* H. M. Hopkins Collection, Central Texas Conference Archives, James and Eunice West Library, Texas Wesleyan University, Fort Worth, Texas. (Used courtesy of the Central Texas Conference of the United Methodist Church Archive.)

McDonald, Archie, ed., *Recollections of a Long Life by the Rev. Elijah L. Shettles.* Nashville, Blue and Gray Press, Inc., 1973.

Urbantke, Carl, *Texas is the Place for Me,* Pemberton Press, Austin, 1970.

Moers, Raymond, *Twelve Adventurous Decades: 1875-1990,* Houston, 1991.

CHAPTER 17

# AFRICAN-AMERICANS IN THE MEC AND MC

The Texas and West Texas Conferences of the MEC were created by the division of the Texas Conference in 1874. That division had been prompted by the perceived need to divide the African-American and white organizations. The 1876 General Conference ratified the boundaries of the two African-American MEC conferences in Texas. The Texas Conference included

> *So much of the State of Texas as lies east of a line beginning at the Gulf of Mexico on the east side of Matagorda County, and running along said line and the east line of Wharton and Colorado Counties, to the north point of Colorado County, thence north until* (Houston and Texas) *Central Railroad at Calvert; thence along the line of said railroad to the northern boundary of Texas, excluding Calvert and all the towns on the line of said road.*

The West Texas Conference embraced "so much of the State of Texas as is not included in the Texas Conference."

The boundaries thus set were remarkably persistent, especially compared to the boundaries of the other MEC conferences in Texas. The boundaries lasted even past the 1939 merger with the MECS and MP churches. They were not abolished until the UMC abolished the racially based Central Jurisdiction in 1970. That action had been mandated by the 1968 General Conference, but that conference also allowed the conferences two years to plan for the transition. During those two years (1968 and 1969) the Texas Conference of the former Central Jurisdiction was renamed the Gulf Coast Conference to prevent confusion. There was already a Texas Conference in the South Central Jurisdiction.

The Texas and West Texas Conferences both developed schools, mainly to educate African-American preachers and teachers. Both were founded by the Mission Board of

# Conferences of
# MEC (1874-1939)
## &
# MC (1939-1970)
# (Central Jurisdiction 1939)

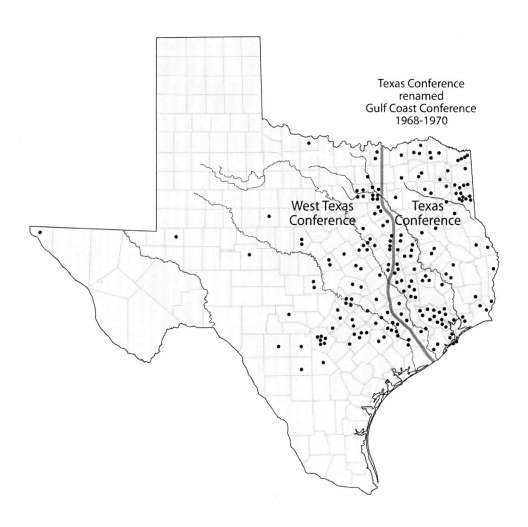

Texas Conference
renamed
Gulf Coast Conference
1968-1970

West Texas
Conference

Texas
Conference

the MEC, and both were beneficiaries of northern philanthropy. Wiley College, in Marshall, was within the bounds of the Texas Conference. It was founded in 1873, chartered in 1882, and renamed in honor of Bishop Isaac W. Wiley who died in 1884. Wiley had been a medical missionary to China before returning to the United States and being elected a bishop. His death occurred in China while on an episcopal visit. Samuel Huston College in Austin was named for Samuel Huston of Iowa who gave $9,000 to the school that opened its doors to receive a class of eighty students in the fall of 1900. Unlike most Methodist schools founded in the latter part of the 19th century, both Wiley and Samuel Huston (Now Huston-Tillotson University) are still in operation.

As might be expected, the Texas and West Texas Conference churches tended to be concentrated in areas of greatest African-American population. As rural African-Americans moved to the cities, the MEC was quite active in establishing neighborhood churches in African-American neighborhoods. In 1938, on the eve of Union, Dallas had six such churches, as did San Antonio. Fort Worth and Marshall had four while Houston was home to thirteen African-American MEC churches.

*References:*

Wilson, James Grant and Fiske, John, eds., *Appleton's Cyclopedia of American Biography, Six volumes,* New York: D. Appleton and Company, 1887-1889.

*Minutes of the General Conference of the Methodist Episcopal Church, 1876.*

*The New Handbook of Texas*

*Journal of the Texas Conference of the MEC 1939.*

*Journal of the West Texas Conference of the MEC, 1939.*

CHAPTER 18

# SPANISH SPEAKING METHODISTS

The Rio Grande Conference of the early 21st century, a Spanish-language conference embracing all of Texas and New Mexico, proudly claims a dual heritage from both the MEC and MECS branches of Methodism. The MEC stream proceeded mainly from Colorado and was most prominent in northern New Mexico. The MECS stream was most closely tied to Texas and especially the West Texas Conference. Its main activities were along the Texas/Mexico border and also in the states of northern Mexico. Since unification of the two streams in 1939 Spanish speaking Methodists in Texas and New Mexico have ministered to congregations in one of the largest annual conferences in the United States in terms of area.

Methodist attempts to evangelize Tejanos date at least to 1834 and David Ayres' distribution of Spanish-language New Testaments in San Patricio. Records from the 1840s and 1850s show instances of Tejano conversions at camp meetings and participation in churches at Corpus Christi, San Antonio, and the Medina River Valley. When the Rio Grande Mission Conference was struck off from the Texas Conference in 1859, four appointments were made to Mexican missions. Unfortunately two of them were left unfilled. The coming of the Civil War and its disruptions brought an end to the early efforts directed toward Spanish speakers in Texas.

After the Civil War the Rio Grande Mission Conference's name was changed to the West Texas Conference, and it slowly began to increase its efforts. A milestone occurred in 1870 when Alejo Hernandez was licensed to preach in Corpus Christi. The following year he was admitted to deacon's orders at the West Texas Annual Conference and appointed to Laredo.

Hernandez's other appointments included Corpus Christi and Mexico City, but unfortunately he suffered a stroke and died at the young age of 33. In the meantime, Rev. A. H. Sutherland had been directed to begin learning the Spanish language, and in 1874 the West Texas Conference created a Spanish speaking district with Sutherland as Presiding Elder. Charges in that district included Corpus Christi, San Diego, Laredo,

Brownsville, and Conception and Presenas. Three Mexican Methodists, Doroteo Garcia, Felipe Cordova, and Fermin Vidaurri, filled those charges. Sutherland vigorously expanded the work of the district so that the next year (1875) San Antonio and Rio Grande City were added to the appointments. The Rio Grande City charge was especially important because the pastor assigned there, Rev. Clemente A. Vivero, also preached at Roma, Mier, and Carmargo.

By 1880 the Spanish speaking district in the West Texas Annual Conference had grown so that it was split into two new districts, the San Antonio and San Diego Districts. The General Conference of 1882, as had the General Conference of 1878, authorized the establishment of an annual conference to be known as the Mexican Border Mission Conference. Its boundary was designated as the same as the West Texas Annual Conference.

By the time the Conference was organized in 1885 such boundary restriction was obsolete. The four district seats included San Antonio, El Paso, Monclova, and Monterrey. The next year Sutherland, as P.E. of the El Paso District, went even further west into Sonora. By 1889, the last year of the existence of the original Mexican Border Mission Conference, its appointments stretched from Guaymas and Mazatlan on the Pacific to Corpus Christi, Texas, on the Gulf of Mexico. Other Texas charges included El Paso, Presidio, Fort Davis, Del Rio, Rio Grande City, San Diego, Laredo, San Antonio, Lodi, San Marcos, Medina, and Bandera. The 1889 Minutes also reported schools in Laredo, Monterey, Nogales, Saltillo, Chihuahua, and Durango. The entire conference reported 1,819 members.

The General Conference of 1890 responded favorably to a petition from the MBMC that it be divided. Accordingly a new conference, the Northwest Mexican Missionary Conference was created to include Chihuahua, Durango, Sinaloa, Sonora, Baja California, and Texas west of the Pecos River. The redrawn Mexican Border Mission Conference would now include Coahuila, Nuevo Leon, Tamaulipas, and Texas east of the Pecos River. The same General Conference created the New Mexico Annual Conference and also used the Pecos River as a boundary. That portion of Texas west of that river became part of the New Mexico Annual Conference, and the West Texas Conference gave up churches in El Paso and other trans-Pecos towns.

The 1890 boundaries were in effect until 1914. As a result of a consultation between missionaries and officials of the Board of Missions held in Laredo in February 1914 the boundaries were redrawn. The years since 1890 had seen huge changes for the borderlands. Railroad and mining activity on both sides of the border had increased developments in both industry and commercial agriculture. The Mexican Revolution had spurred Mexican immigration to the United States. The international border was the scene of tension, violence, and increasing military activity. Spanish speakers in Texas were subjected to worsening racism as discriminatory policies were hardened into institutional form. The reorganization approved by the 1914 General Conference created three new entities, two of which would be bi-national:

1. The Texas Mexican Mission would include churches in Texas east of the Pecos River.
2. The Mexican Border Conference would include Tamaulipas, Nuevo Leon, Coahuila, Chihuahua, Durango, and Texas west of the Pecos River, and New Mexico.
3. The Pacific Mexican Mission would include California, Arizona, Sinaloa, Sonora, and Baja California.

The bi-national organizations lasted only one quadrennium, 1914-1918. Relations between the United States and Mexico during that period were marked by hostilities such as Pancho Villa's raid on Columbus, New Mexico, in 1916. The punitive expedition launched in response, release of the Zimmerman telegram, and many other incidents created problems for Methodist missionaries and mission schools in Mexico. On the other hand, the influx of Mexican immigrants to Texas fleeing the revolutionary turmoil created new opportunities for missionary service and evangelism north of the Rio Grande. Lydia Patterson Institute (for boys) and Effie Eddington School (for girls) in El Paso had a special mission to children of Mexican refugees. The old Laredo Seminary, now named Holding Institute, also had a special mission to Mexican children uprooted by revolution. In 1917 the Mexican Methodist Institute (later Wesleyan Institute) was established in San Antonio. In 1921 it was followed by the Valley Institute in Pharr. The MECS was redirecting its missionary activities from Mexico to the safer locations to which its clients had removed themselves. The directory of missionaries in the *Southern Methodist Handbook* for 1915 lists 35 missionaries appointed to Mexico. Twenty-one of them have addresses in the United States, including eight in El Paso. The *Handbook* also gives the year of initial appointment for each missionary. No appointments are listed for Mexico for 1913-1915.

The 1918 General Conference responded to the turmoil in Mexico by separating Mexican and United States Methodist organizations. Texas east of the Pecos was already in the Texas Mexican Mission Conference. Texas west of the Pecos was part of the Mexican Border Mission Conference with only five appointments in the United States: two in El Paso, Marfa, Toyah, and Alamagordo. That section of the trans-Pecos became part of the new Western Mexican Mission along with California, New Mexico, and Arizona. The 1914-1918 quadrennium also saw a struggle between the MECS Board of Missions and several powerful bishops. As described by Robert W. Sledge in *Hands on the Ark: The Struggle for Change in the Methodist Episcopal Church, 1914-1939,* the organization of conferences in Mexico was the main source of conflict. Bishop Walter Lambuth and staff members of the Board of Missions were in favor of a plan to assign different territories in Mexico to different denominations and thus reduce competition. Bishop Elijah Hoss and several other bishops objected to such a plan. Sledge reports that "the result was an impasse in the guidance of the Mexican missions."

# Spanish Speaking Methodists

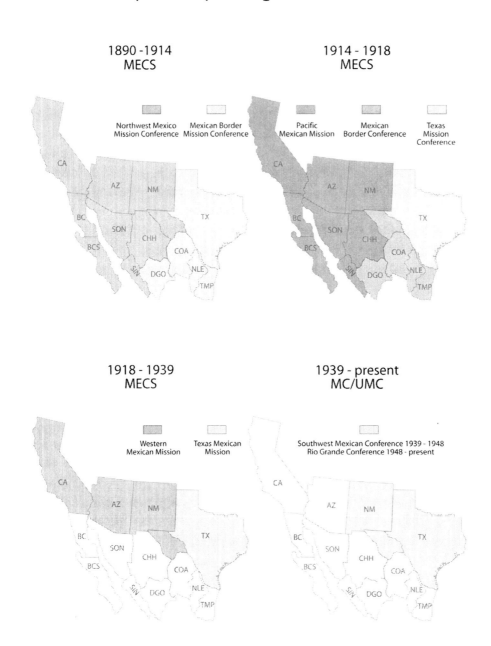

### 1890 -1914
### MECS

Northwest Mexico Mission Conference   Mexican Border Mission Conference

### 1914 - 1918
### MECS

Pacific Mexican Mission   Mexican Border Conference   Texas Mission Conference

### 1918 - 1939
### MECS

Western Mexican Mission   Texas Mexican Mission

### 1939 - present
### MC/UMC

Southwest Mexican Conference 1939 - 1948
Rio Grande Conference 1948 - present

In 1930 both the Texas Methodist Mission Conference and the Western Mexican Mission Conference became annual conferences. Unification in 1939 brought together the Texas Mexican Conference, the Texas portion of the Western Mexican Conference, and the Spanish speaking churches in New Mexico that had been part of the Methodist Episcopal Church into a new conference—the Southwest Mexican Conference. The name chosen at that time was an unfortunate one. Many New Mexicans claimed a Spanish rather than Mexican heritage. Many church members in the conference, although rightfully proud of their Mexican ancestors, could point to several generations of their families living in Texas rather than Mexico. In 1948 the conference name was changed to the Rio Grande Conference.

In 1968 as the racially based Central Jurisdiction was being eliminated, it was necessary to state unequivocally that the Rio Grande Conference was based on language rather than ethnicity. The *Journal of the General Conference* stated "The Rio Grande Annual Conference is not a conference constituted on the basis of race; it is primarily a language conference."

## The MEC

The Methodist Episcopal Church started a modest effort at evangelism in New Mexico soon after the United States acquired that territory as a result of the Mexican War. Benigno Cardenas, a former Roman Catholic priest from New Mexico, became a Methodist and along with Revs. Nicholson and Hansen constituted a mission to New Mexico from about 1853 to 1856. That effort was discontinued, but in 1865 a presiding elder of the Colorado Conference, Rev. John L. Dyer, actually moved to Elizabethtown, New Mexico and preached in northern New Mexico. In 1868, the Colorado Conference created the New Mexico-Rio Grande District with Dyer as presiding elder. In 1872 the General Conference authorized the organization of a New Mexico Mission to serve both Spanish and English speaking Methodists. In 1884, at the request of long-time missionary Thomas Harwood, the mission was divided into English and Spanish speaking missions. In 1889 the English Mission reported ten charges served by eight pastors, as well as appointments to Albuquerque College and a mission to the Navajo Indians. The Spanish Mission that same year had twenty-five appointments. Both the English and Spanish Missions included appointments in El Paso, Texas.

The Women's Home Missionary Society of the MEC also had a great interest in New Mexico. By 1892 it had established schools in Dulce, Las Vegas, Candelaria, and Albuquerque.

By 1892 the New Mexico Mission had prospered enough to change its status from a mission to a mission conference. The next 15 years saw expansion of educational and publishing efforts of the New Mexico Mission Conference under Rev. Thomas Harwood, Superintendent of the mission. In 1907, the seventy-eight year old Harwood was shifted away from the superintendency to run the Boy's School. A period of decline followed, and in 1915 the Spanish speaking mission was reduced to a district in the English speaking mission. That re-organization was followed in 1923 by the creation of the Southwest Spanish Mission in which the Spanish speaking churches of New Mexico, Arizona, Colorado, and Kansas were joined into a new organization. That effort failed to prosper, and in 1931 Spanish speaking churches in New Mexico were added to the Latin American Mission centered in southern California. Once again, the new organization was unworkable, and in 1936 the Spanish speaking New Mexican congregations were attached to the New Mexico English Mission. The final reorganization came in 1939 and unification with the MECS and MP churches. Spanish speaking churches in all of Texas and New Mexico were included in the Southwest Mexican Conference (later Rio Grande Conference). Only four ministers from the Spanish speaking New Mexican MEC joined the new conference when it was organized.

## The EUB

The United Brethren in Christ, a predecessor denomination of the Evangelical United Brethren, also organized evangelical and educational efforts among Spanish speaking persons in northern New Mexico. The short lived North Texas Mission Conference of the UBC (1908-1914) supported Miss Mellie Perkins of Dumas, Texas, as she established a school for Spanish speaking children in Velarde, New Mexico, in 1912. Although the North Texas Mission Conference was dissolved in 1914, the school at Velarde became the basis for the establishment of a high school, the McCurdy School, at Espanola, New Mexico. That school continues under the auspices of the General Board of Missions of the UMC.

*References:*

*Minutes of the Rio Grande Mission Conference of the MECS, 1859, 1861, 1864, 1865.*

Nanez, Alfredo, *History of the Rio Grande Conference of the United Methodist Church,* Bridwell Library, Southern Methodist University, 1980.

"Mexican Revolution" in *New Handbook of Texas.*

*Southern Methodist Handbook, 1915,* Nashville, Southern Methodist Publishing House, 1915.

*Journal of the General Conference of the Methodist Church, 1968.* Page 1228.

Sledge, Robert Watson, *Hands on the Ark: The Methodist Episcopal Church, South: 1914-1939,* Commission on Archives and History, the United Methodist Church, Lake Junaluska, North Carolina, 1975.

Barton, Paul, *Hispanic Methodists, Baptists, and Presbyterians in Texas,* Austin, University of Texas Press, 2006.

Polson, Marvin M., and Dale, William J., "A Summary of the Histories of the Annual Conferences of the former Evangelical United Brethren Church within the bounds of the South Central Jurisdiction of the United Methodist Church", paper presented to the Historical Workshop of the South Central Jurisdiction, Oklahoma City, OK, June 17-18, 1968. Typescript in Bridwell Library of the Perkins School of Theology, Southern Methodist University.

www.mccurdy.org/about_mccurdy/mccurdy_school_history.html

CHAPTER 19

# GERMAN CONFERENCES

The MEC, and later the MECS, were quick to recognize German immigrants to both the United States and Texas as prime candidates for evangelistic efforts. German speaking Wesleyans in the Evangelical Association and United Brethren maintained close ties with English speaking Wesleyans in the Methodist Episcopal Church. Although many of the pre-Civil War German immigrants were free-thinking agnostics who were emigrating in part to escape the abuses of established religion, Methodism was not tainted with the brush of establishment. Besides the agnostics, Lutheran, and Roman Catholic German immigrants, there were also pietistic evangelical Germans for whom Methodism was an attractive option. Even though Methodism made significant strides in the immigrant Texan German community, its effectiveness was limited by the rift between the MEC and MECS. Just as many German immigrants to Texas were placed in a difficult position when confronted with decisions to support the Confederacy or the Union, many also had to decide whether to affiliate with the MEC or the MECS. In both cases one feels empathy for persons caught up in a conflict not of their own making.

Cincinnati, Ohio, assumed an early leadership role among German speaking Methodists. William Nast, of that city, was converted, became a missionary to German immigrants, and founded a newspaper, the *Christliche Apologete*. After the 1844 division, Nast remained with the MEC. Another MEC preacher, Henry Young (originally Heinrich Jung) found himself attached to the Mississippi Conference as missionary to the Germans in New Orleans. In 1845 he was appointed missionary to Texas and soon thereafter established churches in both Galveston and Houston. Thanks to the efforts of Young, Charles Goldberg, Edward Schneider, Charles Rottenstein, and others both the Texas Conference and the Rio Grande Mission Conference of the MECS had German districts before the Civil War. Texas Conference appointments were Galveston, Houston, Bellville, Industry, Round Top, Bastrop, and Victoria. Rio Grande Mission Conference appointments were New Braunfels, Fredricksburg, New

Fountain, Yorktown, Goliad, San Antonio, and Llano Circuit. The combined membership of all German charges was 601 in 1861.

One German Methodist minister's career is worthy of note because it illustrates how fluid denominational loyalties were among Texas Germans. Henry Bauer, a member of the Ohio Conference of the MEC, came to Texas as a missionary to enslaved Texans. Sectional tensions in 1845 were strong enough so that slave holders would not allow a member of the MEC, or for that matter other northerners, to associate with slaves. Bauer's mission to the slaves was a failure, but he did not return to Ohio. Instead in 1848 he joined the Texas Conference of the MECS and received an appointment as missionary to the Germans. He terminated that relationship, moved to Industry, and organized a United Brethren church. Bauer again felt the missionary urge, and in 1854 moved to Nicaragua to serve a German immigrant colony there. He offered his UB church in Industry first to the Lutheran Church and then to the MECS so that they would have a pastor. The MECS accepted the church and appointed Frederick Vordenbaumen to that charge.

The end of the Civil War brought new opportunities for evangelism in the South by the MEC. African-American freedmen were the most obvious targets for MEC efforts, but northern Methodists also looked upon Texas Germans as potential members. An important factor that already linked Texas Germans to the MEC was the fact that many of them, while they were still members of the MECS, used literature from William Nast's MEC publishing offices in Cincinnati. The MECS had too few German speakers to justify extensive publishing efforts.

The minutes of the Annual Conference of the MECS held in Galveston in October 1866 reveal that the charges formerly in the Rio Grande Mission Conference had been transferred to the Texas Conference. They also reveal difficulty in supplying those charges because of the location of six German pastors. The six pastors who located were among the most distinguished in the conference. Presiding Elder Carl Biel was pastor at Industry, the largest church in the German District. Peter Moelling had edited a Texas edition of *Der Christliche Apologete* until 1861. Most of the six had been serving churches near Biel's church in Industry. On August 22, 1866, that congregation voted to change its affiliation from the MECS to the MEC.

When Bishop Matthew Simpson organized the Texas Mission Conference of the MEC in Houston, January 3-5, 1867, three German pastors were admitted on trial. Two of them, Carl Biel and Edward Schneider had located from the MECS the previous October. The third, Carl Urbantke, had been led to the ministry at the Industry church. The following year, two more of the former MECS pastors, Gustavus Elley and Peter Moelling, were admitted to the MEC.

Changing their affiliation from the MECS to the MEC was an act of considerable courage. The MEC was strongly associated with Unionism and abolitionism in the minds of southern whites. MEC preachers had actually moved south with Union armies and occupied buildings which had formerly housed MECS congregations. The

# German Conferences

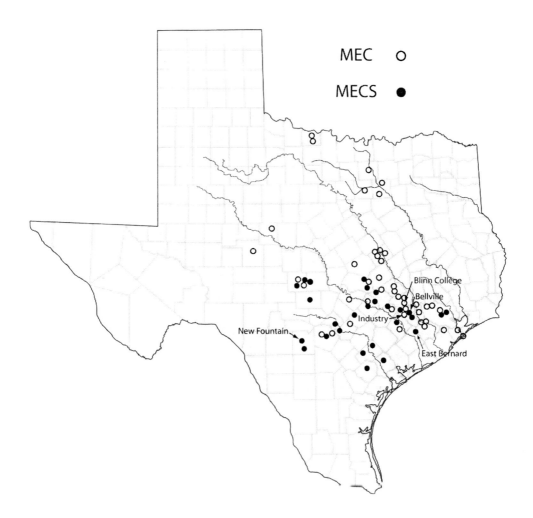

MEC ○

MECS ●

Blinn College

Bellville

Industry

New Fountain

East Bernard

January 1867 organizing conference in Houston had been presided over by Bishop Matthew Simpson, well known for his close relationship with Abraham Lincoln. The three German pastors at the conference were outnumbered thirtyfold by African-American men joining the Texas Mission Conference. While the rigidity of social segregation known as "Jim Crow" did not develop until the 1890s, whites who voluntarily participated in biracial associations in the 1860s subjected themselves to severe social sanctions and even physical danger.

The German District of the Texas Conference ("Misson" was dropped in 1869) of the MEC continued to grow, mainly as congregations, either wholly or in part, switched affiliation. The process was painful, especially when church properties were in dispute. At Industry, for example, members of the new MEC church brought suit in a state court to obtain title to the church property from the MECS congregation that now occupied the property. Such disputes contributed to continuing ill will between members of the two denominations. On the other hand, some communities found ways to cooperate. At Bellville, just fifteen miles from the bitter dispute at Industry, the MEC and MECS congregations shared facilities.

As African-American membership in the Texas Conference grew rapidly and German membership in that same conference grew slowly, tensions arose. A movement to allow racially based conferences began to grow. All great issues in Methodism eventually find their way to General Conference. The 1872 General Conference in Brooklyn, New York, saw passionate debate on the issue of racially defined conferences. On one side were delegates who argued for a vision of brotherhood and equality that was true to the Gospel message of universality in Christ. Proponents of racial conferences pointed to the need to accommodate to local conditions. The General Conference compromised by allowing Texas to divide, but only upon approval by a supermajority. Accordingly, an enabling resolution was passed on June 4, 1872, "that the Texas Conference be and is hereby authorized to divide into two more conferences during the coming year, 2/3 of the members of said conference voting in favor thereof, and the Bishop concurring." Although the Texas situation appeared to be solved, the issue continued into the 1876 General Conference. That conference resolved by a 199 to 97 vote that before a conference could divide into racial conferences a majority of white members and a majority of colored members must agree to the division.

The Texas Conference quickly took advantage of the enabling resolution. A plan was approved which authorized Texas and West Texas Conferences for African-Americans, the Austin Conference for English speaking whites, and the Southern German Conference for German Methodists. That latter conference was organized at Industry on January 15, 1874. Its composition was revealing. Five of its thirteen charter members had been MECS pastors. Four were transfers from northern conferences, and four men were entering from German Texan congregations. With the exception of Edward Schneider who was Swiss, all the preachers had been born in various German states. The boundaries of the new conference included the German churches in New Orleans. The Southern German Conference remained in existence until 1926. Assimilation into the larger English speaking culture and fewer immigrants from Germany decreased the need for German language churches. A merger with the Southern Swedish Missionary Conference and the English speaking Gulf Conference resulted in a new conference, called the Southern Conference which included some charges in Oklahoma.

A continuing legacy of the Southern German Conference is Blinn College in Brenham. The conference recognized the need for an educated clergy, but the MEC schools to train young German pastors were located inconveniently in the north. Blinn began when the preacher appointed to the Brenham church, Carl Urbantke, taught a class of three students in the church building in 1883. Only four years later the Mission Institute, as it was called, received financial support from Christian Blinn of New York, who was travelling through Texas by rail. The Conference renamed the school Blinn Memorial College in gratitude. The presence of Blinn strengthened the MEC in Washington, Austin, and Fayette Counties as students served pastorates while enrolled. Almost 100 preachers were trained at Blinn. Elevation to junior college status in 1927 as public high schools became more common was not enough to provide a continuing flow of students. Merger with Southwestern University, a MECS institution, in 1930 was also an attempt to put Blinn on a stronger financial footing which failed. When church funding was discontinued in 1933, Blinn was left as a private junior college. Its future was finally assured in 1937 when Washington County voters created a junior college district with taxing authority. Blinn continues as a public college with more than 10,000 students on three campuses. It proudly honors its German Methodist heritage in "Old Main" constructed in 1906 one block from the MEC church in which it began, lovingly preserved by the Presbyterians who now occupy that building.

### Germans in the MECS

Just as the 1872 General Conference of the MEC authorized a German conference for Texas which was organized in January, 1874, the 1874 General Conference of the MECS also authorized a German speaking conference in Texas. With that authorization, the German charges that had been part of German districts in the Rio Grande Mission Conference and the Texas Conference before the Civil War and in the Texas Conference during and immediately after the Civil War were organized into the German Mission Conference of Texas and Louisiana. The organizing conference was held at Houston on December 16, 1874 with sixteen preachers becoming charter members of the conference.

The merger of the Louisiana churches into the English speaking conference in that state in 1886 provided the occasion to rename the conference "German Mission Conference." Another name change at the General Conference of the MECS in 1918 to "Southwest Texas Annual Conference" was accompanied by permission to merge its work with the Texas and West Texas Conferences. The last session of the conference was held at New Fountain in October 1918. There were 1,800 members served by 22 preachers and 18 local preachers when it merged. Two churches in Houston (Bering Memorial and Beneke Memorial) and one in East Bernard fell within the bounds of the Texas Conference. All others became part of the West Texas Conference (now named the Southwest Texas Conference.) The former German Mission Conference charges were all placed in a special district called the Southwest District with a former German Mission Conference member as presiding elder. Eventually the German charges in that special district were assimilated into the West Texas Conference.

The German Mission Conference of Texas and Louisiana authorized a school at its first session. Fredericksburg College operated in the closing years of the 19th century until its sale to the city of Fredericksburg for use as a public school. Southwestern University also attracted German Texan Methodists because of its proximity to the majority of MECS German churches.

An examination of the German churches in the MEC and MECS reveals spatial differentiation. To use Terry Jordan's terms, German Methodists on "the Rim of the Desert" were more likely to be MECS, and German Methodists in the "Cotton Kingdom" were more likely to be MEC. The MECS membership was concentrated in the Colorado and Guadalupe River basins while the MEC membership tended to be farther east in the Brazos and San Jacinto watersheds. German Methodists in Washington, Austin, Fayette, Fort Bend, Waller, and Harris Counties were much more likely to be affiliated with the MEC. As a matter of fact, the MECS church at East Bernard mentioned above as only one of three to be in the bounds of the Texas Conference, was that far east only because in 1893 the congregation moved *en masse* from near Weimar, bringing their pastor and church building with them. On the other hand, Medina, Llano, Mason, and other western counties tended to be more MECS. There were several towns that had German churches of both branches, but they tended to merge over time as the reasons for separation receded into the past. For example, the MECS church in Industry was abandoned in 1903 and the members simply moved to the MEC church.

*References:*

*Journal of the General Conference of the Methodist Episcopal Church, 1872, 1876.*

Anon., *The One Hundred Fiftieth Anniversary of the Industry United Methodist Church, Industry, Texas,* n.d. (1997)

Douglass, Paul F., *German Methodism: Biography of an Immigrant Soul, Cincinnati, Methodist Book Concern, 1939.*

Schmidt, Bruno Carl, *A History of the Southern German Conference,* B.D. thesis, School of Theology, SMU, 1935

Borchardt, Craig William, *German Lutheran Transplants and Methodist Converts in Austin and Washington Counties, Texas, 1860-1930,* Ph.D. dissertation, Texas A&M University, 1996.

*Minutes of the Texas Mission Conference of the MEC, 1867, 1868.*

*Minutes of the Texas Conference of the MEC, 1869.*

*Minutes of the Texas Conference of the MECS, 1861, 1865, 1866.*

Radetzky, F. W., *"Our German Work: a Few Dates and Condensed Facts," in Texas Methodist Centennial Yearbook,* Olin W. Nail, ed., 1934.

*Kurze Gesichichte der Suedlich-Deutchen Konferenz zum 50jaehrigen Jubilaeum, 1922.*

*Urbantke, Karl Texas is the Place for Me, Ella Urbantke Fischer, translator, Austin, The Permberton Press, 1970.*

*New Handbook of Texas*

Jordan, Terry, *German Seed in Texas Soil,* Austin, University of Texas Press, 1966.

Schmidt, Charles F., *History of Blinn Memorial College, 1883-1934,* San Antonio, Lodovic Printing Co., 1934.

CHAPTER 20

# SOUTHERN SWEDISH MISSION CONFERENCE

Organized efforts to promote Swedish immigration to Texas began in 1847 when Swante Swenson, a Swede who had been living in Texas since 1838, offered to pay passage for Swedes willing to work on his Texas farms. The first group of immigrants arrived in 1848 and began working on farms in Fort Bend County. Swenson relocated to a ranch just east of Austin, and his fellow countrymen moved with him. Swenson and his uncle, Swante Palm, continued to encourage Swedish immigration. Eventually Travis and Williamson Counties had significant numbers of Swedes, most of whom lived in small farming communities.

Swedish Texas Methodism dates from 1871 when C. C. Charnquist arrived in Austin and began the work of the church as part of the MECS. Upon Charnquist's move to Kansas in 1880, the congregation switched its affiliation to the MEC.

A second wave of Swedes immigrated to Texas in the 1890s. These immigrants tended to come not from Sweden, but from the Great Lakes region of the United States. Travis and Williamson Counties continued to lead the state in Swedish population, but the newer immigrants also found homes in other parts of the state including the Rio Grande Valley and Coastal Plains.

In 1896 the Austin Conference of the MEC created a Swedish District with O. E. Olander as superintendent. In 1912 the Austin Conference was dissolved and the Southern Swedish Mission Conference was created. Most of the churches that made up the Southern Swedish Mission Conference were in Williamson and Travis Counties. The two largest churches were in Georgetown and Austin, the respective county seats. Smaller churches existed in the area at Decker, Manda, Hutto, and Taylor. Churches also existed in Galveston, Crosby, Houston, Brady, El Campo, Waco, Lyford, Dallas, Fort Worth, and Kenedy.

In 1926 the MEC merged the Southern (German) Conference, the Gulf Conference (white, English speaking), and Southern Swedish Mission Conference into a new conference called the Southern (United) Conference.

99

# Southern Swedish
## Mission Conference MEC
## 1912 - 1927

Although the Southern Swedish Mission Conference never had as many as 2,000 members, it provided support for two institutions. The first was Seaman's Bethel which provided hospitality at the port of Galveston. Much of the expense of the Bethel was underwritten by the Swedish Consul, Mr. Adoue. The other institution, located in Austin, was Texas Wesleyan College, which came into existence with the appointment of a board of trustees in 1909. The first building on the twenty-one acre campus was situated between 24th and 26th streets and Waller Creek and Red River Street (The site is currently occupied by the University of Texas School of Law.) and was completed in time for the first students to enroll in January 1912. Texas Wesleyan College served its constituents until the 1930s. Economic difficulties and continuing assimilation of Swedish Texans into the majority culture reduced enrollments. In 1935 the trustees changed the name to Texas Wesleyan Academy and discontinued academic instruction in 1936. The Academy continued to offer music instruction until 1956.

Unlike most church colleges which are forced to cease operation, Texas Wesleyan College enjoyed considerable assets. Its proximity to the University of Texas and that university's desire to expand made its campus valuable. In 1931 the trustees sold the grounds to the University of Texas for $135,000 and retained the right to use the buildings. In 1936 the trustees loaned $100,000 to Texas Wesleyan College in Fort Worth, a MECS institution. Texas Wesleyan College filed suit against Texas Wesleyan Academy in an attempt to cancel the debt. The courts eventually ruled in favor of the College and a compromise was agreed upon that most of the Academy's assets would be turned over to the College. A portion of the assets, though, was reserved for funding college scholarships for Swedish Methodist Texans. That fund provided scholarships until 1977.

Counties with largest population born in Sweden, 1910 Census:

> Travis – 1,061
> Williamson – 798
> Galveston – 440
> Harris – 237
> Tarrant – 237
> Wharton – 234

*References:*

*The New Handbook of Texas*

Journal of the 12th Annual Session of the Southern Swedish Mission Conference.

Journal of the 15th Annual Session of the Southern Swedish Mission Conference.

Protokoll fordt vid Sodra Svenska Missions-Konferensens of the Metodist Episkopal Krykan.

Westerberg, T. J., "Svenska Metodistkyrkan I Texas" and "Svenska Hogskolor: Texas Wesleyan College", in *Svenskarne I Texas I Ord Och Bild: 1838-1918*, Severin.

13th U.S. Cenus, 1910

CHAPTER 21

# THE EVANGELICAL UNITED BRETHREN CHURCH

The Evangelical United Brethren Church (EUB) was formed on November 16, 1946, by the merger of the Evangelical Association and the United Brethren in Christ. Both churches claimed a German Wesleyan heritage. Their early history is summarized in the *Discipline:*

> As The Methodist Episcopal Church was in its infancy, two other churches were being formed. In their earliest years they were composed almost entirely of German-speaking people. The first was founded by Philip William Otterbein (1726–1813) and Martin Boehm (1725–1812). Otterbein, a German Reformed pastor, and Boehm, a Mennonite, preached an evangelical message and experience similar to the Methodists. In 1800 their followers formally organized the Church of the United Brethren in Christ. A second church, The Evangelical Association, was begun by Jacob Albright (1759–1808), a Lutheran farmer and tilemaker in eastern Pennsylvania who had been converted and nurtured under Methodist teaching. The Evangelical Association was officially organized in 1803. These two churches were to unite with each other in 1946 and with The Methodist Church in 1968 to form The United Methodist Church.
>
> 2000 *Discipline*

Both of the predecessor denominations organized churches in Texas. The Evangelical Association responded to appeals from Rev. Frederick Vordenbaumen (MECS) of Houston and Rev. August Arnold (MEC) of San Antonio to send preachers to serve German speaking Texans. After a visit to Texas by EA Bishop J. J. Escher in 1879, the Board of Missions authorized mission stations in Galveston and San

# Evangelical United Brethren
## Churches at Time Of
## EA, UB Merger
## (1946)

Antonio. Rev. J. M Gomer of the Indiana Conference volunteered for Galveston and Rev. Daniel Kreh of the Canada Conference for San Antonio. By 1887 the mission had grown to seven charges and 253 members. That same year, on November 25, the work was organized into the Texas Annual Conference at Temple. The seven charges were at Galveston, Temple, San Antonio, Sherman-Denison, Post Oak (southeast of San Antonio), and near Wichita Falls. As immigrants from the north arrived in Texas in the period from 1890 to 1914, the EA organized churches to serve them. Lissie and El Campo, both on the coastal plains, and Henrietta and Bowman in north Texas all added EA churches. The number of new churches was unsustainable. Following World War I the pattern was that of retrenchment and consolidation. As reported in the 1947 *Proceedings*, ". . . the Texas Conference history has not been very encouraging from the viewpoint of a rapid growth in churches or membership . . . the early years were not stable years, although some churches were becoming well established. Others were abandoned and never taken up again. "

The United Brethren Church had an even smaller membership in Texas than did the Evangelical Association. That denomination had organized a North Texas Conference in 1908 and ratified the organization at the General Conference in 1909. The North Texas Conference consisted of New Mexico, the Texas Panhandle, and the three counties in Oklahoma that make up that state's panhandle.

A Texas charge, Middlewater in Hartley County, existed, but most of the churches were in either Oklahoma or New Mexico. The North Texas Conference of the UB dissolved in 1913 after never holding an annual conference in the state for which it was named.

When the EA and UB merged in 1946, the Texas Conference had seven charges, the same number as the EA's organizing conference in 1887. Those seven included First El Campo, Oaklawn in Houston, First Lissie, Zion Post Oak, First San Antonio, First Temple, First Wichita Falls. The total membership reported was 1,247. First San Antonio was the largest church with 356 members.

In 1968 the Methodist Church and the Evangelical United Brethren Church merged creating the United Methodist Church.

*References*:

Marvin M. Polson and William J. Dale, "A Summary of the Histories of the Annual Conferences of the former Evangelical United Brethren Church within the bounds of the South Central Jurisdiction of the United Methodist Church," pamphlet in collection of Bridwell Library, SMU.

*Proceedings of the Fifty-ninth Annual Session Texas Conference of the Evangelical Church*, 1946.

*Proceedings of the Sixtieth Annual Conference of the Evangelical United Brethren Church*, 1947.

*Journal of the Texas Conference of the Evangelical United Brethren Church, Sixty-ninth Annual Session, 1956.*

www.umc.org

CHAPTER 22

# THE CREATION OF THE
# METHODIST CHURCH IN 1939

The creation of the Methodist Church in 1939 by the unification of the MEC, MECS, and MP denominations was one of the most significant events in the history of Methodism. Nineteenth century disputes over church governance and slavery were finally resolved, and the unified church looked forward to greater avenues of witness and service in a denomination no longer encumbered by regionalism. Many Methodists believed that their denomination most closely approximated a sort of American national religion that Robert Bellah later termed "American Civil Religion." Methodists were the most widely distributed denomination in the United States. Roman Catholics predominated in New England, southern Louisiana, and the Southwest. Lutherans constituted a majority in Scandinavian and German ethnic enclaves. Mormons constituted an absolute majority of the population in Utah. Baptists and Presbyterians remained divided into northern and southern branches, but Methodists after unification had almost complete "coverage" of the United States.

Methodists were also representative of "average" America in terms of social class. The Holiness Movement of a previous generation, although deeply rooted in Methodism, had spawned new pentecostal denominations. Methodist defections to those denominations had come mainly from the lower economic classes, thereby making Methodism even more middle class than it had been. Socialist challenges to capitalism as enunciated by the Social Gospel preachers of a previous generation had also faded. The northern and southern branches of the church that merged were very much alike. They were solidly middle class and moderate throughout both urban and rural areas. Methodists looked like a "snapshot" of America.

When one dug a little deeper, however, one was able to find that at least one regional difference did exist and demanded some sort of compromise. That difference was what to do about African-Americans? The MEC and the MECS, although almost identical in doctrine and polity, differed in implementing segregation of African-

105

# Creation of the Methodist Church in 1939

## South Central Jurisdiction*

* also included Southwest Mexican (now Rio Grande)
and Oklahoma Indian Missionary Conferences

## Central Jurisdiction

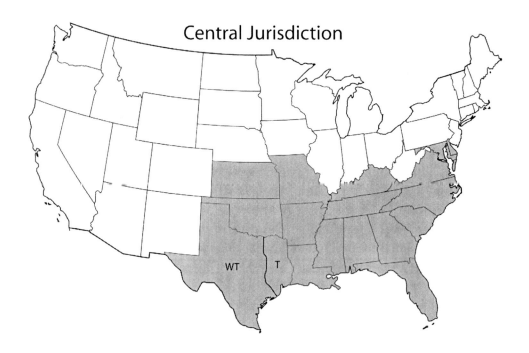

American and white Methodists. The MECS sponsored the creation of a new denomination, the Colored Methodist Episcopal Church (CME). By 1890 Bishop Keener could boast to the General Conference of the MECS, ". . . we have now a solidly white church, for which we thank God." The minutes of the General Conference report that applause followed Bishop Keener's declaration. The MEC, on the other hand, created African-American mission conferences as early as 1864. By 1925, when the South Florida Conference was founded, there were nineteen African-American annual conferences in the MEC. Two of those, the Texas and West Texas Conferences, were in Texas. Any plan of union had to deal with those nineteen conferences. A majority of the delegates of the MECS **and** the MEC would not even consider any unification arrangement that did not honor racial segregation. The solution, just as had been the case in the creation of the United States of America by the constitution, was federalism. In the case of the United States it was dividing powers between the federal government and the states. In the case of Methodism, it meant creating new geographic entities and investing them with one very important power.

The new geographic entity created by unification was the Jurisdiction. The United States was divided into six jurisdictions. Five of the jurisdictions were based on geography—Northeast, Southeast, North Central, South Central, and Western. The sixth jurisdiction, the Central Jurisdiction, included the nineteen African-American conferences that had formerly been part of the MEC. Election of bishops was transferred from the General Conferences to Jurisdictional Conferences. Such elections would constitute the only real power of the jurisdiction. Ultimate authority about doctrine and polity would remain with the General Conference.

The assumption that some sort of jurisdictional plan would be necessary for unification was so widely held that several proposed jurisdictional plans were proposed. In 1920 a plan was tendered that put Texas in a jurisdiction with Missouri, Arkansas, Louisiana, Oklahoma, New Mexico, and Arizona. In the final plan, though, the white and Spanish speaking Texas conferences were included in the South Central Jurisdiction along with Missouri, Kansas, Nebraska, Arkansas, Louisiana, Oklahoma, and New Mexico. The Oklahoma Indian Missionary Conference with two churches in Texas (Dallas and near Paris) would also be part of the South Central Jurisdiction. The two African-American conferences in Texas became part of the Central Jurisdiction.

The creation of the jurisdictions eased MECS fears. Methodist bishops had church-wide authority. There were more Methodists in the North than the South. It was therefore conceivable that an African-American could be elected bishop and assigned to a southern conference. If the power to elect bishops were transferred from the General Conference to the Jurisdictional Conference, no such episcopal assignment would occur.

The creation of the South Central Jurisdiction would enhance the chances of white Texans to be elected bishop, and the creation of the Central Jurisdiction would guarantee the election of African-American bishops. Two Texans, Willis King and Edward Kelly were elected bishops in 1944 by the Central Jurisdiction.

The certain prospect of electing African-American bishops was little solace to African-American Methodists who saw institutional racism strengthened by the juris-dictional system. African-American delegates to the Uniting Conference at Kansas City in 1939 recognized the creation of the Central Jurisdiction for what it was—a monumental humiliation. There were forty-seven African-American delegates. Thirty-six of them voted against the Plan of Union, the other eleven abstained.

The humiliation deepened at the first General Conference of the newly-formed Methodist Church in 1940 when the Committee on Special Days recommended that the offering for African-American Methodist colleges be divided between historically black MEC colleges such as Wiley College and Colored Methodist Episcopal Church colleges.

Although African-American and white Methodists shared denominational affili-ation after 1939, there was practically no interaction between the churches and church members in the Central and South Central Jurisdictions. Some church institutions such as SMU and Mount Sequoyah would be connected to the jurisdiction, and since the jurisdiction was all white, those institutions could be also. Until the Central Jurisdiction was dissolved in 1970, white and African-American Methodist Texans operated almost completely in separate spheres.

Although the jurisdictional system had been enacted to deal with race, there were also important geographic implications for Texas. As members of the MECS, the Texas annual conferences had been the southwestern extension of a region that was anchored in Virginia, Tennessee, Alabama, the Carolinas, and Georgia—well to the east of Texas. The interposition of Roman Catholic Louisiana and relatively small population states of Arkansas and Mississippi meant that MECS membership assumed a sort of dumbbell shaped distribution. Texas's substantial Methodist population made it a substantial southwestern anchor, but the real core of the MECS was east of the Mississippi—as reflected in membership, institutions, site of the quadrennial General Conferences and election of bishops. Of the 24 sessions of the General Conference of the MECS, seven were held in cities later to be included in the South Central Jurisdiction. The following chart of membership in MECS annual conferences in 1939, the year of unification, shows clearly that the majority of MECS membership (and therefore votes at General Conference) was well to the east of Texas.

### Fifteen largest MECS annual conferences, 1939

*(Italics indicate conferences whose territory was included in the South Central Jurisdiction.)*

| | |
|---|---|
| Virginia | 168,780 |
| Western North Carolina | 161,780 |
| North Georgia | 156,978 |
| North Alabama | 142,933 |

| | |
|---|---|
| North Carolina | 129,481 |
| Holston | 122,700 |
| *Texas* | 118,405 |
| South Georgia | 116,316 |
| Memphis | 97,007 |
| *Central Texas* | 96,902 |
| Tennessee | 96,823 |
| Baltimore | 96,556 |
| Alabama | 95,602 |
| *North Texas* | 93,559 |
| *Oklahoma* | 88,324 |

The creation of the jurisdictions and the placement of Texas in the South Central Jurisdiction changed that situation. After 1939 Texas delegates would constitute a larger percentage of the conferences which elected bishops. The historic cultural and economic ties with Louisiana, Arkansas, New Mexico, Oklahoma, and Missouri would be enhanced. With the exception of the Methodist Kansas wheat farmers who settled the northernmost counties of the Texas Panhandle, Texas Methodism had few historic ties with Kansas and Nebraska. Those states had large Methodist populations, but they had been in the MEC, and therefore mainly unknown to Texas Methodists. Oklahoma also had a large MEC population, so much so that after unification, its territory was divided into two conferences, East and West. Even with the inclusion of Kansas and Nebraska, the South Central Jurisdiction's boundaries were geographically coherent. They showed a new identity, less southern and more southwestern.

*References:*

Moore, John M., *Long Road to Methodist Union,* New York, Abingdon Press, 1943.

MECS, *Minutes of the Annual Conferences, and Methodist Year Book,* 1939.

MC, *Minutes of the Annual Conferences,* 1940.

MECS, *Minutes of the General Conference,* 1890.

Thomas, James S. *Methodism's Racial Dilemma: The Story of the Central Jurisdiction,* Abingdon, Nashville, 1992.

CHAPTER 23

# THE MP CHURCH
# ON THE EVE OF UNION

The proposed Plan of Union was the most important item to come before the Texas Annual Conference of the Methodist Protestant Church as it met in 1936. The General Conference of the MP Church had already overwhelmingly approved the Plan as it met in High Point, North Carolina, earlier in the year. Annual conferences had been instructed by the General Conference to vote on the issue as they met the following fall.

Two powerful men in favor of Union were in attendance as the members of the conference, both clergy and lay, met to debate the issue. Rev. J. A. Richardson, president of the Texas Annual Conference, had been a delegate to the General Conference and now presided over the debate. The president of the General Conference, Dr. J. H. Straughn, had come to Texas to lend his influence to the cause of Union. Although the majority sentiment favored Union, that feeling was not unanimous. Rev. M. B. Howell, pastor of the MP Church in Corsicana, argued that the democratic principles upon which the Methodist Protestant Church had been founded would be sacrificed as the episcopal system of the MECS and MEC churches would continue in the new Methodist Church. Methodist Protestant members of the Commission on Church Union had argued for term episcopacy as a compromise but failed in that effort. When the issue of Union finally came to a vote at the Texas Annual Conference, it passed by a wide margin. It was obvious to all that the Texas heritage of the MP Church would continue in a different form.

The Texas Annual Conference by the 1930s consisted of fewer than thirty preachers serving about 3,500 members in about 70 churches, eight of them designated as "station" and the rest charges on a circuit. Such figures revealed that the MP Church was declining in membership as the population of Texas increased. Greater efficiency had been achieved by consolidating conferences. The conference boundaries in the 1936 Constitution and Discipline of the Methodist Protestant Church delimited the

# Methodist Protestant Church
## 1939

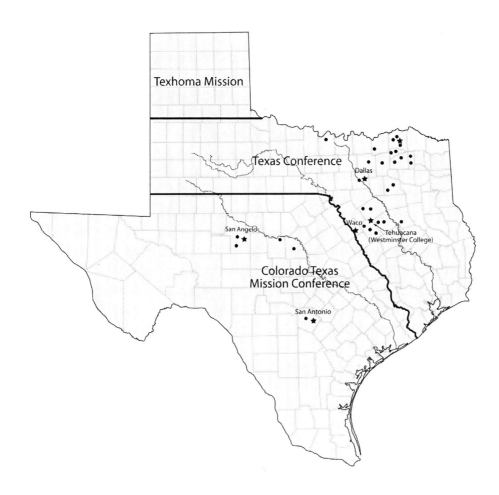

Texhoma Mission

Texas Conference

Dallas

Waco

Tehuacana
(Westminster College)

San Angelo

Colorado Texas
Mission Conference

San Antonio

Texas Conference boundary as "the entire state of Texas, except that portion of the panhandle north of a line from Childress, Texas, to the New Mexico border." North of that line was the Texhoma Mission. Texas west of the Brazos was the "Colored Mission" named the Colorado-Texas Mission Conference. Methodist Protestants diagnosed their lack of growth. Their core constituency had been very small rural churches served by relatively uneducated pastors. The founding of Westminster College in 1895 was intended to upgrade the educational level of the pastors, but the increasing urbanization of Texas meant that the pool of potential members was shrinking.

An examination of the Minutes of the Eighty-Eighth Session of the Texas Annual Conference of the Methodist Protestant Church shows that attempts were being made to increase the MP urban presence. Churches in Dallas, Paris, San Angelo, and Corsicana all boasted over 100 members as did Tehuacana, home of Westminster College. Most of the appointments, though, followed the traditional pattern of churches being points on a circuit. An examination of the location of the MP churches reveals their strength in those areas of Texas heavily influenced by immigration from the Upper South. MP churches did not exist in areas settled by immigrants from Europe or the northern United States such as the Coastal Plains and Rio Grande Valley.

Fears about loss of distinctive identity after Union were well-founded. The disparity in membership between the MP and the MECS meant that the MC would have much more of a MECS "flavor" after Union. Westminster College in Tehuacana became a Methodist Church institution in 1939. It ceased operations in 1950. The most important legacy of the MP Church were the lay members and clergy who continued on in the MC after Union. One of the preachers, Kenneth Copeland, was elected to the office of bishop in 1960.

*References*:

Copeland, Kennard Bill, *History of the Methodist Protestant Church in Texas*, Commerce, *Commerce Journal*, n.d.

*Minutes of the 88th session of the Texas Annual Conference of the Methodist Protestant Church, 1935.*

*Constitution and Discipline of the Methodist Protestant Church, 1936.*

# CHAPTER 24

# A TYPICAL CIRCUIT OF
# THE MID-TWENTIETH CENTURY
### (DeKalb Circuit of the Texarkana District of the Texas Conference)

Improvements in transportation during the twentieth century caused huge changes in Texas Methodism. The planting of churches in suburbs made possible first by streetcars and then by autos is discussed in another chapter. Transportation improvements were also significant in rural areas. Regular train and bus service enabled college and seminary students to serve appointments many miles from their campuses. A young man (No women were admitted to elder's orders until later.) did not have to choose between beginning his ministry and obtaining higher education. Rural churches benefited by having a larger pool of potential ministers from which to draw. The senior author of this *Atlas* has provided a memoir of his ministry on the DeKalb Circuit which he served as a nineteen-year old junior at SMU.

DeKalb Circuit in Bowie County Texas clustered around DeKalb in the Texarkana District of the Texas Conference. There were five churches on the circuit

> Austin Chapel – three miles east southeast of DeKalb
> Dalby Springs – ten miles south of DeKalb
> Hubbard (Lawrence Chapel) – four miles south of DeKalb
> Oak Grove – four miles west of DeKalb
> Spring Hill – twelve miles north-northwest of DeKalb

In April 1941 while I was in my third year of college, I was appointed pastor of this circuit, serving until November when annual conference met. These churches had been grouped as a circuit for less than five years. Some of the churches had been on other circuits and some were served by the pastor of First Methodist DeKalb. First Methodist Church DeKalb requested a full-time pastor so the DeKalb Circuit was organized. The total annual salary from these five churches was $633. Spring Hill, the most prosperous church, accepted one-half that amount and, as a result, had services twice

# DeKalb Circuit

of the Texarkana District
of the Texas Conference
early 1940's

Oklahoma

Arkansas

● Spring
  Hill

● Oak Grove

  ● DeKalb

Hubbard ●   ● Austin Chapel

● Dalby Springs

Bowie County

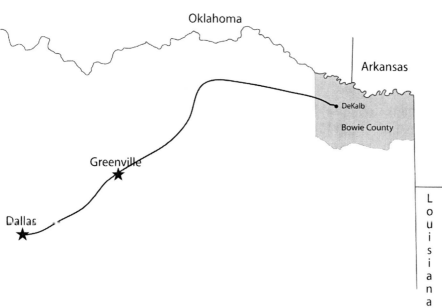

Oklahoma

Arkansas

● DeKalb

Bowie County

Greenville

Dallas

Louisiana

per month, morning and evening. Another Sunday was given to Dalby Springs, and another to Hubbard. Services at Oak Grove were held only one afternoon per month, and Austin Chapel had services once per month on a Saturday night. Its contribution to the total salary was $50. The fifth Sunday of a month was rotated among the churches. One dollar in every ten collected for the preacher's salary was given to the presiding elder.

In addition to the appointment, I was also enrolled in SMU with a schedule that included Saturday morning classes. After my last class I would walk from campus to Greenville Avenue and flag down a Greyhound bus that would leave Dallas around noon and arrive in DaKalb about 5 o'clock. All of the churches on the circuit served farm families. Some owned a few acres. Others were tenants. They grew cotton and corn and most had a few acres of tomatoes which were shipped green from DeKalb. On Saturdays they came to town for their shopping. The streets of DeKalb were filled with these families so that I never failed to find some family from the community where I was to preach the following morning ready to take me home and to church the next morning. When I had a Saturday evening or Sunday afternoon service, they would help me find transportation to keep that appointment. Following the Sunday night service, someone would drive me back to town where I would catch a bus in DeKalb headed for Dallas sometime before midnight. I would usually arrive back in Dallas a few hours before sunrise and have a couple of hours of sleep before meeting my Monday morning Greek class. Although an understanding Greek professor, Dr. John Strayer McIntosh, gave me a respectable grade in the course, that schedule gave me an excuse for not becoming an outstanding Greek scholar.

My appointment was the result of my seminary friend, Harold Fagan, who was serving the Mount Pleasant Circuit, taking me to see Presiding Elder L. W. Nichols on Easter weekend in April 1941. P. E. Nichols appointed me to take the DaKalb Circuit immediately. My first Sunday was April 20, 1941. I rode the bus from Dallas to DeKalb and went to a café operated by Ocie McBeth. Joe Gay met me there and took me to his home at Spring Hill to spend the night. The next morning I preached to ninety people at Spring Hill on "The Meaning of the Resurrection" using Colossians 3:1 as my text. That afternoon Joe Gay took me to Oak Grove where I preached to fifty people on "Friends of Jesus" from John 15:14. Spring Hill also had an evening service with about fifty people in attendance to hear "Man's Values Versus God's Values" based on Proverbs 14:12. Following that service one of the members took me back to DeKalb to wait for the bus that would take me back to Dallas.

When the semester ended in May, I gave full time to the churches for the summer. I took a room in the Austin Hotel, an old building whose first floor was occupied mainly by the Post Office and an insurance company. That room was mainly a place to clean up, change clothes and occasionally spend a night. I spent most nights in the homes of church members. The cost for the room was $10 per month. The bath was at the end of the hall.

All five churches had revivals during that summer. My father, Rev. W. W. Hardt, came and assisted me at Dalby Springs and a weekend revival at Austin Chapel. College friends Ike Killingsworth and Archie Fleming shared in services at Hubbard and Oak Grove. I did the preaching at Spring Hill. During the revival at Oak Grove the congregation planned a social event at the home of postmistress, Mrs. T. D. Butram. I was touched and humbled during that social as members of the congregation presented me with wrapped packages. When I opened them, I found clothes such as shirts that had been left behind by young men who had left for military service and well-worn socks in patterns I never would have chosen for myself. After all the packages were opened, I was handed a list. Each of the items of clothing had been listed and beside it was an estimate of its value. The total value represented about one-half of my estimated salary from that church. I was then told that I could count the value of the used clothing toward my salary.

My pastoral records contain the names of twenty-one people who were received into membership of the churches of the DeKalb Circuit during the revivals that summer. Two of the churches, Hubbard and Spring Hill, gave special offerings to the pastor in addition to the anticipated regular salary. The other three churches made special offerings to pay the conference claims and apportionments.

During the second week of July the Texarkana District Camp was scheduled at Camp Kelleyville, near Jefferson. Because Methodist camping had been such an inspiring part of my life, I was determined that some of our young people would attend that camp. I borrowed a car and took five young people to camp. When we arrived, carpenters were still building the only building at the camp. It served as dining hall, meeting room, kitchen, and floor space for sleeping mats. Most of the activities were conducted under the trees. Although I was a pastor, I was not much older than many of the campers. I was enrolled in the class on marriage and family taught by the pastor of First Methodist Church of Jefferson, Rev. L. A Reavis, Jr. When he stressed the importance of pastors avoiding romantic entanglements with members of their congregations, I felt he was focussing the class on me. In each of the five congregations I served, there was someone who was making suggestions about some woman in the church who would make a good wife. Those suggestions ranged from very young teenagers to divorced women a decade older than I, and many between those ages.

On my twentieth birthday, July 14, 1941, I was invited to preach at the vesper service. I spoke on Jesus' invitation "Follow Me."

My service to the five churches was not my only responsibility. I had been elected president of the Texas Conference Youth at an assembly held at Lon Morris College in Jacksonville. The position carried the expectation that I would attend the Jursidictional Conference of Methodist Youth held at Mount Sequoyah, Fayetteville, Arkansas, in late August. I arranged for a high school student from Texarkana, Wayne Banks, to fill my appointment for one Sunday, and I rode an old school bus to Fayetteville. After the conference ended, I traveled with other conference presidents to Baker University in

Baldwin, Kansas, to attend the first national meeting of Methodist youth following the unification of northern and southern Methodism. Upon the conclusion of that conference Francis Christie, President of the North Arkansas Conference Youth, and I hitchhiked through Missouri and Arkansas. We arrived in Conway, Arkansas, and Hendrix College in the middle of the night and spent half a night in a dormitory there. The next morning I continued hitchhiking alone to Texarkana and made it back to DeKalb in time to prepare for my Sunday preaching assignments.

Most of my time in the summer of 1941 was spent visiting families who were members of the five churches I served. I wore a hat to make me look more mature and also to keep the sun off since I mainly walked to my visits in homes and fields. As I walked the dirt roads of Bowie County, automobile drivers would offer me rides. That gave another chance to cultivate relationships with people in the community.

Although the salary seems meager by today's standards, it was actually the most money I had ever had. I had no car. I ate most meals with church families. My hotel room was only $10 per month. I returned to school that fall with enough money to pay my tuition and make loans to two other students to help pay their tuition. While I had preached for nearly three years in special services or even revival meetings before April 1941, the DeKalb Circuit ushered me into a new world of responsibility of being "pastor in charge." I will be forever grateful for what I learned while serving the DeKalb Circuit from April to November of 1941.

*Afterword:* Three of the churches on the DeKalb Circuit have been discontinued. Dalby Springs remains an active congregation, served by the preacher who also serves Omaha. The church building there may be the oldest church building still in use by an active congregation in Texas. Hubbard is also an active congregation. It is served by the pastor from DeKalb.

*References:*

Hardt, John Wesley, Pastor's Record Book, Archives, Bridwell Library, Perkins School of Theology, SMU, Dallas.

CHAPTER 25

# TEN LARGEST
# METHODIST CHURCHES IN TEXAS,
# THE TWENTIETH CENTURY

## 1900

| STATEWIDE | CONF. | MEM. |
|---|---|---|
| CORSICANA, FIRST | NWT | 893 |
| WACO, FIFTH STREET | NWT | 723 |
| DALLAS, FIRST | NT | 722 |
| HOUSTON, SHEARN | T | 707 |
| WEATHERFORD, FIRST | NWT | 675 |
| WAXAHACHIE, FIRST | NWT | 648 |
| GEORGETOWN, FIRST | NWT | 624 |
| SAN ANTONIO, TRAVIS PARK | WT | 621 |
| SHERMAN, TRAVIS ST. | NT | 614 |
| AUSTIN, TENTH ST | T | 576 |

## 1910

| STATEWIDE | CONF. | MEM. |
|---|---|---|
| FORT WORTH, FIRST | CT | 1,708 |
| BEAUMONT, FIRST | T | 1,490 |
| SAN ANTONIO, TRAVIS PARK | WT | 1,353 |
| SAN ANGELO, FIRST | WT | 1,047 |
| FORT WORTH, POLYTECHNIC | CT | 1,010 |
| GEORGETOWN, FIRST | CT | 949 |
| WAXAHACHIE, FIRST | CT | 941 |
| DALLAS, TRINITY | NT | 929 |
| STAMFORD, ST. JOHN | NWT | 926 |
| AMARILLO STATION | NWT | 907 |

## 1920

| STATEWIDE | CONF. | MEM. |
|---|---|---|
| HOUSTON, FIRST | T | 2,179 |
| DALLAS, FIRST | NT | 2,147 |
| FORT WORTH, FIRST | CT | 2,143 |
| SAN ANTONIO, TRAVIS PARK | WT | 1,751 |
| PARIS, FIRST | NT | 1,634 |
| AMARILLO, POLK ST | NWT | 1,642 |
| BEAUMONT, FIRST | T | 1,432 |
| DALLAS, GRACE | NT | 1,400 |
| WICHITA FALLS, FIRST | NT | 1,313 |
| HOUSTON, ST. PAUL'S | T | 1,288 |

## 1930

| STATEWIDE | CONF. | MEM. |
|---|---|---|
| HOUSTON, FIRST | T | 5,017 |
| DALLAS, FIRST | NT | 4,040 |
| SAN ANTONIO, TRAVIS PARK | WT | 3,863 |
| FORT WORTH, FIRST | CT | 2,890 |
| WICHITA FALLS, FIRST | NT | 2,869 |
| AMARILLO, POLK STREET | NWT | 2,698 |
| LUBBOCK, FIRST | NWT | 2,599 |
| WACO, AUSTIN AVE. | CT | 2,482 |
| PORT ARTHUR, TEMPLE | T | 2,250 |
| DALLAS, TYLER STREET | NT | 2,212 |

## 1940

| STATEWIDE | CONF. | MEM. |
|---|---|---|
| HOUSTON, FIRST | T | 4,468 |
| SAN ANTONIO, TRAVIS PARK | SWT | 3,852 |
| DALLAS, FIRST | NT | 3,751 |
| FORT WORTH, FIRST | CT | 3,453 |
| DALLAS, HIGHLAND PARK | NT | 3,178 |
| AMARILLO, POLK ST | NWT | 3,026 |
| TYLER, MARVIN | T | 2,639 |
| LUBBOCK, FIRST | NWT | 2,479 |
| PORT ARTHUR, TEMPLE | T | 2,469 |
| BEAUMONT, FIRST | T | 2,452 |

## 1950

| STATEWIDE | CONF. | MEM. |
|---|---|---|
| HOUSTON, FIRST | T | 6,028 |
| DALLAS, HIGHLAND PARK | NT | 5,635 |
| SAN ANTONIO, TRAVIS PARK | SWT | 4,521 |
| FORT WORTH, FIRST | CT | 4,033 |
| DALLAS, FIRST | NT | 3,966 |
| AMARILLO, POLK ST | NWT | 3,614 |
| DALLAS, TYLER ST. | NT | 3,599 |
| TYLER, MARVIN | T | 3,262 |
| HOUSTON, ST. PAUL'S | T | 3,219 |
| EL PASO, TRINITY | NM | 3,064 |

## 1960

| STATEWIDE | CONF. | MEM. |
|---|---|---|
| DALLAS, HIGHLAND PARK | NT | 8,756 |
| HOUSTON, FIRST | T | 6,051 |
| FORT WORTH, FIRST | CT | 5,564 |
| DALLAS, FIRST | NT | 5,450 |
| LUBBOCK, FIRST | NWT | 5,328 |
| AMARILLO, POLK ST. | NWT | 4,671 |
| DALLAS, LOVERS LANE | NT | 4,634 |
| SAN ANTONIO, TRAVIS PARK | SWT | 4,460 |
| EL PASO, TRINITY | NM | 4,003 |
| HOUSTON, ST. PAUL'S | T | 3,997 |

## 1970

| STATEWIDE | CONF. | MEM. |
|---|---|---|
| HOUSTON, FIRST | T | 9,663 |
| DALLAS, HIGHLAND PARK | NT | 8,705 |
| DALLAS, LOVERS LANE | NT | 7,171 |
| LUBBOCK, FIRST | NWT | 5,960 |
| DALLAS, FIRST | NT | 5,931 |
| HOUSTON, ST. LUKE'S | T | 5,796 |
| HOUSTON, ST. PAUL'S | T | 5,434 |
| FORT WORTH, FIRST | CT | 5,289 |
| HOUSTON, MEMORIAL DRIVE | T | 4,092 |
| AMARILLO, POLK STREET | NWT | 4,008 |

## 1980

| STATEWIDE | CONF. | MEM. |
|---|---|---|
| HOUSTON, FIRST | T | 11,715 |
| DALLAS, HIGHLAND PARK | NT | 9,799 |
| DALLAS, LOVERS LANE | NT | 8,011 |
| FORT WORTH, FIRST | CT | 6,496 |
| HOUSTON, ST. LUKE'S | T | 6,206 |
| HOUSTON, MEMORIAL DRIVE | T | 6,150 |
| RICHARDSON, FIRST | NT | 6,147 |
| LUBBOCK, FIRST | NWT | 5,581 |
| DALLAS, FIRST | NT | 5,407 |
| ARLINGTON, FIRST | CT | 4,253 |

## 1990

| STATEWIDE | CONF. | MEM. |
|---|---|---|
| HOUSTON, FIRST | T | 13,632 |
| DALLAS, HIGHLAND PARK | NT | 11,740 |
| FORT WORTH, FIRST | CT | 9,473 |
| HOUSTON, MEMORIAL DRIVE | T | 8,264 |
| HOUSTON, ST. LUKE'S | T | 8,180 |
| RICHARDSON, FIRST | NT | 6,873 |
| DALLAS, LOVERS LANE | NT | 6,442 |
| LUBBOCK, FIRST | NWT | 5,581 |
| ARLINGTON, FIRST | CT | 4,900 |
| DALLAS, FIRST | NT | 4,889 |

## 2000

| STATEWIDE | CONF. | MEM. |
| --- | --- | --- |
| DALLAS, HIGHLAND PARK | NT | 12,612 |
| HOUSTON, WINDSOR VIL. | T | 12,449 |
| HOUSTON, FIRST | T | 12,315 |
| FORT WORTH, FIRST | CT | 10,854 |
| HOUSTON, ST. LUKE'S | T | 7,218 |
| PLANO, CUSTER ROAD | NT | 6,234 |
| RICHARDSON, FIRST | NT | 5,845 |
| HOUSTON, MEMORIAL DR. | T | 5,687 |
| ARLINGTON, FIRST | CT | 5,514 |
| HOUSTON, WOODLANDS | T | 5,024 |

It is not surprising that Methodist church membership in Texas should reflect trends in Texas population during the same period. The overall pattern for both the Texas population and large membership Methodist churches during the 20th century is the same, constant significant increase reflecting first urbanization and then suburbanization, punctuated with booms and busts related to petroleum discoveries and war time industrialization.

## 1900

The ten largest Methodist churches, as reported in the Journals of the various conferences, were located on either side of a line stretching from Sherman to San Antonio with only Shearn (First) Methodist Church in Houston as an exception. The largest Texas Methodist church was Corsicana First, benefiting from that city's population increase after an oil discovery in 1895. The federal census of 1900 had reported that 13 of the 15 most populous counties of Texas were also in that same region so it is not surprising that the largest Methodist churches should be located there. The ten largest churches were equally located in five large cities and five smaller cities. In the pre-automobile era the size of the city was less important that the population density and the transportation technology which the members used to go to church. Corsicana and Waxahachie had mule-drawn city transit systems (Corsicana converted to electric trolleys in 1902.). Sherman and Denison were joined by an interurban electric rail line in 1901. Such urban services in relatively small cities were based on the prosperity of the cotton/railroad economy that benefited the Blackland Prairie more than any other region. Because the boundaries of the annual conferences cut across the Blackland Prairie east-west, each of the five conferences wholly in Texas had at least one church in the top ten list. When examining the membership of the ten largest churches, one notices that there is relatively little difference between the largest (Corsicana with 893 members) and the tenth (Austin, Tenth St. with 576).

## 1910

The conference journals which reported membership for 1910 revealed huge changes had taken place in the decade since 1900. Beaumont First had become the second largest Methodist church in the state, thanks to the petroleum discoveries at Spindletop. Perhaps even more striking was the appearance in the list of ten largest by western churches. Fort Worth with two of the largest ten churches, Amarillo, Stamford, and San Angelo all reflected the land development boom of the first decade of the twentieth century. Railroad companies had been awarded tracts of public land as a incentive to lay track. Those tracts were now being subdivided into farms, and the railroads were conducting vigorous sales campaigns to induce immigration to western Texas. The middle years of the decade were significantly wetter than normal, and the resultant bumper crops attracted even more immigrants, mainly farmers abandoning exhausted farms in eastern Texas. Western Texas was later to become dominated by two other denominations—the Southern Baptists and the Christian Church, but in the first years of settlement the Methodist appointive system provided an advantage. Methodist preachers could be appointed to the new towns springing up along the railroad developments and be there ready to organize the immigrants as they arrived. The Baptist pattern was for a congregation to form and then call a pastor. The Methodist appointive system thus provided a head start over other denominations.

Another factor helps explain why the churches in smaller cities in the western part of the state appear on the ten largest list for 1910. Urban Methodists in the first decade of the 20th century responded to increasing population by founding numerous new churches. In Houston, for example, Harrisburg, Brunner Ave., Heights (later renamed Grace), and South End (later renamed St. Paul's) were all founded in 1905. Before the decade ended, Lorianne St. and Trinity were also founded. Dallas had even more new churches during the same time span as Oak Cliff ('02), Grace and Clark's Chapel ('03), Colonial Hills and Grand Ave. ('05) Cochran and Maple Ave. ('06), Fairland, Wesley Chapel, Forest Ave., and West Dallas Churches ('08) became new charges. Government Hill, Alamo, and Laurel Heights were founded in San Antonio in the decade. Fort Worth was only slightly behind Dallas in founding churches as North Fort Worth, Riverside, Central, Rosen Heights, Diamond Hill, Weatherford Street, Brooklyn Heights, Boulevard, and McKinley Ave. Churches all came into being in the first decade of the 20th century. The general pattern was that a group of members from one of the older, more established churches agreed to move their membership to one of the new churches and provide a nucleus of leadership for that new church. As a result, new churches in the new cities of West Texas actually surpassed many of the older churches in the older cities in membership.

## 1920

The federal census of 1920 reported that Harris, Dallas, Bexar, and Tarrant Counties were the most populous Texas counties. Those four counties were to remain the largest Texas counties throughout the rest of the twentieth century. The largest Methodist churches in Texas would also be concentrated in those counties for the rest of the twentieth century. The four dominant cities of the four largest counties, Houston, Dallas, San Antonio, and Fort Worth were located in four different conferences. Although all four were in the same state, significant cultural, demographic, and economic differences existed between the four. Those differences were reflected in the Methodist churches of each city. Houston, while transforming itself from a cotton and lumber town to the nation's most important petroleum city, was the most southern of the four cities. Its traditional immigration base was the lower South. It is thus no coincidence that of the fifteen men to serve as senior pastor of First Methodist Houston during the 20th century, six had roots in Georgia, another three in Tennessee, and one each in both North Carolina and Alabama.

Dallas was developing into the dominant commercial and transportation hub of the entire Southwest. Its connections were to the Midwest-to Kansas City, St. Louis, and Chicago, rather than to the South. The business elite who wielded power in Dallas tended to have a grander vision than did community leaders elsewhere in Texas. From the very beginning, for example, SMU would be much more than a Texas university— its appeal would be to the whole South (especially the South west of the Mississippi River. Dallas leaders also pointed to Dallas as the logical site for other centralized efforts of the church such as the publishing endeavors. Fort Worth was, by necessity, westward looking since the presence of Dallas precluded influence to the east. Its railroads and livestock industry tied it economically to the Plains, but Methodist geography did not conform to economic and social realities. Fort Worth was tied instead to the Blackland Prairie and Temple, Waco, and Georgetown because of the Central Texas Conference boundaries. In 1920 San Antonio was still coming to terms with the implications of the great influx of Mexican immigrants coming to Texas as a result of the Mexican Revolution. Although the population of San Antonio was growing rapidly, very few of the newcomers were welcomed into the existing Anglo Methodist churches.

Besides the churches in the four largest counties, churches in Paris, Beaumont, Wichita Falls, and Amarillo reported membership over 1000.

## 1930

The Journal figures for 1930 report that the four largest churches from 1920 had all remained in the top four. Houston First, under the leadership of A. Frank Smith, had more than doubled its membership so that it now exceeded Dallas First by almost one thousand members. All four of the largest cities witnessed the shift from streetcar suburbs to automobile suburbs during the 1920s. Even though neighborhood churches were established in the 1920s (e.g. Englewood, Glen Garden, Forest Hill in Fort Worth; Woodlawn Place in San Antonio; Trinity Heights, Cockrell Hills, Brandon Ave., Lakewood in Dallas; Bellaire, Ludtke, Fulbright in Houston), the central business district of each city remained dominant in terms of employment, commerce, and church membership. Other large churches besides those in the four largest cities also benefited from population growth. Wichita Falls First more than doubled its membership thanks in large part to the construction of refineries to take advantage of oil from the Burkburnett Oil Field. Temple Church in Port Arthur similarly benefited from refinery construction as it became the ninth largest Methodist church in Texas in 1930. Lubbock First achieved the top ten rank for the first time in 1930. Lubbock County population had grown from 3,624 in 1910 to 39,104 by 1930. It had positioned itself as the main marketing center for cotton and sorghum as improved irrigation technologies opened the fertile soils of the High Plains to farming.

## 1940

The 1930s provided a reminder that population growth is never inevitable. The Great Depression slowed the urbanization of Texas and also the growth of urban Methodist churches. Houston First retained its status as the largest church in Texas Methodism in spite of a membership loss of over 500 members from 1930 to 1940. Dallas First and San Antonio's Travis Park also experienced membership decline. Both agriculture and petroleum, the two mainstays of the Texas economy suffered in the 1930s. Many Lower Plains and High Plains counties that had been developed into farms were hit by drought and dust storm, and lost population as farms were abandoned. The abandonment of farms created a ripple effect in the cities and towns of West Texas as banks, implement dealers, other businesses and churches were all forced to cut back. As the Great Depression decreased the demand for petroleum products, the East Texas Oil Field was brought in within the bounds of the Texas Conference. The oil discovery there further depressed the price of oil. On the other hand, the population boom in East Texas swelled the membership of churches in Tyler, Longview, Henderson, Gladewater and other towns in the vicinity. Marvin Church in Tyler appeared on the ten largest churches list for the first time as a result of the boom.

Another newcomer to the list of ten largest was a hint of things to come. Highland Park Church in Dallas reported a membership of 3,178 which placed it fifth in the state. Highland Park had been established on the southern edge of the SMU campus and profited from its association with the university and from the housing developments which soon surrounded the SMU campus. It was blessed with the appointment of Rev. Marshall Steel in November 1936. He served in that pulpit until December 1957.

## 1950

The war years of the 1940s produced the most intense surge of urbanization of any period in Texas history. An agency of the state government estimated that at least 350,000 rural Texans moved to the cities in the first eighteen months of World War II. Thousands of immigrants also poured into Texas from other states as they sought employment in war-related industries. Although every part of the state, from Dumas to Midland to Laredo to Alice to Texarkana, was impacted, the greatest population increase was in the major metropolitan areas. The Houston area saw the construction of refineries and factories to produce gasoline, aviation fuel, rubber, tin, magnesium, naval vessels, and other materiel. Aircraft production became a specialty of the Dallas-Fort Worth area. While less military production occurred in San Antonio, that city became home to thousands of military personnel as its bases expanded. Much of the growth in Houston, Dallas, and Ft. Worth was in suburban cities which were part of the metropolitan area but had their own identity. In the Houston area those suburbs included, among others, Baytown, Pasadena, Texas City, LaPorte, and Galena Park. In the Dallas-Fort Worth Metroplex they included Arlington, Euless, Bedford, Garland, and many others. The growth was staggering. Garland, for example, had reported a population of 2,233 in 1940. Its 1950 population was 10,571.

Little housing had been built during the war as the metropolitan areas swelled with immigrants. The pent up demand for housing was satisfied mainly by huge expanses of tract homes in subdivisions along the transportation arteries leading in to Dallas, Houston, Fort Worth, and San Antonio. Methodist officials were eager to plant churches in the new subdivisions. Developers were amenable to making choice building lots available for church construction. Methodists in each of the conferences institutionalized church expansion under the rubric of missions. Mission boards at both the city and district level raised money for the purchase of building sites at pre-development prices and then made those sites available to new congregations as population increased enough to warrant a church. Sometimes these programs such as Room to Grow (Houston), Church Builders Club (Galveston), Board of Church Extension (Dallas) and New Church Fellowship (Beaumont) also supplemented pastoral salaries until the new churches were established. In a 1960 report Room to Grow reported raising $447,330 and establishing twenty-one new churches from 1954 to 1960.

Not all of the new churches of the post World War II building boom succeeded. Some of the new churches were located in neighborhoods that failed to live up to their promise. Sometimes, in their enthusiasm to build new churches, mission boards built churches too close to each other. Two of the churches of the post World War II building boom, however, quickly became two of the largest churches in their respective conferences. St. Luke's in Houston and Lover's Lane in Dallas were founded immediately after World War II in affluent neighborhoods with help from established congregations. Both quickly had membership rolls of over a thousand.

The list of ten largest churches in Texas Methodism for 1950 showed most of the same churches as ten years before including Marvin in Tyler and Polk Street in Amarillo. Dallas, however, now had three of the ten largest churches. Tyler Street Methodist, which had barely survived the Depression, reported 3,599 members. Highland Park, had surpassed Dallas First by more than 1000 members. Commercial activity was following the population to the suburban housing developments. The establishment of new churches in the suburbs provided a church home for people unwilling to drive to the central business district on Sunday. In 1950 few "downtown" church leaders appeared concerned about deteriorating position of the central business district vis-à-vis the suburbs, but the new status of Highland Park relative to First Dallas was a sign that huge changes were coming.

## 1960

The journals of 1960 reported that Highland Park of Dallas had increased by an astounding 3,100 members since 1950 to become the largest Methodist church in

Texas. In addition, Lover's Lane, only a few miles away and only fifteen years old, was now the seventh largest Methodist church in Texas. Other Dallas churches such as First, University Park, Tyler Street, Munger Place, and Oak Lawn all grew significantly and all had membership of greater than 2,000. The situation in Houston differed from that in Dallas in one important feature. Houston First's membership, although the largest in the Texas Conference and second largest in the state, had grown by only 23 members in the 1950s. Houston First had been a prominent arena in the battle over alleged Communist influence in the Methodist church during the McCarthy Era. That distraction hindered church growth, but downtowns in general and downtown churches in particular were facing competition from suburban development—a process that would continue through most of the second half of the twentieth century. The downtown church obviously could not compete with the suburban churches in terms of convenience. To be sure, the drive from the suburbs for Sunday morning worship was generally traffic-free and easy, but getting back downtown during the week for committee meetings, Bible study, youth activities, and numerous other functions became more and more difficult. Downtown churches often grappled with the problem of parking. This was one area the suburban churches enjoyed considerable advantages. While a downtown church might feel lucky to own an entire city block, many of the suburban churches were sited on multi-acre campuses with hundreds of parking places. Since few new church buildings had been constructed during the 1930s and 1940s because of the Great Depression and World War II, many downtown congregations worshiped in buildings constructed in the first third of the twentieth century. (Beaumont First 1907, Houston First 1910, Highland Park Dallas 1927, Dallas First 1926, Austin First 1928, Fort Worth First 1930) Many of those buildings were Akron Style or Gothic Revival architectural masterpieces. On the other hand, they had been built to accommodate roughly one-third of the membership and traffic patterns of the streetcar era when parking was hardly a consideration. Even if adjacent property became available, it made little economic sense to buy expensive city lots to be used only for parking a few hours per week. Retrofitting sanctuaries to accommodate modern lighting, air conditioning, and sound systems also presented problems for downtown churches.

The 1950s had witnessed an increase in religious activity in general. Many service personnel returned from World War II with personal commitments to live religious lives. The anxieties of the Cold War and Atomic Age influenced some people to look for stability and comfort in church. Anecdotal evidence suggests that as the Baby Boomers arrived, the decision of where to place a family's church membership was often determined by the quality of the church's children's activities. As with parking, the suburban churches often had an advantage over the downtown churches in this regard. They generally had newer Sunday School facilities, more room for playgrounds, gymnasiums, and access to suburban stay-at-home moms willing to volunteer in Vacation Bible School, Cherub Choir, Mother's Day Out child care, and other children's programs. It is easy to see why church leaders in many downtown churches contemplated relocation.

## 1970

The membership figures for 1970 show increasing dominance of the Houston and Dallas/Fort Worth metropolitan areas. Six annual conferences in Texas had at least one church on the list of ten largest churches in 1960. In 1970 eight of the ten largest churches were from the Houston and Dallas/Fort Worth areas. Houston First was once again the largest Methodist church in Texas. An episcopal election in 1960 created a vacancy in that pastorate that was filled by Charles Allen, a transfer from Georgia. Rev. Allen's engaging preaching style resonated both with old time Houstonians and recent arrivals to the city. In Dallas, meanwhile, Highland Park reported a membership decline from 1960 while Lovers Lane increased by 2,500 members during the same period. Lubbock First continued to lead the Northwest Texas Conference and was the fourth largest Methodist church in Texas. Lubbock had established itself as the dominant regional center for agribusiness, medicine, education, and service industries for western Texas and eastern New Mexico. Other churches to report greater than 4,000 membership in 1970 were Dallas First, St. Luke's, St. Paul's and Memorial Drive in Houston, First in Fort Worth, and Polk Street in Amarillo.

## 1980

Immigrants continued to pour into Texas and Texas Methodist churches during the 1970s. The formation of a cartel to limit production of petroleum drove the price of oil to record levels, and Texas was the acknowledged leader in petroleum exploration. As the price of oil increased, there were ripples throughout the economy as banking, construction, housing, transportation, communications, and engineering sectors all enjoyed increased prosperity. Increased employment in those sectors encouraged immigration both from the rest of the United States and from foreign countries. The large cities of Texas became even larger. The federal census of 1980 revealed that Harris County had increased from 1.7 to 2.4 million. Even greater percentages of increase were recorded in the first tier of counties surrounding the metropolitan areas. Fort Bend County grew from 52 to 130 thousand. Montgomery County from 49 to 150 thousand. Denton County almost doubled as it grew to 143 thousand. Collin County more than doubled from 66 to 144 thousand.

Population growth was so great during the 1970s that both the downtown churches ("First" in most cities), the near-downtown churches (St. Luke's in Houston; Highland Park and Lovers Lane in Dallas), and the more distant suburban churches all reaped the benefits. Houston First reported an astounding 11,715 members in 1980. Highland Park was approaching 10,000 while Lovers Lane topped 8,000. Richardson First and Arlington First attained membership that placed them in the ten largest churches in Texas Methodism. Lubbock First was the only one of the ten largest not to be in either the Houston or Dallas/Fort Worth metropolitan areas.

# 1990

A comparison of the ten largest churches in 1980 and 1990 reveals several changes in rank but no changes in the churches that composed the list. Houston First now counted 13,632 members and Highland Park 11,740.

An examination of church membership figures at the annual conference level reveals changes underway in the 1980s not apparent in the statewide large church statistics.

By 1990 nine of the ten largest churches in the Texas Annual Conference were in the Houston metropolitan area. Marvin in Tyler was the only exception. The largest churches in the Texas Conference continued to be in Houston—First, Memorial Drive, St. Luke's and Chapelwood. What the 1990 statistics revealed, though, was a progression to more distant suburbs. The churches relatively close to downtown Houston, St. Paul's, Westbury, Bellaire, and Fairhaven, had been replaced on the top ten list by more distant churches, Windsor Village, Clear Lake, Bear Creek, Klein, and Kingwood. A similar situation occurred in the North Texas Conference in which the greatest gains were achieved by churches in suburban Richardson, Plano, and Carrolton. Dallas First and Lovers Lane both lost membership during the decade, and Wichita Falls, traditionally a strong city for the conference, no longer had a church among the ten largest in the conference. In the Southwest Texas Annual Conference, San Antonio Alamo Heights now had more than twice the membership of Travis Park. San Antonio Coker, Colonial Hills, and University all had more members than Travis Park which had been the largest church in the conference for decades. (Travis Park's membership was approximately one-third what it had been only a generation earlier.) Austin First continued to be the largest Methodist church in the capital city, but University and St. John's both lost membership in the decade. By 1990 the Northwest Texas Conference no longer had representatives on the top ten list from the smaller cities such as Plainview, Vernon, Big Spring, and Pampa. All of the ten largest churches were located in the urban areas of Lubbock, Amarillo, Abilene, and Midland. A similar situation occurred in the Texas charges of the New Mexico Conference. Throughout most of the 20th century Pecos, Fort Stockton, and Monahans had been among the ten largest churches. By 1990 nine of the ten largest churches were in either El Paso or Odessa.

Although much attention was devoted to the relationship and possible competition between the inner city and suburban Methodist churches, the greater challenges of the last third of the twentieth century were not intramural. Instead they came from larger cultural and religious developments.

The first of these challenges was a change in the nature of the immigration swelling the populations of the Texas cities. During the first part of the 20th century, Texas urban growth was fueled especially by immigrants from rural areas of Texas and the rest of the South and later by Rust Belt to Sun Belt migration. A significant number of these immigrants were already Methodist or at least favorably disposed toward

Methodism. The growth of the suburban churches already noted in many cases followed a relatively simple formula—provide an attractive, convenient building with a competent staff and newcomers will affiliate. In the last third of the 20th century, however, the nature of the immigration changed. The metropolitan areas continued to swell with new arrivals, but those new Texans were more likely to be from Asia, Africa, or Latin America and were not predisposed to Methodist affiliation. Even with hundreds of thousands of Spanish speaking immigrants, the Spanish language Rio Grande Conference experienced stagnant membership, usually reporting about 15,000 members.

The other challenge in the last third of the 20th century was the rise of very large nondenominational and Southern Baptist churches throughout Texas cities. Pundits soon christened such very large churches "megachurches." They tended to have some characteristics in common—a compelling preacher, excellent music, a television ministry, and a conservative outlook on theology, social issues, and politics. Methodists were divided over a response. On the one hand, it was obvious that some Methodist preachers wished to imitate many of the Megachurch traits. Other Methodists, however recalled the traditional emphasis upon class meetings and intimacy that came with smaller groups. One aspect of Megachurches certainly clashed with traditional Methodism. The conference structure of Methodism had tended toward compromise and moderation as delegates from the entire church met every four years to determine Discipline and practice. The Megachurches —both nondenominational and Southern Baptist—acted without such moderating influences. They were very often the extension of one man's personality and ideology rather than the product of a conciliar process. The temptation to follow a similar path existed in the very large Methodist churches. For example, their pulpits were often filled outside the normal appointive system. On the other hand, many of the very large Methodist churches heartily embraced the traditional connectional system, especially in supporting the missions and institutions of the church.

## 2000

The annual conference journals for 2000 confirmed that all of the ten largest Methodist churches in Texas were in either the Houston or Dallas/Fort Worth metropolitan regions. Each region had five of the largest churches. Houston Windsor Village had reported a membership of 4,052 in 1990. In 2000 it reported 12,449. Highland Park had grown to 12,612 to become the largest Methodist church in Texas. Houston First also reported membership of greater than 12,000 while Fort Worth First was also over 10,000. Both Houston First and Windsor Village had redefined the idea of church facilities. Windsor Village offered worship services at three different locations. Houston First, after a failed attempt to relocate from downtown Houston, built a second church plant in western Houston and conducted worship services at both locations. Previous generations of downtown Methodists had been generous in

128

supporting new congregations as Texas cities expanded. That process had previously resulted in independent congregations. Houston First's two campuses represented an innovation.

Houston First was the only church that was on the list of largest churches in both 1900 (as Shearn Church) and 2000. The 2000 list was made up mainly of churches that did not even exist in 1900. The largest churches of 2000 offered their communities much more than Sunday worship. They offered a full schedule of activities for all ages and life situations. One could find music, recreation, support groups, drama, scouting, education, fitness, hobbies, travel opportunities, self-help, and many other activities. Perhaps it is no coincidence that the churches with the most programs were also the fastest growing. Houston Windsor Village's ministries extended to employment and housing. Although it had some Megachurch aspects, in some ways Windsor Village was more like a 1900 church. The large downtown churches of the early 1900s often supported a Wesley House which provided educational, health, housing, and employment services to immigrant and impoverished populations. Downtown churches of the early 1900s tended to reflect the social class of the (white) population of city fairly well.

One aspect of the suburbanization of the Methodist church has been a narrowing of its constituency. The suburban churches, often called "neighborhood" churches, did tend to reflect their neighborhoods. Since Texas residential patterns conformed to economic, racial and social class patterns, Methodist churches tended to be relatively homogeneous in terms of race, class, and economic status. While such homogeneity provides comfort, it does not provide challenge. As Texas cities are experiencing an upsurge in central-city residents moving into loft apartments and townhouses, downtown churches now stand in the path of population growth after experiencing decades of population decline.

*References*:

Grimes, Lewis Howard, *Cloud of Witnesses: a History of First Methodist Church, Houston, Texas*, Wilkinson Printing Co, Dallas, 1951.

*New Handbook of Texas*

Vernon et al., *Methodist Excitement*.

Vernon, Walter N., *Methodism Moves Across North Texas, Historical Society of the North Texas Conference, Nashville, 1967*.

Crenshaw, Rosa Dieu and Ward, W. W., *Cornerstones: A History of Beaumont and Methodism 1840-1968*, First Methodist Church, Beaumont, 1968.

Carlton, Don. E. *Red Scare*, Austin, Texas Monthly Press, *1985*.

West, C. A. ed., *Texas Conference Methodism on the March, 1814-1960*, Nashville, Parthenon Press, 1960.

Johnson, Doris Miller, *Golden Prologue to the Future: A History of Highland Park Methodist Church*, Nashville, Parthenon Press, 1966.

www.hpumc.org

www.fumcdal.org

www.fumcftw.org

www.fumcaustin.org

www.firstmethodist-houston.org

www.kingdombuilder.com

CHAPTER 26

# WOMEN'S MISSIONARY SOCIETY PROGRESSIVE ERA INSTITUTIONS

The last years of the 19th and first years of the 20th century witnessed the transformation of the United States by industrialization, urbanization, and immigration. These forces posed challenges and opportunities for the Protestant denominations, none more so than Methodism. The circuit rider and camp meeting system had produced explosive growth when the United States was a rural nation. New institutions were needed as the nation became more urban. Some Christian reformers boldly seized the opportunity to serve and witness in the new environment. They brought their faith to the social ills of the day. Their concerns included poverty, assimilation of immigrants, child nutrition, industrial safety, illiteracy, public health, and problems of young single women away from home at either university or urban employment. Although not all activists in these areas were motivated by their religious beliefs, many were. Their movement became known as the Social Gospel and helped shape the aims and accomplishments of the Progressive Era.

The two most visible expressions of Progressive Era social activism in Texas Methodism featured intense involvement of women. The first expression was the campaign for the prohibition of alcoholic beverages. Women were involved at all levels in the prohibition movement, especially in such organizations as the Women's Christian Temperance Union and the Anti Saloon League. The other expression was the establishment of institutions by the Woman's Missionary Societies of the various conferences. Women in the MEC, the MECS, and the MP Church all followed a similar pattern—the establishment of a foreign missionary society followed by a home missionary society. The foreign missionary societies raised money and recruited

### Year of Establishment

|  | Foreign Missionary Society | Home Missionary Society | Office of Deaconess |
|---|---|---|---|
| MEC | 1869 | 1880 | 1888 |
| MECS | 1878 | 1890 | 1902 |
| MP | 1879 | 1893 | 1908 |

missionaries for destinations such as China, Brazil, and Mexico. The home missionary societies supported work in the United States—including Texas home missionary societies also encouraged churches to build or buy parsonages. All three churches also created the office of deaconess a few years after the creation of the Missionary Societies.

Since women were excluded from full ordination by the MEC and MECS (Anna Howard Shaw was ordained by the MP church in 1880.), the office of deaconess provided an opportunity for full-time Christian vocation to women. Many of the deaconesses worked in the mission institutions. Although they were not full annual conference members, they often moved among the various missions. In their memoirs deaconesses often spoke of their "appointments" and being sent to various mission schools and Wesley Houses. Eugenia Smith, for example, worked in Wesley Houses in Thurber, Fort Worth, and Houston during her long and distinguished career. The various schools, settlement houses, and other institutions were financed and adminis-tered by the Missionary Societies, and therefore provided women with much more autonomy than did institutions administered by the annual conferences. The Missionary Society was a truly grassroots organization. Societies were organized in local churches. Those local church organizations often formed societies for younger women, and even infants were enrolled on a "Cradle Roll." The local societies did more than raise money to support foreign missionaries and deaconesses. The minutes of the various churches are full of references to sending boxes of household items such as linens and cookware, cases of home-canned vegetables, fruit, and meat, and clothing and sewing supplies. Deaconesses would give reports to Annual Conferences, and they would also visit local churches to inform members of the work and raise funds to continue.

In 1910 the Foreign and Home Mission Societies of the MECS were merged into the Woman's Missionary Council. The 50 years Jubilee of the founding of the Woman's Foreign Missionary Society in 1878 was celebrated in 1928 with the publi-cation of commemorative histories by each of the conference organizations. The various Texas conferences could point with pride to their various projects.

## METHODIST EPISCOPAL CHURCH SOUTH

**West Texas Conference**

**Laredo Seminary-Holding Institute** traced its origins to 1880 when Mrs. Joseph Norwood and Mrs. A. H. Sutherland began teaching a small number of Mexican girls in their homes. The following year the MECS sent Misses Annie Williams and Rebecca Toland to Laredo to establish a school. The first building was constructed in 1882 and classes opened for four students. Miss Nannie Holding became principal in 1883. After her retirement in 1913, the school was renamed in her honor.

The **Wesley Community House** in San Antonio opened in 1913 when deaconesses Mrs. Almeda Hewitt and Miss Ella Bowden were employed to provide social services to Mexican and Mexican-American residents of San Antonio.

The **Valley Institute** was opened in 1921 in Pharr as a boarding school for Mexican girls. Although it had been begun by the Board of Missions of the MECS, in 1926 it was transferred to the Women's Missionary Society of the West Texas Conference in return for the facilities on the Pacific coast serving Asian immigrants.

Also within the bounds of the West Texas Conference was **Kirby Hall**, a women's dormitory at the University of Texas. The hall was named for Mrs. Helen Kirby, first dean of women at the University of Texas and for twenty-five years president of the conference Woman's Missionary Society. Kirby Hall was owned by Woman's Missionary Societies of the Texas, North Texas, West Texas, Central Texas, and Northwest Texas Annual Conferences. Kirby Hall on the Southern Methodist University campus was named for Mrs. Kirby's son, R. H. Kirby.

## Central Texas Conference

The **Rebecca Sparks Home** (later **Inn**) in Waco was established in 1900 as a cooperative home for working women. In 1901 Mattie Wright was appointed to Waco. She organized Christmas basket distribution and newsboy clubs, but her greatest accomplishment in Waco was expanding the Rebecca Sparks Home. Cooperative homes filled the need for lodging for young single women who had moved to the city seeking employment. On April 15, 1903, Mattie Wright became the first deaconess in the MECS, when she was consecrated in Atlanta, Georgia, by Bishop Hendrix. Her career after her Waco assignment included positions in St. Louis, Missouri, Houston, Texas, and San Francisco, California.

A special concern of Progressive Era reformers was assimilating or "Americanizing" recent immigrants. That concern was mixed with both hope and fear. The hope was that souls would be saved and misery alleviated. The fear was that Roman Catholic, Orthodox, and Jewish immigrants would become a majority in what had been a majority Protestant nation. Reformers also feared that immigrants would be subject to manipulation by political bosses, and immigrant ghettos would serve as reservoirs of disease that might spread to the larger community. It is not surprising, therefore, that many of the Woman's Missionary Society concerns included ministries to immigrant populations. There were two such notable ministries in the Central Texas Conference.

# Women's Missionary Society MECS Institutions Progressive Era

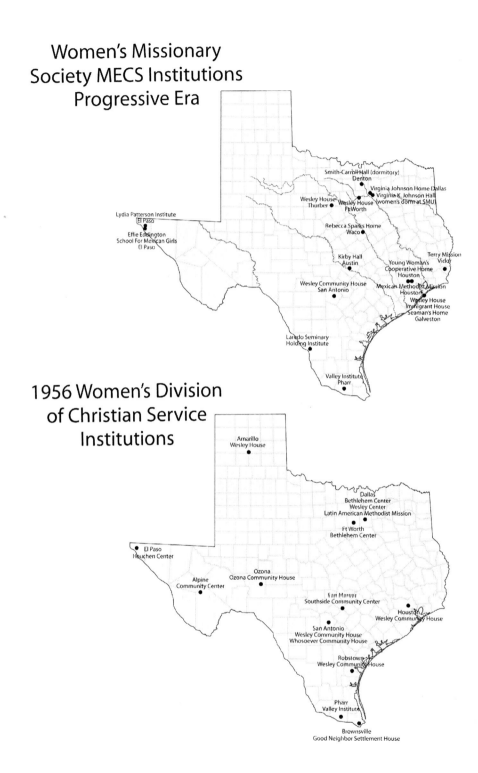

Smith-Carroll Hall (dormitory)
Denton

Virginia Johnson Home Dallas
Virginia K. Johnson Hall
(women's dorm at SMU)

Wesley House
Thurber

Wesley House
Ft Worth

Lydia Patterson Institute
El Paso

Effie Eddington
School For Mexican Girls
El Paso

Rebecca Sparks Home
Waco

Kirby Hall
Austin

Terry Mission
Vidor

Young Woman's
Cooperative Home
Houston

Wesley Community House
San Antonio

Mexican Methodist Mission
Houston

Wesley House
Immigrant House
Seaman's Home
Galveston

Laredo Seminary
Holding Institute

Valley Institute
Pharr

# 1956 Women's Division of Christian Service Institutions

Amarillo
Wesley House

Dallas
Bethlehem Center
Wesley Center
Latin American Methodist Mission

Ft Worth
Bethlehem Center

El Paso
Houchen Center

Alpine
Community Center

Ozona
Ozona Community House

San Marcos
Southside Community Center

Houston
Wesley Community House

San Antonio
Wesley Community House
Whosoever Community House

Robstown
Wesley Community House

Pharr
Valley Institute

Brownsville
Good Neighbor Settlement House

The first was at Thurber where the coal mines had attracted a labor force of "8,000 foreigners representing 18 nationalities." Eugenia Smith went to Thurber in 1908 and first organized a Sunday School. She secured the donation of a building from the Texas and Pacific Railway which became **Marston Hall**, a Wesley House. Smith directed most of her mission efforts to Italian, Mexican, and Bohemian immigrants. Eventually a church was founded in Thurber to supplement the work of the Wesley House.

In 1911 Smith moved to Fort Worth to head the **Jerome Duncan Wesley House** which served the multi-ethnic community that had grown up around the meat-packing plants north of downtown Fort Worth. As in Thurber, a Sunday School led to the establishment of a church. The Jerome Duncan Wesley House provided educational and charitable services including maternal education, child care, and nutrition education.

**The Texas Conference**

The Texas Conference missionary activity was concentrated on the coastal plains, that part of the conference most affected by foreign immigration. Mattie Wright transferred to the Texas Conference in 1907 to establish the **Young Woman's Co-Operative Home** in Houston. The home was located just a few blocks north of downtown Houston. The work prospered, and was soon expanded to an old hotel on North Main Street. Although Shearn Church had provided the initiative in starting the work, McKee Street Church was nearer the facilities, so its pastor and membership became deeply involved in the sponsorship of the Home. Even though the institution was a project of the Woman's Missionary Society, its board of directors was consisted of elite businessmen including bankers S. F. Carter and J. T. Scott. The Home provided much more than a residence for young working women. It had a full program of cultural and recreational activities including a glee club, basketball team, a library, and a swimming club.

Across the street from the Young Woman's Co-Operative Home was the **Mexican Methodist Mission**. That institution provided child care, Vacation Bible School, sewing classes, English language instruction, and similar educational programs. They used the old McKee Church building to house these programs.

The **Galveston Wesley House** began in 1905 as a project of First Methodist Church when Deaconess Elizabeth Taylor opened a sewing class in the Sunday School classrooms of that church. The next year a City Mission Board was created, and the work was expanded. They rented a house and organized a kindergarten and Sunday Schools. The nature of the work changed in 1908 as the Wesley House changed to the **Galveston Immigrant Home**. Still later the work was expanded by the creation of the **Seaman's Home**. Immigrants and seamen had different needs. Representatives from the Home would meet immigrant ships, help the immigrants through U.S. Immigration, send telegrams to relatives announcing their arrival, and secure rail passage out of Galveston to their desired destinations. Some immigrants were detained as they arrived. The Home provided lodging until the detainee was either deported or admitted. Sometimes unaccompanied children arrived on the immigrant ships as did young women betrothed to immigrants already in the country. Deaconesses took special care of these immigrants. The Seaman's Home looked after both the spiritual and physical needs of the sailors. Church services were held for seamen passing through Galveston. The Home provided Christian literature in German, Spanish, Italian, Swedish, and French. The Home also served as a hiring hall for seamen seeking employment. As the U. S. Immigration Service and labor unions provided more of the services the Home had provided, the Home was closed, and in its place a missionary was appointed as Port Missionary.

In 1906, a Japanese immigrant, Kichimatsu Kishi, planted an agricultural colony in Orange County near Vidor. Although the colonists were disappointed when salt water intrusion made rice farming difficult, they switched their efforts to truck farming. The switch to truck farming meant an increase in demand for labor. That demand was met by Mexican and Cajun workers. The result was a tri-ethnic community of Japanese, Cajun, and Mexican families. The **Terry Mission** was established to serve these families. A chapel was built in 1924 under the direction of Deaconess Cleta Kennedy. The director in 1928, Virginia Hicks, not only summed up the work of the mission, but she also captured in a few words the spirit of the Progressive Era women's efforts when she wrote, "Surely we have a melting pot where God is molding us into His Likeness and we are sharing in bringing His Kingdom to pass on earth."

## Northwest Texas Conference

The Northwest Texas Conference did not have within its borders the same opportunities for service as did the other conferences. The women of the Northwest Texas Conference directed most of their efforts to assisting other conferences in the state and also the national work of the Council. Because of its proximity to Thurber and Fort Worth, women of the Northwest Texas Conference supported the Central Texas Conference Wesley Houses there.

NWT women also showed a special interest in Scarrit College in Nashville, Tennessee, through a scholarship fund and also by participating in fund-raising drives for the College's program in training missionaries. The NWT Conference did establish two programs within its own boundaries. In 1916 Mrs. Tom Delaney took several girls camping in the Palo Duro Canyon. A girl's camping tradition was established that resulted in the 1926 authorization to purchase 315 acres of land in the Palo Duro Canyon for use as a campground. The other program was the support of a "Student Secretary" at West Texas State Teachers College in Canyon. The Student Secretary led religious and social life at the college for women students.

## North Texas Conference

The **Virginia Johnson Home** grew out of efforts initiated by Virginia Johnson, a member of First Methodist Church, Dallas, and president of her circle in the Missionary Society, the King's Daughters. In 1893 the King's Daughters opened Sheltering Arms in response to a prostitute's plea for help. The mission of the Ann Browder Cunningham House, as the home was renamed, was to provide shelter for unwed mothers, prostitutes who wished to change their lives, and young women who wished to avoid prostitution. Although the Cunningham House closed in 1911, Johnson was able to raise enough funds to build The Virginia K. Johnson Home and Training School in Oak Cliff. The Home continued to provide shelter for unwed mothers and prostitutes, but it also expanded its program to include Bible study, homemaking and business education. It closed in 1941. Virginia Hall on the SMU campus was also named for Virginia Johnson. **Smith-Carroll Hall** was a dormitory for female college students in Denton.

## New Mexico Conference

**Lydia Patterson Institute** was named for a member of Trinity Methodist Church in El Paso. In May 1906 Lydia Patterson secured approval from the Women's Missionary Society of her church to begin teaching Mexican and Mexican-American children in the pastors' homes. The Effie Eddington School for Mexican Girls already existed, and after Ms. Patterson's death in 1909, her husband, Millard Patterson, decided to establish a school as a tribute to her service. The Institute, which opened in 1913, combined the Eddington and Trinity efforts into a single school. The opening of the Institute coincided with the Mexican Revolution. The influx of Mexican refugees and Methodist missionaries forced out of Mexico meant that Lydia Patterson Institute had a larger client base and also more trained teachers to serve them. The Institute flourished through the 1920s, suffered a downturn during the 1930s, but recovered to continue its vital mission of service and education to the present.

## Other Mission Work

In addition to schools, Wesley Houses, and dormitories, Women's Missionary Society members raised money for parsonages for churches without them. When World War I stimulated the construction of military bases in Texas, the Missionary Societies organized to provide services to the soldiers at San Antonio, Waco, and Fort Worth. Those services included cooperating with the Y.M.C.A. and the Red Cross to provide hospitality, recreation, and practical services such as mending clothing for the young men stationed at those bases. Women also corresponded with families of soldiers confined in the camp hospitals. In a curious note, the 8th Annual Meeting of the Woman's Missionary Council (1918) reported a call for volunteers to protect "our American girls in the vicinity of the encampments."

## METHODIST EPISCOPAL CHURCH

Women of the MEC also established institutions in Texas. Most notable was the King Industrial Home in Marshall. The Home, near the campus of Wiley College, provided sewing, dressmaking, and other domestic training to as many as fifty young African-American women at a time. Most of the support of the King Industrial Home came from the Central Ohio Conference. In 1898 Marguerite J. Tripp opened the Mission School in El Paso to serve Spanish speaking children. Later the Gregory Houchen Settlement House was supported by MEC women.

MEC women also attempted to build an orphanage for African-American children at Harrisburg, about six miles east of Houston. Although the grand plan for a fifty-three acre campus with an industrial school never developed as planned, Mrs. Isabella Howells and her husband did have a school there for several years beginning in 1888.

*References:*

Raymer, Robert G. "The Development of Christianity in the Southwest," *The Methodist Quarterly Review,* June, 1927.

Anon. *An Exhibit of the Industrial Homes, Missions, and Deaconess Homes of the Woman's Home Missionary Society of the Methodist Episcopal Church: Souvenir of the Twentieth Anniversary, 1880-1900,* n.d.

*The New Handbook of Texas*

*Report of the tenth annual session of the Texas Conference Woman's Home Mission Society Methodist Episcopal Church, 1907.*

*Eighth Annual Meeting of the Woman's Missionary Council, 1918.*

Burton, Mrs. Gabie Betts, compiler, *History of the Northwest Texas Conference Woman's Missionary Society Methodist Episcopal Church South,* 1928.

Brown, Mrs. T. A., compiler and writer, *Our Golden Jubilee: Historical Sketch of the Woman's Missionary Society West Texas Conference Methodist Episcopal Church South,* 1928.

The Jubilee Committee Woman's Missionary Society, *History of Woman's Work Texas Annual Conference: 1878-1928,* 1928.

Anon., *Historical Sketch of the Woman's Missionary Society Central Texas Conference Methodist Episcopal Church South,* 1928.

Anon. *"The History of Lydia Patterson Institute,"* n.d. from the files of Lydia Patterson Institute.

Holding, Nannie Emory, *A Decade of Mission Life in Mexican Mission Homes,* Nashville, Methodist Episcopal Church, South, 1895.

CHAPTER 27

# BOHEMIAN AND ITALIAN MISSIONS

As was discussed under the topic of Woman's Missionary Society institutions, missions to immigrants constituted one of the main activities of Progressive Era Methodist activists. Mexican and Japanese missions were mentioned in that discussion. Bohemian and Italian missions were annual conference efforts rather than the Woman's Missionary Society projects. In both cases conferences sponsored a handful of immigrant pastors in missionary efforts among their countrymen. Both Bohemian and Italian immigrants to Texas were overwhelmingly Roman Catholic, and the missionary efforts produced few successes.

Although Texas had been home to Czech immigrants since the days of the Republic, the first decade of the 20th century saw an increase in immigration from Bohemia and Moravia. Discomfort under Austrian rule, the availability of good farm land in Texas, and relatively cheap steamship fares to Galveston all prompted many Czechs to come to Texas. The older Czech settlements had tended to be in Austin, Fayette, Lavaca, and Washington Counties. The newcomers added to those populations and also pressed on to Blackland Prairie settlements in Williamson, Bell, McLennan, Hill, Ellis, and Kaufman counties.

Most Czech immigrants had been Roman Catholic in their homeland, and they remained true to that faith in Texas. Czechs who were Protestant usually attended churches affiliated with the Unity of the Brethren.

Southwestern University became involved in the Bohemian Mission from 1907 to 1912 as the Reverend Vaclav Cejnar divided his time between preaching to Bohemian communities and providing language instruction at the university. There was little demand for the instruction among the general student body, but Cejnar recruited students from Bohemia, including several of his own family members. The April 29, 1909, *Texas Christian Advocate* included a photograph of Cejnar with his students with the article, "Southwestern University as a Factor in the Evangelization of the Foreigner in Texas."

# Bohemian & Italian Missions

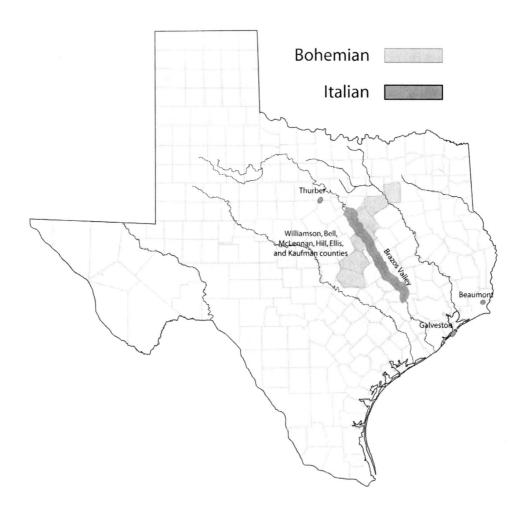

Bohemian
Italian

Thurber

Williamson, Bell,
McLennan, Hill, Ellis,
and Kaufman counties

Brazos Valley

Beaumont

Galveston

Appointments to the "Bohemian Mission" appear in the Journals of the Texas Conference from 1914 through 1918 and of the Central Texas Conference from 1917 to 1920 as follows:

**1914**  J. M. Vondracek Bohemian Missionary to the Marlin District

Joseph Dobes Bohemian Missionary to the Navasota District

**1915**  Both men reappointed

**1916**  Both men reappointed , William Brichta to the Navasota District

**1917**  Henry Ibser appointed to the Bohemian Mission of the Marlin Districh

William Brichta to the Bohemian Mission of the Navasota District

J. M. Vondracek to the Bohemian Mission of the Brenham District

Joseph Dobes transfers to the Central Texas Conference

**1918**  Brichta reappointed

Joseph Dobes appointed to the Georgetown District (Temple) of the Central Texas Conference

Henry Ibser appointed to the Fort Worth District of the Central Texas Conference

Vondracek withdrawn after he "joined a sister church"

**1919**  Dobes and Ibser reappointed, Brichta withdrawn "has joined another church"

**1920**  Ibser reappointed, Dobes goes to the new nation of Czechoslovakia as a missionary

This last appointment was a point of special pride. The dismemberment of the Austrian Empire after World War I created the opportunity to send American-educated missionaries back to an independent Czechoslovakia. As assimilation took place, the Bohemian Mission work was folded into the English speaking church.

## Italian Mission

Many of the same forces that attracted Czech immigrants to Texas in the first decade of the 20th century also encouraged Italians to immigrate. In 1903 one finds the establishment of an Italian mission at Galveston in the Texas Conference Journal. In 1904 that mission is shifted to Beaumont, but in 1908 it was back in Galveston under the direction of Rev. S. Pantaleone who held Sunday afternoon services in First Methodist Church. The coal mines at Thurber also had enough Italian miners to warrant special attention there. The *Texas Christian Advocate* reported an Italian population of 3,000 there in 1909, served by missionary D. Maurini.

In 1915 the Texas Conference received Francisco Zito as a transfer from the Central Texas Conference and appointed him to the Italian mission in the Navasota District. Zito had been converted from Roman Catholicism at a MEC mission in Florence in 1891. He was ordained by the MEC in 1905 and served Italian immigrants in Florida and New Orleans. He continued at Bryan until 1922. Bruno Martinelli who was received on trial that same year assumed responsibilities for the Bryan church as Zito took an extended leave of absence to return to Italy. Zito died in Rome in 1926.

### Counties with greatest foreign born population, Census of 1910

| Italian | Austrian (Czech) |
|---|---|
| Harris 1,057 | Lavaca 2,480 |
| Galveston 1,030 | Fayette 2,477 |
| Erath 720 | Williamson 1,462 |
| Brazos 627 | McLennan 895 |
| Jefferson 478 | Bell 854 |

*References:*

*New Handbook of Texas*

*Texas Conference and Central Texas Conference Journals*

Cannon III, James, *History of Southern Methodist Missions,* Nashville, Cokesbury Press, 1926.

Jones, William B., *To Survive and Excel: The Story of Southwestern University, 1840-2000,* Georgetown, Southwestern University, 2006.

Barcus, John M., "Southwestern University As a Factor in the Evangelization of the Foreigners in Texas," *Texas Christian Advocate,* April 29, 1909.

*13th U.S. Census, 1910*

CHAPTER 28

# SCHOOLS

Establishing schools was a prominent feature of Texas Methodism from the 1840s through the first decades of the 20th century. Both Littleton Fowler and Martin Ruter lobbied the Congress of the Republic of Texas for a university charter and land appropriation. Methodists were so eager to have an educational institution that the first one, Rutersville College, actually preceded the establishment of an annual conference.

One factor that encouraged Methodists to establish schools was the absence of public schools. The charge against the Mexican government in the Texas Declaration of Independence, *"It has failed to establish any public system of education . . .."* was basically true even though private schools with some public assistance had operated briefly in San Antonio and Nacogdoches. There were private schools in Mexican Texas, some of which had religious connections. Baptist preacher Thomas J. Pilgrim established Austin Academy at San Felipe in 1829, and in October 1835 Lydia McHenry and Ann Ayres opened a school at the Ayres house, Montville, near present-day Burton.

Denominational rivalry was another stimulus to the creation of schools. Methodists, Presbyterians, Baptists, and Roman Catholics established schools in pre-Civil War Texas. Rivalry between Presbyterians and Methodists in San Augustine was perhaps the most famous since its pernicious effects included the closing of each denomination's San Augustine school. Presbyterian and Methodist schools also existed in the 1850s in Goliad and Huntsville. (Aranama and Paine College in Goliad and Austin College [men only] and Andrew Female College in Huntsville)

The governance and curricula of those schools varied greatly. Many of the "Methodist" schools were Methodist because the proprietor/principal/teacher was a Methodist preacher who solicited his students from Methodist families, was under appointment, and received a "board of visitors" who were Methodists. Annual conference journals occasionally report that the president of such-and-such a school was allowed to address the conference, and the conference members were urged to send young people to that school. Other schools were founded by districts, annual conferences, and cooperative efforts of annual conferences. In some cases Methodist churches or districts assumed ownership of schools from their proprietors. The curricula of Methodist schools in the 19th century varied from high school through junior college, four-year college, and comprehensive university. Colleges often had a preparatory department which taught high school subjects. The *Second Annual Catalogue of Rutersville College*, 1841 specified a course of study that was divided into seven departments: Moral Science and Belles Lettres, Mathematics, Ancient Languages and Literature, Modern Languages, Natural Science, Preparatory Department, and Female Department. Women could take courses in any of the other departments, and in addition could take piano, painting, and drawing. Although the *Catalogue* states that the president would lecture to the student body on Moral Science and Natural Philosophy semi-weekly, adherence to Methodist doctrine was not a requirement for admission or degree. The Congress of the Republic of Texas, in granting a charter and land to Rutersville, insisted that references to sectarianism be omitted from that charter. Other denominations established "Bible Colleges", but Methodist schools, were organized to provide a general "classical" education—not ministerial education. Methodist preacher education was mainly through self-study of the texts required in the "course of study." The result of such a policy was fortuitous in that the educated men and women who constituted the lay leadership of the annual conferences often formed deep bonds of friendship with the clergy while they were classmates.

Unfortunately the zeal to establish schools often exceeded the ability of Methodists to maintain them. As John H. McLean, who had been intimately associated with several schools, wrote in retrospect, "Our fathers overdid the school business." ("Our Early Schools," *Texas Methodist Historical Quarterly*, vol. II, #1, July 1910.) Methodists could not sustain all the schools. The Civil War was particularly devastating to the cause of Methodist schools in Texas. At Soule University, for example, most of the student body enlisted in the Confederate Army. The economic disruption accompanying the war meant hard times for education, and most of the schools closed.

Compiling a comprehensive list of all the Texas Methodist schools poses a formidable challenge to historians. Some schools such as Soule University have left voluminous documentary evidence of their work. Others are represented only by passing references in Methodist histories and a few lines in annual conference journals. Information in the charts was derived from a variety of sources.

*(Note: Schools which have Texas Historical Commission historical markers are indicated with an "HM." The full text of those markers can be read at www.thc.state.tx.us/)*

# Pre Civil War, Methodist Episcopal Church and Methodist Episcopal Church South

| | | |
|---|---|---|
| Rutersville College | Rutersville, Fayette County HM | Founded in 1840 by Methodists who bought a league of land near present day LaGrange. The college was chartered by the Republic of Texas with no reference to denomination affiliation. It continued until 1856 when its facilities were used by the Texas Monumental and Military Institute. |
| McKenzie Institute (College) | Clarksville, Red River County HM | Founded in 1841 and privately owned by J. W. P. McKenzie until deeded to church. Chartered in 1848. Closed in 1868. |
| Wesleyan College | San Augustine, San Augustine Co.; HM | Chartered in 1844, closed in 1847. |
| Fowler Academy | Henderson, Rusk County | Founded by East Texas Conference of the MECS in 1850. Building later used by the Henderson Male and Female Academy. |
| Chappell Hill Female College | Chappell Hill, Washington County HM | Began as Chappell Hill Institute in 1850, chartered in 1852 as Chappell Hill Male and Female Institute (non-denominational, co-ed), acquired by Methodists in 1854 who split men's department off to form Soule. Closed in 1912. |
| Gilmer Female Institute | Gilmer, Upshur County | Gilmer Masonic Female Institute founded in 1851. Taken over by Gilmer Methodist Church in 1852, East Texas Conference received charter in 1856. Closed in 1857. |
| Bastrop Academy | Bastrop, Bastrop County HM for school's extant bell | Opened 1851, chartered 1853, co-ed. closed in 1872 with property going to public schools. |
| Andrew Female College | Huntsville, Walker County 2 HM | Founded 1852, chartered 1853, closed 1879 with opening of Sam Houston Normal Institute. James Follansbee, first president, followed by Thomas H. Ball, R. T. Heflin, John Patton, and P. C. Archer. |
| Paine Female College | Goliad, Goliad County | Founded 1852 with classes held in Jesse Hord's house. Became Paine Male and Female Institute in 1862. Closed 1877. |
| Starrville Female High School | Starrville, Smith County HM for town | Chartered 1856. Presidents included M. H. Porter and John T. Kennedy. |
| Soule University | Chappell Hill, Washington Co., (Medical Branch in Galveston, Galveston County); HM | Created in 1856 by Texas Conference of the MECS from Male department of Chappell Hill Male and Female Institute. Closed c. 1887. |
| Galveston Medical | | College operated from Nov. 1865 until 1873 as branch of Soule. The law school authorized for Houston never opened. |
| Port Sullivan Male & Female Academy | Port Sullivan, Milam County | 1860 |
| San Saba College | San Saba, San Saba County | Founded as San Saba Masonic College in 1860, chartered in 1863, donated to the MECS in 1879, rechartered in 1885 as "San Saba College." Closed as church school in 1886. |

*cont.*

| | | |
|---|---|---|
| Waco Female Institute (College) | Waco, McLennan County | Successor to Waco Female Seminary (est. 1857) and Waco Academy, Chartered 1860, closed 1895. |
| (Sylvia Academy) | Daingerfield, Morris County | Girls School operated by Miss Margaret Wethred who had begun school at Clarksville as female counterpoint to McKenzie. Moved to Daingerfield and then to Paris where it became Paris Female Seminary. |
| Stovall Academy | Nechesville, Anderson County | Rev. John Adams, president. |
| Name unkown; referred to in conf. minutes as "our school" | Leesburg, Camp County | Rev. I. W. Clark |
| Bastrop Military Inst. | Bastrop, Bastrop County HM | Successor to Bastrop Academy. |
| Guadalupe Male and Female College | Seguin, Guadalupe County | Successor to failed Guadalupe High School Association, 1858 to 1865? Also known as Seguin Male and Female College. J. W. Phillips, president. |
| Murry Institute | Ore City, Upshur County; HM | Rev. Joshua Clark 1853-1861. |
| Fairfield Female Institute (College) | Fairfield, Freestone HM | H. V. Philpot, est. 1856, chartered 1860. Was also Baptist during some of its existence. |
| Methodist Female Inst. | Tyler, Smith County | Mentioned by Thrall. |

After the Civil War, Texas Methodist education became even more complex as schools were founded by the Freedmen's Aid and Southern Educational Society of the MEC, the Woman's Home Missionary Society of the MEC, and the Woman's Home Missionary Society of the MECS, the AME, CME, Free Methodists, and Methodist Protestants. Debt, fire, and competition from public schools plagued Methodist schools in the 19th century. One could choose almost any one of the schools to illustrate the desperation that often followed several years after the enthusiasm of a school's founding. For example in its report to the October 1878 session of the Northwest Texas Conference, the trustees of Waco Female College reported that the mortgage indebtedness (at 18% interest!) would result in foreclosure by January 31 of the following year. That same year in the North Texas Conference, W. F. Easterling, Chairman of the Education Committee wrote, "Finally, your committee feel that they must in candor make for the Conference, and for the church at large, the humiliating confession that we have not properly appreciated and discharged our obligations in relationship to . . . (education) . . . our institutions of learning are living at a 'poor dying rate.'"

The example of failed and failing institutions all around them did not deter Texas Methodists from starting even more colleges. College building in western Texas came immediately upon the heels of settlement. The removal of Native Americans and construction of rail lines across much of western Texas resulted in dramatically increased population in the areas near the rail lines. Settlement of western Texas differed in many respects from settlement into eastern Texas only few decades earlier. Settlement in western Texas was much more likely to be shaped by commercial interests working in concert—the subdivision of ranches into farms by land development companies, the disposal of bounty lands by the railroad corporations, and the platting and sale of town lots by city developers. Town site developers were, in particular, eager to see schools and churches erected. The Townsite Company of Odessa, for example, recruited ten Methodist Episcopal Church families from Pennsylvania and gave them a lot for the construction of Odessa College. Similarly, Clarendon citizens gave the North West Conference of the MECS four acres and a building to house Clarendon College. The Texas border with Mexico was also a focus for school building during the same period as Woman's Missionary Society schools for Mexican children were established. The eastern portion of Texas became the scene of college building by the "other branches of the vine." Most numerous were the institutions of the MEC. Schools for African-Americans were established in Austin and Marshall. A German college in Brenham and a Swedish one in Austin served linguistic minorities. Fort Worth, Alvin, and Port Arthur also had MEC colleges for English speaking white students.

| Coronal Institute | San Marcos, Hayes County HM | Founded 1868, purchased by Rev. Robert Belvin in 1871. San Marcos District purchased it in 1875, closed in 1917. |
|---|---|---|
| Sherman Male and Female High School | Sherman, Grayson County | 1866. North Texas Conference acquired deed in 1873, Name changed to North Texas Female College in 1874. Closed in 1886. Reopened in 1888 as North Texas Female College and Conservatory of Music. Name changed to Kidd-Key College and Conservatory in 1919. Closed in 1935. Kidd-Key ex-students recognized as SMU alumnae. |
| Canaan Institute | Grayson County | Circa 1867, J. R. Coles, administrator. |
| Kidd-Key College | | See Sherman Male and Female High School. |
| Marvin College | Waxahachie, Ellis County HM | Founded by Northwest Texas Conference in 1869. Incorporated in 1873, Lost to creditors in 1878, but repurchased for church. Sold 1884. |
| Parker Institute | Whitt, Parker County | Founded 1881, North West Texas Conference acquired it in 1884. Closed in 1893. |
| Southwestern University | Georgetown, Williamson Co. 3 HM | Opened as Texas University in 1873 under sponsorship of the five MECS conferences in Texas. Name changed in 1875. As successor to Rutersville, Wesleyan, Soule, and McKenzie it claims title as oldest university in Texas. |

*cont.*

| | | |
|---|---|---|
| Paris Female Seminary | Paris, Lamar County | Established by Rev. James Graham by at least 1861. John McLean was president 1869-1870. |
| Central College | Sulphur Springs, Hopkins County | Began as Sulphur Springs District High School in 1877. Chartered in 1883.,Changed name to Eastman College in 1895. |
| Belle Plain College | Belle Plain, Callahan County HM | Founded in 1881 by Northwest Texas Conference. Mortgage holder foreclosed in 1889. College closed in 1892. |
| Holding Institute | Laredo, Webb County | Laredo Seminary founded by MECS in 1880. Closed in 1983. Reopened as community center in 1987. |
| Alexander Collegiate Institute | Danville/Kilgore/Jacksonville, Gregg, Cherokee Counties HM at Kilgore location | Founded as New Danville Masonic Academy in 1854. Moved to Kilgore and renamed Alexander Collegiate Institute in 1873. Acquired by East Texas Conference in1875. Moved to Jacksonville in 1895. Renamed Lon Morris College in 1924. |
| Centenary College | Lampasas, Lampasas County HM | Founded 1883 by local Methodists. Rev. Marshall McIlhaney was first president. First year's enrollment was 174. Closed in 1895. |
| Fredericksburg College | Fredericksburg, Gillespie County; HM | Operated 1876-1884 by German Methodist Church of Fredericksburg. |
| Midlothian College (Whitten Institute) | Midlothian, Ellis County | Began as private boarding school, Polytechnic Academy and later Whitten Academy and Whitten Institute. 1892-1900, Became part of public schools in 1903. |
| Weatherford College | Weatherford, Parker County | Established 1873 as Granbury High School. Added junior college and moved to Weatherford in 1889. Organized as junior college in 1921. |
| Clarendon College | Clarendon, Donley County | Founded by Northwest Texas Conference of the MECS in 1898, became a junior college, closed in 1926. |
| Westmoorland College | San Antonio, Bexar County | Established 1873 under charter issued to Masonic Lodge in 1869. Name changed to Cleveland College in 1884. Renamed Weatherford College after 1889 merger with Granbury College. |
| Franklin District High School | Pilot Point, Denton County | Named for Dr. M. B. Franklin. .Reported five teachers and 165 students in 1890. |
| Granbury Institute (High School) | Granbury, Hood County | Founded as private elementary and high school in 1873. Became Methodist in 1880. Reported 8 teachers and 350 students when moved to Weatherford and merged with Cleveland College to become Weatherford College.  *cont.* |

| | | |
|---|---|---|
| Honey Grove High School | Honey Grove, Fannin County | Reported 6 teachers and 210 students in 1890. |
| Laredo Seminary | Laredo, Webb County | See Holding Institute. |
| Centerville High School | Centerville, Leon County | 1882 Texas Conference Journal recommended that Centerville High School be designated as the District High School of the Presiding Elder District in which it is located. This was year Leon County, among others, was transferred from the North West Texas Conference back to the Texas Conference. |
| Dallas Female College | Dallas, Dallas County | |
| Mitchell College | Huntsville, Walker County | F. C. Mitchell was agent for this college and also for Andrew Female College in 1879 journal. It occupied the buildings of Austin College which the Presbyterians had relocated to Sherman. Reported 64 students. Three conference members elected to board of trustees. |
| San Antonio Female College | San Antonio, Bexar County | Listed as appointment with Alamo College in 1861. Jesse Boring was president of both Alamo and SAFC, Robert Belvin was appointed principal of SAFC. |
| Alamo College | San Antonio, Bexar County | Listed as appointment in 1861. Jesse Boring was president of Alamo College and also of San Antonio Female College. Civil War prevented opening. |
| Central Texas College (University Training School 1901) | Blooming Grove, Navarro County | Organized in 1902 under auspices of "Corsicana Methodist Conference", closed in 1912. |
| Stamford College | Stamford, Jones County | Organized by Northwest Texas Conference in 1907 as Stamford Collegiate Institute, name changed to "College" in 1910. Closed in 1918. |
| Whitesboro Male and Female Academy | Whitesboro, Grayson County | Circa 1870 |
| Bethel Academy | Collin County | William Allen, principal, circa 1870. |

*cont.*

| | | |
|---|---|---|
| Johnson's Point High School | Johnson's Point, Kaufman County | A. H. Brewer, principal, circa 1870 |
| Seth Ward College | Plainview, Hale County HM | Plainview District bought Central Plains College and Conservatory of Music (founded 1907) from the Holiness Church (Nazarenes) in 1910 for $32,000. Closed in 1916. |
| Southern Methodist University | Dallas, Dallas County 8 HM | In 1911 an Educational Commission chose Dallas as site for a new university to be named Southern Methodist University and hired Robert S. Hyer from Southwestern University as President. The 1914 General Conference designated it for all MECS conferences west of the Mississippi River. The affiliation changed to the South Central Jurisdiction of the MC in 1939. |
| Meridian Junior College | Meridian, Bosque County | 1907—Meridian Training School founded by George F. Campbell. In 1909 affiliated with the Gatesville District of the MECS. In 1920 assumed by the Central Texas Conference, closed in 1927 due to three fires. |
| Valley Institute | Pharr, Hidalgo County | Woman's Missionary Society |
| Lydia Patterson Institute | El Paso, Texas | Founded in 1913 as high school. Successor to Effie Eddington School for Mexican Girls. |
| Wesley College | Terrell, Kaufman County, and Greenville, Hunt County 2 HM at Greenville location | Toon College founded in 1897, became Terrell University School in 1902 ownership to the North Texas Conference in 1905 as North Texas (University) Training School. Became Wesley College in 1909, closed in 1911. Reopened in Greenville by Greenville Development Company in 1912. Last term was 1937-38. |
| Cherokee College | Cherokee, San Saba County | Founded 1911 by Llano District of the MECS. Then to Lampasas District. Operated until at least 1918. Building sold in 1921 to public schools. |
| McMurry College | Abilene, Taylor County 2 HM | Northwest Texas Conference chartered in 1921. Opened in 1923. Became McMurry University in 1990. |
| Texas Woman's College | Fort Worth, Tarrant County | Successor to Polytechnic College and predecessor to Texas Wesleyan College. |
| Polytechnic College | Fort Worth, Tarrant County | Established by Northwest Texas Conference in 1890. Hiram Boaz became president in 1902. Became Texas Woman's College in 1914. |
| Texas Wesleyan University | Fort Worth, Tarrant County 2 HM | Successor to Polytechnic College (est. 1890) which became Texas Woman's College in 1914. In 1935 it became coeducational and was renamed Texas Wesleyan College. On January 1, 1989, it became Texas Wesleyan University. |

*cont.*

| | | |
|---|---|---|
| Lon Morris College | Jacksonville, Cherokee County | Successor to Alexander Collegiate Institute when name change occurred in 1924. Owned by Texas Conference. |
| Owensville High School | Owensville, Robertson County | Mentioned by Thrall, 1871 journal reported J. F. Cox appointed there. |
| Cedar Mountain Academy | Dallas County | Mentioned by Thrall. |
| Johnson's Point | Kaufman County | Mentioned by Thrall. |
| Daniel Baker College | Brownwood, Brown County | Daniel Baker College was founded by Presbyterians in 1888. In 1929 it became independent, and in 1946 was acquired by Southwestern University. That relationship was dissolved in 1949. |

## Methodist Episcopal Church

| | | |
|---|---|---|
| Wiley College | Marshall, Harrison County HM | Founded by Freedman's Aid Society of the MEC.1873 Chartered in 1882. |
| Immanuel Institute | Brenham, Washington County | Operated 1876-1878, by Southern German Conference of the MEC, predecessor of Blinn College. |
| Blinn Memorial College | Brenham, Washington County 2 HM | Founded as "Mission Institute" in 1883 by the Southern German Conference of the MEC. Name changed to "Blinn Memorial College" in 1888. Became a junior college in 1927. In 1930 it became a department of Southwestern University. In 1933 became a public junior college. |
| Samuel Huston College | Austin, Travis County 2 HM | Freedman's Aid Society of the MEC. Purchased property in 1883. Opened in 1900. Merged to become Huston-Tillotson College in 1952. |
| Fort Worth University | Fort Worth, Tarrant County | Chartered as Texas Wesleyan College by MEC in 1881, name changed to Fort Worth University in 1889. After unsuccessful attempt to merge with Polytechnic in 1911, its assets were divided among Port Arthur College, Texas Wesleyan College (Austin) and new MEC college being opened in Oklahoma City. |
| Alvin College | Alvin, Brazoria County | 1900 General Conference Journal: "A school has been started at Alvin, Tex., under the auspices of the Austin and Gulf Mission Conferences." Reported 5 teachers and 100 students. *cont.* |

| | | |
|---|---|---|
| Texas Wesleyan College (Institute) | Austin, Travis County | Board of trustees named in 1909 by the Southern Swedish Conference of the MEC. First classes held in 1912. Name changed to Texas Wesleyan Academy in 1935. After 1936 only music classes conducted. All classes discontinued in 1956 |
| Port Arthur College | Port Arthur, Jefferson County | Business College founded in 1909. Became part of Lamar University in 1975. |
| Odessa College | Odessa, Ector County | Odessa Townsite Company donated $12,000 which was matched by MEC. Austin Conference of MEC established school in 1891. Fourteen students. Fire forced closing after one session. |
| Rutersville School | Rutersville, Fayette County | MEC, Southern German Conference appointed John Plueneke professor. |
| West Texas Conference Seminary | (Austin, Travis County ?) | West Texas Conference appointed Thomas M. Dart president and member of the Simpson Quarterly Conference. Simpson charge was in Austin |

## African Methodist Episcopal

| | | |
|---|---|---|
| Paul Quinn College | Austin, Travis County; Waco, McLennan County; Dallas, Dallas County HM at Waco location | Founded by AME preachers in Austin in 1872 as Connectional High School and Institute for Negro Youth. Moved to Waco in 1877 and to Dallas in 1990 Also known as Waco College. |
| Bishop Ward Normal and Collegiate Institute for Negroes | Hunstville, Walker County | Effort of Presiding Elder C. Porter who founded school in 1883. Named for Bishop T. M. D. Ward (1823-1894) |

## Methodist Protestant Church

| | | |
|---|---|---|
| Westminster College | Seven Points, Collin County and Tehuacana, Limestone County | Founded in 1888 as Seven Points College. Became Methodist Protestant in 1895 and renamed "Westminster" in 1902 and moved to Tehuacana. Briefly associated with Southwestern. Campus sold to Congregational Methodist Church in 1950. |

## Colored (later Christian) Methodist Episcopal Church

| | | |
|---|---|---|
| Texas College | Tyler, Smith County | Founded in 1894 by Colored Methodist Episcopal Church Named Phillips College from 1909-1912. Original name restored 1913. |

## Congregational Methodist

| Congregational Methodist Bible School, also known as Westminster Bible Institute | Dallas, Dallas County, Tehuacana, Limestone County | In Dallas from 1944 until 1953. In Tehuacana from that date until 1972 when it was moved to Florence, Mississippi. Renamed Wesley College in 1976. |
|---|---|---|

## Free Methodist

| | Lawrence, Kaufman County | Free Methodist seminary operated from 1889 until 1892 |
|---|---|---|
| Free Methodist Seminary | Campbell then McKinney, Collin County | Established in 1910 relocated to McKinney in 1918, closed in 1922. |

## Nazarene

| | Pilot Point, Denton County | Seminary merged with Central Nazarene College sometime after 1911. |
|---|---|---|
| Central Nazarene College | Hamlin, Jones County | Chartered 1911, opened in 1911 with J. E. L Moore as president. Merged with Bethany Peniel College in Bethany, Oklahoma in 1929. |
| Central Plains College and Conservatory of Music | Plainview, Hale County | Originally named Central Plains Holiness College. Opened Sept. 18, 1907, with 159 students. Sold to Plainview District of the NWT Conference in 1910 who renamed it Seth Ward College. |

## Post Civil War Methodist Episcopal Church South

Methodist educational leaders could not ignore the dismal survival rate of their schools. It took little reflection to realize that it would be wiser to concentrate educational efforts into a few stronger schools than to continue to provide inadequate support to many weak schools. Plans to strengthen struggling schools usually involved relocation and/or consolidation. The criteria for choosing a site for a school location or relocation changed through the 19th century. A continuing factor was community support. The cultural and economic advantages that would accrue to the town selected as the school location were obvious. In April 1855 the commissioners appointed by the Texas Conference to locate a university entertained proposals from San Felipe, Richmond, and Waco. Chappell Hill was selected as the site for Soule University because its citizens had raised $50,000 in notes and pledges to support a Methodist college. In several other instances colleges were located because vacant buildings were

153

available because some previous school had failed. Three other factors influenced school-location decisions in the 19th century:

First, there was an initial bias in favor of rural locations over urban ones. Rutersville College, for example, was located in the town of Rutersville whose townsite was controlled by Methodists. They could, and did, prohibit alcohol from Rutersville. John H. McLean, writing later of the decision to locate Southwestern University at Georgetown, said that the Williamson County site was ". . .free from the grosser forms of vice incident in large cities." As Texas became more urban in the late 19th and early 20th centuries, the anti-urban bias was dropped. The institutions were forced to follow students and wealth to the cities.

The second location factor was a health factor. Even before the link between mosquitoes and disease was established near the turn of the 20th century, everyone was aware that the coastal plains were unhealthy. Parents would not send their children to schools in the "fever belt." Even the rumor of a yellow fever epidemic in 1867 was enough to send the Soule student body fleeing. In the early 20th century, the MEC did establish schools at Port Arthur and Alvin on the coastal plains, but that was only after public health measures had eliminated the threat of yellow fever and decreased the malaria hazard. These two biases, anti-urban and anti-coastal plain, help to explain why two of the most prominent Texas cities, Galveston and Houston lacked Methodist schools even though both cities had strong Methodist churches and laity such as Mr. and Mrs. Walter Fondren, Harry C. Weiss, Eddy Scurlock, Arthur and Evie Jo Wilson, R. E. and Vivian Smith, W. L Moody, Jr., and Herman Brown who became legendary in Texas Methodist educational philanthropy. (In the late 20th century Methodist education finally came to Houston and Galveston. Perkins School of Theology offered extension courses that met in Houston and Galveston. First United Methodist, Houston, also opened Wesley Academy which provided education through the 8th grade.)

The third factor in college location was transportation. The determining factor for settlement during the heyday of founding Methodist schools was the routes chosen by railroad surveyors. Many towns were deserted when they were bypassed by the rails while others sprang up, especially where two rail lines crossed. Two excerpts from college catalogs illustrate how important railroads were to college location:

> *Jacksonville is beautifully located in the fruit belt of East Texas, at the intersection of the Cotton Belt* (St. Louis and Southwestern), *and the International and Great Northern Railways. These, with their connecting lines, render it easily accessible from every part of East Texas. The location is healthful. The large amounts of fine fruits produced in the immediate vicinity makes it possible, at a slight*

*expense, for everybody to have an abundance of fresh or canned fruit the year round.*

*Annual Register*,
28th session of the Alexander Collegiate Institute
1899-1900

*Location: Chappell Hill is one of the most refined and cultured towns to be found in Texas. It is situated 10 miles from Brenham on the Austin Branch of the H and TC RY* (Houston and Texas Central) *and an equal distance from Hempstead. Thus we have easy connections with the railroads from all points. Chappell Hill is located on a high rolling prairie. The community is almost completely free from malaria. The surrounding country with its farms, together with its wooded hills, and pastures interspersed therein, dotted here and there with the magnificent residences, is one of the most beautiful scenes in southeast Texas.*

Regular Session of the 55th Session
1908-1909 of Chappell Hill Female College

The scenic attractions of Chappell Hill were insufficient. The Texas Conference, in an attempt to broaden the base of support for Soule University, granted the East Texas Conference the privilege of naming ten of the twenty-five trustees. Even with that measure, Soule did not fulfill the vision of the "Central" university. That torch was passed first to Southwestern which had the support of all the MECS annual conferences in Texas, and later to Southern Methodist University with an even greater regional support. The stories of the location decisions that resulted in Georgetown and Dallas as seats for the central university are told in other chapters. One more critical period needs to be considered for an understanding of school location as part of the history of Texas Methodist schools—the Great Depression of the 1930s.

The economic and social hardships of the 1930s created problems for both public and denominational schools. In 1932 the five annual conferences of the MECS entirely within Texas named delegates to the Joint Commission on Methodist Educational Work in Texas. The Commission was charged with investigating the status of the ten MECS schools in Texas and making recommendations for their future direction.

The Commission found that only Southern Methodist University was operating on a reasonably sound financial basis. Recommendations for the other nine colleges included closing Weatherford College (Weatherford), Kidd-Key (Sherman), Texas Woman's College (Fort Worth), and Wesley College (Greenville). Blinn (Brenham) and Westmoorland (San Antonio) would be merged with Southwestern, if Southwestern were to become solvent. If Southwestern could not become solvent, it would either continue as a women's junior college in Georgetown, move to the

Westmoorland campus in San Antonio, or be merged with SMU. No recommendations were made for changing Lon Morris (Jacksonville) or McMurry (Abilene).

The report of the Commission contains many references to location. Much of the blame for the economic distress of the schools was blamed on the concentration of schools in North Texas. The hope was that one (and only one) Methodist school would survive in each of the five conferences and would, therefore, solve that problem.

The Commission's recommendations were not implemented *in toto*. Southwestern University was able solve its debt problem and remain in Georgetown. Wesley College and Kidd-Key College were closed. Weatherford College and Blinn survived as public junior colleges when association with Southwestern proved unworkable. Westmoorland provided the campus for Trinity University's relocation to San Antonio from Waxahachie. Texas Woman's College was able to survive by becoming co-educational as Texas Wesleyan College.

The reorganization of the 1930s and 1940s and the 1939 Union brought two former MEC colleges into the new Methodist Church. The result was that all five of the United Methodist annual conferences completely within Texas have at least one, but no more than two, institutions of higher education within their boundaries:

| | |
|---|---|
| Texas Conference: | Lon Morris College at Jacksonville and Wiley College at Marshall |
| North Texas Conference: | Southern Methodist University at Dallas |
| Central Texas Conference: | Texas Wesleyan University at Fort Worth and Southwestern University at Georgetown |
| Southwest Texas Conference: | Huston-Tillotson University at Austin |
| Northwest Texas Conference: | McMurry University at Abilene |

The Texas portion of the New Mexico Conference contains a high school, Lydia Patterson Institute at El Paso.

*References:*

Evans, C. E., *The Story of Texas Schools*, Steck Company, Austin, 1955.

Stowell, Jay S., *Methodist Adventures in Negro Education*, The Methodist Book Concern, New York, 1922.

Sinks, Julia Lee, "*Rutersville College*," *Quarterly of the Texas State Historical Association, vol 2, number 2*.

Selecman, Charles C., "*One Hundred Years of Methodist Education*," in Nail, ed., *Texas Methodist Centennial Yearbook*.

*New Handbook of Texas*

MECS and MEC Annual Conference *Journals*

Urbantke, Carl, *Texas is the Place for Me*, Pemberton Press, Austin, 1970.

Thrall, Homer S. *History of Methodism in Texas*, E. H. Cushing, Publisher, Houston, 1872.

Phelan, Macum, *A History of Early Methodism in Texas*, Cokesbury Press, 1924.

Phelan, Macum, *The Expansion of Methodism in Texas*, Van Nort, 1937.

*Texas Historical Commission* www.thc.state.tex.us/

Kenney, M. M., *"Recollections of Early Schools," Quarterly of the Texas State Historical Association*, vol. 1, #4, October, 1898.

Grimes, Lewis Howard, *A History of Perkins School of Theology*, SMU Press, Dallas, 1993.

*Catalog of the second session of Rutersville College, 1841.*

*Texas Christian Advocate*, April 6, 1855.

McLean, John H., *Reminiscences, Nashville, 1922.*

Cody, C. C., *The Life and Labors of Francis Asbury Mood*, Chicago, 1888.

*Regular Session of the 55th Session , 1908-1909 of Chappell Hill Female College.*

*Annual Register, 28th session of the Alexander Collegiate Institute, 1899-1900.*

Martin, Robert L., *The City Moves West: Economic and Industrial Growth in Central West Texas*, Austin, UT Press, 1969.

Blodgett, Jan, *Land of Bright Promise: Advertising the Texas Panhandle and South Plains, 1870-1971*, Austin, UT Press, 1988.

*Report of the Joint Commission on Methodist Educational Work in Texas, C. M. Montgomery, Chair, 1933.*

Spellman, Norman, *Growing A Soul: The Story of A Frank Smith*, Dallas, SMU Press, 1979.

Hardt, John Wesley, ed., *Cecil Peeples: A Twentieth Century Giant*, Dallas, UMR Communications, 1999.

Cody, C. C., *"Soule University," Texas Methodist Historical Quarterly*, vol. 2, no. 3, Jan. 1911.

McMullen, William C., *"A Descriptive History of Wesley College,"* Doctor of Education dissertation, North Texas State University, 1987.

Winfield, Mr. and Mrs. Nath, *All Our Yesterdays: A Brief History of Chappell Hill*, Texian Press, Waco, 1969.

Bentley, F. Edward, *"Soule University from 1872 to 1887", The Chappell Hill Historical Review, vol III, 1997.*

*Journal of the General Conference of the MEC. 1900.*

Baldwin, John W., *An Early History of Walker County, Texas*, M. A. Thesis, Sam Houston State Teacher's College, 1954.

Smith, Boyce O., *A History of the Andrew Female College*, Thesis, University of Texas, 1930.

Wright, Richard R., *Centennial Encyclopedia of the African Methodist Episcopal Church*, Book Concern of the AME Church, 1916.

Jones, William B., *To Survive and Excel: The Story of Southwestern University, 1840-2000*, Georgetown, 2006.

Milhouse, Paul, *Oklahoma City University: A Miracle at 23rd and Blackwelder*, Oklahoma Heritage Association, 1984.

CHAPTER 29

# SOUTHWESTERN UNIVERSITY, A CENTRAL UNIVERSITY

One of the main activities of Texas Methodists in the mid-19th century was founding schools. Unfortunately the enthusiasm for founding schools all too often faded as the difficulties of maintaining schools became apparent. The governance of Methodist schools was a hodgepodge. Some were district efforts, others were conference institutions, and still others represented the efforts of a single individual who happened to be Methodist. The high hopes on which Methodist schools were founded were seldom fulfilled. The problems of debt, fire, epidemics, and Civil War meant that most of the early Texas Methodist schools lasted only briefly.

Some Methodists came to realize that their educational efforts often relied on too small a base of support and came to the conclusion that a central university, supported by all the Texas Methodist conferences would remedy that defect. The leader in the movement to create a central university was Francis Asbury Mood, a South Carolinian who had come to Chappell Hill to assume the presidency of Soule University in 1868. Mood found the situation at Soule so desperate that within a year he had come to the conclusion that it would be better to start a new university than to try to revive an existing one. Mood presented his plan for the five Texas conferences to unite behind a single university to the Soule University Board of Trustees on October 4, 1869, and immediately began working toward that goal. Robert Alexander warned him of the "impossibility to unite the five Texas conferences on anything," but Mood was not dissuaded. He attended all five of the 1869 annual conferences meeting in Henderson, Paris, Weatherford, Goliad, and LaGrange and secured favorable action on his plan from each session.

The annual conferences authorized an organizing convention to meet at Ryland Chapel in Galveston in April 1870. At that meeting plans were made to go ahead with the organization of a central Methodist university to be named the Texas University. Mood had secured assent on the general proposition to establish a central university,

# Siting A Central University

Southwestern University
Administration Building 1896

31°North Latitude

Site
chosen

but significant pitfalls lay in the implementation of the plan. The siting of the university was one of the most formidable of those pitfalls. Several cities were eager to be selected as the site and enjoy the prestige and economic benefits that would thus accrue. Mood realized that as long as the site was not named, the contending cities would enthusiastically support the project in the hope that their city would be chosen. A meeting of the convention in charge of the project met in Waxahachie in April 1871. Partisans of that city mounted a campaign to locate the university there at Marvin College. Mood resisted what was called "the catastrophe of premature location."

Mood also had to contend with rumors that he intended for Soule University to serve as the central university. Since epidemic disease had been one of the main problems for the older universities, it was widely assumed that coastal cities would not even be considered. This thinking was codified in resolution form at the 1872 annual conferences as

> *They shall have authority to name the locality where the university shall be established; provided it be north of 31° north latitude, the counties of Bell, Williamson, Burnet, and Travis excepted.*

Ten cities presented petitions to try to obtain the university. Mood visited Fairfield, Calvert, Fort Worth, Salado, Belton, Waco, Austin, and Georgetown. The regents chose Georgetown as the site. Rev. John H. McLean later wrote

> *For beauty of scenery and healthfulness, Georgetown is not easily surpassed. . . . Being an inland town, it is well protected against contagion . . ..*

The Texas University opened in Georgetown in 1873. In 1876 the Regents changed the name to Southwestern University.

*References*:

C. C. Cody, *The Life and Labors of Francis Asbury Mood*, Chicago, F. H. Revell, 1886.

McLean, Jno. H. *Reminiscences* Nashville, Smith and Lamar, 1918.

Jones, Ralph Wood, *History of Southwestern University, Austin*, Jenkins Publishing Co., 1973.

*Journal of the Texas Annual Conference* 1872.

Jones, William B., *Southwestern University: To Survive and Excel, 1840-2000*, Georgetown, 2006.

Mood, Francis Asbury, *For God and Texas: Autobiography of Francis Asbury Mood, 1830-1884*, Edited by Mary Katherine Metcalf Earney, Dallas, Listo Publications, 2000.

CHAPTER 30

# SOUTHERN METHODIST UNIVERSITY

The notion of centrality had been important in siting decisions for both Soule University and Southwestern University. Other considerations such as community support, transportation, healthy environs, and insulation from the temptations of urban life also played important parts. School founders weighed those considerations from the founding of Rutersville in 1840 all through the 19th century. In the first decade of the 20th century, however, some Texas Methodists called for the creation of a university consisting of several colleges. The old standards that had been used in locating preparatory schools and colleges with classical curricula no longer applied. Railroad construction and public health advances had diminished regional differences. Rural location which had once been touted as advantageous came to be seen less favorably because rural communities could offer neither the financial support nor the base of potential students now required.

Much of the change was due to the perceived need for university rather than college education. Not just in Texas, but throughout the United States, lawyers, physicians, dentists, engineers, teachers, and preachers were taking the steps that would result in the professionalization of those occupations. Central to those steps was the establishment of universities for rigorous training, research, and the acquisition of credentials to demonstrate the completion of that training. A successful university would benefit from a large population base from which to draw both students and community financial support. Medical and law schools also employed practicing physicians and attorneys as adjunct faculty. Cities were more likely to be able to provide those professionals.

The increasing desire for a Texas Methodist university coincided with a "golden age" in North Central Texas. On December 24, 1872, the Missouri, Kansas, and Texas Railway crossed the Red River at Denison. The Houston and Texas Central arrived at Dallas earlier that same year. The northern Blackland Prairie, and especially Dallas,

Collin, Denton, Fannin, and Grayson Counties, entered an era of prosperity and population growth as Texas was linked to the rest of the United States through that region. By 1900 Dallas had assumed the dominant position in the northern Blackland Prairie. Delegates to the MECS General Conference of 1902, meeting in Dallas, came to a city that was already parlaying its rail connections with St. Louis, Chicago, and Kansas City into becoming the commercial, banking, and insurance capital of Texas, and much of Oklahoma Territory, Louisiana, Arkansas, and New Mexico Territory. Meanwhile Fort Worth was booming as a result of industrial growth based on processing meat, hides, and grain produced on the western plains. Texas became integrated into the national economy. Dallas and Fort Worth became the hub around which that integration turned. The result was that North Texas dominated Texas in terms of both population and wealth. Its employment base in finance, insurance, and commerce required an educated white-collar work force.

The increasing demand for a university and North Texas's "golden age" created interest in establishing a Methodist university in North Texas. Several options were considered: 1.) Move Southwestern from Georgetown, 2.) upgrade Polytechnic in Fort Worth, 3.) build a new university, and 4.) Move Southwestern to Fort Worth and combine it with Polytechnic. The president of Southwestern at the time was Robert S. Hyer, an eminent physicist as well as a college administrator. Hyer wanted to move Southwestern to Dallas, but could not convince the trustees to do so. After several years of discussion, debate, and letters about the issue in the *Texas Christian Advocate*, the MECS annual conferences of Texas voted in their 1910 sessions to create the Texas Education Commission and invest it with the power to both establish a new university and determine its site.

Since the real debate had been over the establishment of the Commission, when it convened for the first time in January 1911, it was able to proceed rapidly under its chairman, Bishop James Atkins. A handful of towns had competed for Soule. Ten towns competed for Southwestern. In 1911 the stakes were higher. Fort Worth and Dallas were the only cities wealthy enough to be in the running. Both cities offered inducements of cash, pledges, and real estate. The commission chose a site six miles north of downtown Dallas and immediately hired Robert S. Hyer as president. Hyer then chose Hiram Boaz, president of Polytechnic, as vice-president. Much of the success of the new university was due to Boaz's administrative and fund raising talents. The names considered for the university all had some geographic component. *Southern Methodist University* won out over *Southland University*, *Texas Wesleyan University*, and *Trans-Mississippi University*.

Although initially conceived as a project of the five MECS annual conferences wholly within Texas, the fledgling institution enlarged its scope even before instruction began. The German Mission Conference, New Mexico Conference, East Oklahoma, and West Oklahoma Conference all asked to participate, and trustees from those conferences joined the board of trustees in 1913. The General Conference of 1914 named a commission on theological education in the wake of Vanderbilt University's severing its connections with the MECS. Support for seminaries was by no means universal. Only a small handful of Methodist preachers of the era possessed a seminary education. Ministerial education had been mainly "learn by doing" as a junior preacher under the supervision of an experienced preacher and reading the books assigned in the course of study. There was even a tradition of hostility toward seminary education by those who thought it distanced preachers from their parishioners. The MECS Commission recommended two connectional schools of theology, one east of and one west of the Mississippi River. Emory College in Atlanta was the eastern one, and Southern Methodist was the western one since it was the only one in that region. When the 1918 General Conference accepted the commission's recommendations, it meant that annual conferences in Arkansas, Louisiana, and Missouri as well as Texas, Oklahoma, and New Mexico, would all relate to Southern Methodist University.

The Dallas location, with its excellent rail connections to all these states made more sense than ever. After unification in 1939, SMU's connection was to the South Central Jurisdiction. The states named above and Kansas and Nebraska constituted that jurisdiction. It remained the only Methodist seminary in the jurisdiction until St. Paul's School of Theology in Kansas City received its charter in 1958.

Even though its planners did not speak of SMU as a central Texas Methodist university, over the years its School of Theology became a unifying force in Texas Methodism. The School of Theology, named Perkins School of Theology in 1945, not only provided seminary education for preachers in all of the annual conferences in Texas, it expanded its program to include Pastor's Week, Laity Week, and the Course of Study. Its professors served as guest preachers and lecturers in local churches throughout the state, and many Perkins students served student appointments in the various annual conferences.

The SMU Board of Trustees is elected by the South Central Jurisdiction fifty percent of whom must be United Methodist. The College of Bishops nominates three bishops and nine other persons to serve on the Board. Any change in the Board's bylaws or transfer of property constituting the original campus must be approved by the Jurisdiction. (Note: The bishops of a jurisdiction constitute the "college." All UM bishops make up the "Council" of Bishops.)

*References:*

*New Handbook of Texas*

Thomas, Mary Martha Hosford, *Southern Methodist University: Founding and Early Years*, SMU Press, Dallas, 1974.

*"A Brief Resume of the History of Southern Methodist University,"* in Nail, ed., *Texas Methodist Centennial Yearbook, 1934.*

Grimes, Lewis Howard, *A History of Perkins School of Theology,* SMU Press, Dallas, 1993.

Jones, William B., *To Survive and Excel: The Story of Southwestern University, 1840-2000.* Georgetown, Southwestern University, 2006.

CHAPTER 31

# ENCAMPMENTS

The camp meeting was one of the defining institutions of 19th century Methodism in Texas. Families would gather for two or even three week revivals in late summer or early fall while they were waiting for crops to mature. Preachers from nearby churches, often aided by travelling evangelists, led the campers in worship, song, and prayer. Many, if not most, Methodists were members of churches which were points on a circuit which had worship services only once or twice per month. Camp meetings typically had three preaching services per day. An attendee could therefore hear more preaching in two weeks than in the rest of the year. The religious intensity in such an isolated atmosphere often had the desired effect of religious conversion and decisions to devote one's life to full-time church professions. A main camp meeting emphasis was upon young people who had not made a public declaration of their faith or decided upon their life's work.

Camp meetings were so important to the religious and social life of the community that sites were obtained, associations were formed, and primitive facilities were constructed throughout much of Texas in the late 19th and early 20th centuries. Urbanization and the increase in number of churches that had weekly rather than monthly worship services helped to bring an end to most camp meetings.

The late 19th and early 20th centuries was also the period when a youth organization called the Epworth League was formed in the MEC (1889) and MECS (1890) Local churches, districts, and annual conferences formed Epworth Leagues soon after that. In 1896 the state convention of the Texas Epworth Leagues drew 10,000 participants to San Antonio. That particular convention was notable not just for its size. Conventioneers were given an opportunity to go on a special excursion train to Monterrey, Mexico, to observe missionary efforts there and at Laredo Seminary firsthand.

The Texas Epworth League continued its activity into the 20th century. In 1905 it purchased property near Corpus Christi and developed it into a campground called

# Encampments

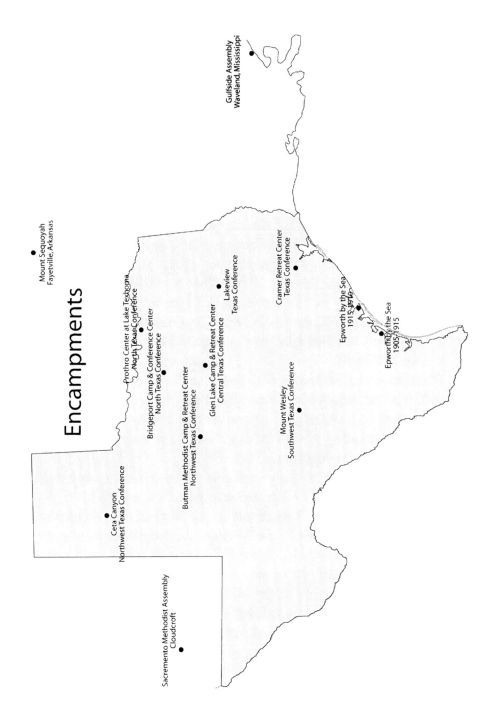

Gulfside Assembly
Waveland, Mississippi

Mount Sequoyah
Fayetville, Arkansas

Prothro Center at Lake Texhoma
North Texas Conference

Bridgeport Camp & Conference Center
North Texas Conference

Butman Methodist Camp & Retreat Center
Northwest Texas Conference

Glen Lake Camp & Retreat Center
Central Texas Conference

Lakeview
Texas Conference

Cramer Retreat Center
Texas Conference

Epworth by the Sea
1915-1918

Epworth by the Sea
1905-1915

Mount Wesley
Southwest Texas Conference

Ceta Canyon
Northwest Texas Conference

Sacremento Methodist Assembly
Cloudcroft

Epworth by the Sea. Campers slept mainly in tents on the beach. In 1915 Epworth by the Sea was sold and similar facilities were developed at Port O'Connor. A hurricane destroyed that camp in 1919, and it was not rebuilt.

There would be no more statewide Methodist encampments after 1919. Each conference would develop its own encampment—especially for youth but not by the League itself.

The Northwest Texas Conference's effort stemmed from an August 1916 camping trip conducted by Mrs. Tom C. Delaney, Conference Secretary of Young People. She took several girls to Rocking Chair Ranch in Collingsworth County and began working toward a conference camp under the auspices of the Woman's Missionary Society. The Woman's Missionary Society and the Northwest Texas Annual Conference combined their efforts, and in 1926 purchased 315 acres in Palo Duro Canyon. This facility, Ceta Canyon, was described as . . ." one of the most beautiful spots with which nature has blessed any country. The towering rock ribbed walls sink abruptly from the level surface above to a cool sparkling stream below, which is fed by many springs and winds along in idle leisure through the heart of the Canyon."

The West Texas (now Southwest Texas) Conference established Mount Wesley at Kerrville during this time. It opened for camping in 1924. The Central Texas Conference bought property at Glen Rose in 1939. The North Texas and Texas Conferences both acquired property in 1947 at Lake Bridgeport and in Anderson County (Lakeview) respectively. In 1962 the North Texas Conference accepted another camp site on Lake Texhoma from the Sherman District. That facility was later renamed the Prothro Center at Lake Texhoma.

The Northwest Texas Annual Conference acquired a second encampment site in 1953 with the gift of 231 acres near Abilene from Mr. Sam Butman, Jr. The Texas Annual Conference also received a gift of property to be used as a retreat center. The Cramer UM Retreat Center, consisting of 18.5 acres of land, three houses, and ponds, is located near Spring in northern Harris County.

Texas Methodists could also point to their relation to three other encampments outside Texas. The New Mexico Annual Conference has owned Sacramento Methodist Assembly since 1931. It is located near Cloudcroft in the Sacramento Mountains. Although that encampment is in the state of New Mexico, it is conveniently close to most of the Texas charges of the New Mexico Annual Conference. The MECS established Mount Sequoyah at Fayetteville, Arkansas, in 1923. That encampment was designed to serve the western constituency of the MECS in much the same way that Lake Junaluska, in the mountains of western North Carolina, served the eastern constituency. After 1939 and the creation of the jurisdictional system, Mount Sequoyah has related to the South Central Jurisdiction, and therefore to Texas Methodists. Bishop Robert Jones of the MEC spearheaded the drive for an encampment for African-Americans who faced exclusion and discrimination in the Jim Crow era. His efforts led to the establishment of Gulfside Assembly, a 140-acre facility in Mississippi.

*References:*

(Epworth) *League Directory*, 1899.

"A Step Over Into Mexico," Jno. J. Tigert, *The Methodist Review*, July-August 1896.

Hardt, John Wesley, *Lakeview: A Story Of Inspiring Unity*, United Methodist Reporter, n.d.

Burton, Gabie Betts, History of the Northwest Texas Conference Woman's Missionary Society, MECS,

Egger, Darris, *Butman Methodist Camp in Mulberry Canyon*, published by the trustees of Butman Methodist Camp and Retreat Center, n.d.

"The Cramer United Methodist Retreat Center", informational bulletin published by the Texas Annual Conference.

www.sacramentoassembly.org

CHAPTER 32

# MECS, MC, UMC
# JOURNALISM AND PUBLISHING

Publishing has been a large part of Methodism from its origins. John Wesley was one of the most prolific authors of the 18th century. Since most preachers received their education by reading the prescribed texts of the *Course of Study*, there was a built-in demand for a publishing and book distribution enterprise to grow up along with the church itself. Methodist circuit riders were often the only sources of reading material in new settlements. Nathan Bangs recorded the statement of a Protestant Episcopal Church member who wished to donate to the rebuilding of the New York City Publishing House after a fire in February 1836. "I have lived heretofore in the new countries; and I remember the time when the people who dwelt in their log cabins had no other books to read but such as they obtained from Methodist itinerants, who carried them around their circuits in their saddle-bags, and after preaching sold them to the people." Book depositories in New York City and Cincinnati supplied the demand for religious texts, pamphlets, and quadrennial editions of the *Discipline*.

Methodist publishing was also intimately connected with missionary endeavors. Employees of the Book Concern conducted the correspondence of the Missionary Society. Denominational newspapers published letters from missionaries in the field. Martin Ruter, who later came to Texas as a missionary, had managed the Cincinnati Book Depository from its founding in 1820 until his assumption of the presidency of Augusta College in 1828. The election of book agents to manage the New York and Cincinnati Book Depositories was a function of General Conference. Several of those elections rivaled episcopal elections in drama. After the creation of the MECS, that denomination's publishing efforts were centered in Nashville, Tennessee.

The first Texas Methodist publishing venture that can be identified is the *Texas Christian Advocate and Brenham Advertiser* launched by Reverend Robert B. Wells in 1847 as a private venture. That newspaper, which contained both denominational and secular news, was short lived. In 1848, Wells' father-in-law, Orceneth Fisher, moved the newspaper to Houston where it was published under the name of the *Texas Christian Advocate*. In September 1848, at a Rutersville camp meeting, both the East Texas and Texas Conferences adopted the newspaper, changed the name to the *Texas Wesleyan Banner*, and appointed Chauncey Richardson as editor. Mounting debts, an overly generous salary for the editor, and inability to attract more than approximately 1,500 subscribers plagued the newspaper. In 1854 the newspaper was moved to Galveston and renamed the *Texas Christian Advocate*. Other *Christian Advocates* of the 1850's included those of the MEC at New York City, Auburn, New York, Cincinnati, Pittsburgh, Chicago, St. Louis, San Francisco, and Salem, Oregon, in addition to *Zion's Herald*, published in Boston and the German-language *Christian Apologist* published in Cincinnati. The MECS published *Advocates* in Nashville, Richmond, Charleston, Raleigh, New Orleans, Memphis, St. Louis, and San Francisco. It, too, published a German-language newspaper, the *Evangelische Apologete*, in Galveston. Both the MEC and the MECS also published Sunday School literature, hymnals, and quarterly journals.

The Civil War blockade of Galveston brought about an evacuation of the presses to Houston and cessation of publication until December 1864. The newspaper returned to Galveston in 1866 where it became the leading denominational newspaper in Texas with a circulation of 10,500 by 1884. That same year G. W. Briggs assumed the editor's duties from Isaac G. John. Both men were preachers first and journalists second. As Briggs wrote when he assumed the editorship, "Being without experience in journalism, it is natural that I should enter upon this work with some trepidation." (*Texas Christian Advocate*, Dec. 27, 1884.) The *Advocate* also had an associate editor in each of the annual conferences of the day. Several of these associate editors such as Homer S. Thrall and Horace Bishop, became quite prominent in the life of the church. As was typical of journalism of that period, the *Advocate* contained both original news articles and articles reprinted from other newspapers—especially other regional *Advocates*. Obituaries of prominent Methodists, pastoral appointments, announcements of camp meetings, vigorous editorials in favor of prohibition and against other social ills, constituted the bulk of the text. Briggs' assumption of the editorship provided an opportunity to state the *Advocate's* goals. The January 3, 1885, issue contained the following message to readers:

*In 1885*

*It will aim to be a Texas Paper fulfilling its great mission as the organ of the Five Texas Conferences and continually concerned for the welfare of the people of the whole state*

*A Methodist Paper: Teaching and defending the doctrines, supporting the institutions and laboring for the prosperity of the Methodist Episcopal Church, South.*

*A Family Paper: providing home reading for laymen as well as preachers, for the young as well as the old, with a carefully edited department for children.*

*A New Paper: Giving full reports of the history of the church throughout the connection and in foreign fields, and reports of such secular news as may be instructive and helpful to its readers.*

*A Literary Paper: Securing contributions from the best pens in Texas, and throughout the Union.*

*A Commercial Paper: Giving full reports of the markets, with editorial comment and interpretation when necessary.*

*A Clean Paper: Permitting nothing sensational, nothing acrimonious, nothing impure, to appear in the columns of either the reading or advertising departments*

*A Fearless Paper: Vigorous and unbending in its defense of the right, and true to its record in opposing wrong.*

*A Progressive Paper: Keeping step with a great and growing Church in a great and growing State.*

Revenues from subscriptions and advertising rarely met production costs and wealthy laymen including Charles Shearn, Jabez Giddings, and David Ayres often subsidized the publication. Ayres, who lived in Galveston, also served as the fiscal agent for the newspaper. The general subscription rate in 1884 was $2 per year, but preachers paid only $1. Preachers were also expected to solicit subscriptions from their members. Pastoral record books well into the twentieth century contain lists of Advocate subscribers in each church served.

In 1887 the paper, now with a circulation of 18,000, moved to Dallas. It assumed a larger role in 1932 when it merged with another journal and expanded its coverage to Oklahoma and New Mexico. It assumed a new name, the *Southwestern Advocate*, to show the new coverage. It retained that name until 1949 when it merged with a national newspaper. Texas subscribers received a newspaper called the *Christian Advocate* that had a supplement that dealt with Texas news. The state supplement was dropped in 1952, and the *Texas Christian Advocate* was reborn, this time published in Fort Worth.

In 1960 the paper was again renamed. It became the *Texas Methodist*. It began publishing local church editions. Subscribers would receive one page of news about their local church activities, and the rest of the paper contained denominational news, both national and international. Local churches which chose to have local church editions were thereby relieved of the burden of printing and mailing church newsletters. Another benefit was the strengthening of denominational ties as information about the church's work was distributed to a wider audience.

Another name change in 1981 resulted in the *United Methodist Reporter*.

At least three German-language newspapers were published to serve the German Texan members of the MECS. Peter Moelling published *Der Evangelische Apologete* in Galveston from 1855 to 1861. After the Civil War J. B. A. Ahrens revived the paper under the name *Der Familienfreund* which was published in New Orleans. In 1894 the German Mission Conference founded *Der Missionsfreund* which lasted until 1932.

The retail operations of the United Methodist Publishing House are conducted by Cokesbury, a name coined by combining the names of Francis Asbury and Thomas Coke, the first two bishops of the MEC. Cokesbury markets devotional and study literature, church supplies, aids to worship, Sunday School literature via catalog, internet, and retail stores in 70 locations in the United States. In 2003 Cokesbury stores were located in Austin, Dallas, Fort Worth, Houston, Lubbock, and San Antonio.

*References:*

www.cokesbury.com/storelocator.aspx

*Texas Methodist Centennial Yearbook*

*New Handbook of Texas*

Stone, William J., Jr., *A Historical Survey of Leading Texas Denominational Newspapers, 1846-1861* Ph.D. dissertation, University of Texas at Austin, 1974.

Bangs, Nathan, *A History of the Methodist Episcopal Church in two volumes New York, 1839.*

*Ladies Repository,* December, 1858.

Nail, Olin W., "History of the *Texas Christian Advocate*," in Nail, Olin W., ed., *The History of Texas Methodism: 1900-1960,* Capital Printing Co., Austin, 1961.

CHAPTER 33

# MINISTRIES TO COLLEGE AND UNIVERSITY STUDENTS

By the last decade of the 19th century the Christian denominations no longer enjoyed monopoly status in Texas higher education. Public institutions such as Texas A&M (1876), Prairie View A&M (1876), the University of Texas (1883), Sam Houston Normal Institute (1879), North Texas Normal College (1899), and Southwest Texas State Normal College (1899) provided alternatives to denominational institutions. Not all Methodists were pleased with the growth of the public institutions. The Methodist colleges were founded to prepare the brightest young people for future leadership roles in both church and civil arenas. Fears that bright young people might fall away from the church led Rev. J. Marvin Nichols of the North Texas Conference to urge his colleagues to preach more sermons steering young men from the state institutions to the Methodist colleges.

> *Men of Texas, the time has come for a determined movement. Methodism in the next generation pivots herself on Christian vs. secular education. Let us ring the welkin. The opposition is aggressive; we must sound the tocsin of war . . . secular education is going to move upon us. Let strong men write for the press. Let every pulpit become the arena. Not to do it means the surrender of our strongest fort.*

The warfare between denominational and secular education envisioned by Rev. Nichols did not occur. Texas's pluralist society could accommodate both private and public institutions. As Methodist students streamed to public institutions, the conferences found ways of ministry that combined the best of public and private education. The actual ministry varied according to level of resources provided and local circumstances. One model for ministry was the Wesley Bible Chair. The first such chair opened at the University of Texas in 1916. A minister appointed to such a position

172

offered Bible classes for which the university awarded academic credit. In addition to the pastor who held the chair, University Methodist in Austin assigned an assistant pastor to full-time student work. That same church gave a lot on which to erect a building to house the work which was supported by all the annual conferences of Texas. The Texas A&M experience was much the same. In 1920 the Boards of Missions of the five MECS conferences completely in Texas began work there. King Vivion, assistant pastor at Bryan, worked as a full-time campus pastor. Meanwhile Texas Methodist women built dormitories at both Austin and Denton.

The precedents set at the University of Texas and Texas A&M became the model for other campuses.

- The Wesley Foundations (the name chosen by the 1926 MECS General Conference) would relate to all the conferences in Texas rather than the conference in whose bounds they fell.
- The Foundations would be staffed by preachers who possessed academic credentials sufficient to offer classes for academic credit.
- The Foundations would relate to one or several of the local churches. Wesley Foundation preachers could hold dual appointments with local churches.
- The Foundations would occupy their own property rather than using rooms in local churches.

Since the administration of the Wesley Foundations was placed in the hands of all the conferences, it became necessary to establish a state wide body. In 1924 the Rev. Glenn Flinn of the Texas Conference appealed to all the conferences to establish a commission for that purpose. The conferences studied the issue, conducted a census of Methodist students at public universities, and authorized the formation of the "Methodist Student Commission of Texas" in 1926. That name was changed to "Wesley Foundation of Texas." Flinn continued to serve as either secretary, chair, or director of the state organization until 1952.

The years immediately after World War II saw a marked increase in both college enrollments due, in part, to the passage of the G. I. Bill and also interest in religious matters. The Interconference Commission on Student Work, which was responsible for campus ministries responded to these post-war developments with a burst of activity. Thirteen new centers were built in Texas. The *Annual Report* of the Texas Methodist Student Movement for 1953-1954 reports activities on 37 Texas campuses. The same sort of rapid growth was occurring not just in Texas, but in other states as well. There were problems associated with the rapid growth. What should be the relationship of the campus work to the churches in the local community? Who should be responsible for financial support? In whose name should title to campus ministries property be held? What should be the relationship between Methodist groups at state universities with Methodist student groups at Methodist colleges? Should Methodists cooperate with other denominations to sponsor interdenominational student organizations?

The General Conference of 1952 brought the campus ministries under the Section of Secondary and Higher Education of the Board of Education. It also formalized the structure of campus ministries for the Methodist Church. The 1952 edition of the *Discipline* had the following provisions concerning campus ministries:

♦ A Campus-Church Relations Committee, or a Wesley Foundation Board of Directors would be established in every college community with a Methodist church.

♦ Religious groups at Methodist institutions would relate to Methodist organizations at non-Methodist institutions through the Methodist Student Movement (MSM).

♦ The Boards of Education of each of the conferences in a state shall create an Interconference Commission on Student Religious Work to coordinate campus ministries in the state.

Standards would be developed for a ministry to be designated a "Wesley Foundation." (Other campus work would be designated "Units of the MSM.")

The 1952 General Conference action made clear that campus ministry was to be directed at the state rather than the conference level. Campus ministries prospered under such an arrangement. Methodist work expanded to include several community colleges, a professional school, state schools, and universities owned by other denominations. Wesley Foundations continue to offer traditional programs such as Bible study, worship, recreation, counseling, and so on. Mission trips, often involving construction or other physical labor, have become a popular program area of the Wesley Foundations. A recent list of campuses with Methodist ministries included the following:

| | |
|---|---|
| Angelo State University, San Angleo | North Texas State University, Denton |
| Austin Community College, Austin | Rice University, Houston |
| Baylor University, Waco | Sam Houston State University, Huntsville |
| Blinn College, Brenham | Southern Methodist University, Dallas |
| Huston-Tillotson University, Austin | Texas State University, San Marcos |
| Lamar University, Beaumont | Southwestern University, Georgetown |
| Lon Morris College, Jacksonville | Stephen F. Austin University, Nacogdoches |
| McMurry University, Abilene | Sul Ross State University, Alpine |
| Midwestern State University, Wichita Falls | Tarleton State University, Stephenville |
| Prairie View A&M University, Prairie View | University of Texas at Austin, Austin |
| Kilgore College, Kilgore | University of Texas at San Antonio, San Antonio |
| Navarro College, Corsicana | University of Texas at Tyler, Tyler |

# Ministries to
# College & University Students

West Texas A&M

Texas Tech

Midwestern State

Texas Women's University • Texas A&M Commerce
North Texas

Texas Wesleyan • Southern Methodist Wiley
UT Arlington Texas Tyler Kilgore
UT Tyler • Tyler CC
• McMurry Tarleton State Corsicana • Trinity Valey CC
• Lon Morris

• UT El Paso

Angelo State • Baylor

Southwestern Texas A&M • Sam Houston State
Austin Community College
Sul Ross State Texas • Prairie View
Huston-Tillotson Blinn
University of Houston
Rice
Texas San Antonio
UT
Medical Branch
University of Houston Victoria

Texas A&M Corpus Christi •

• UT Pan American

University of Texas at Arlington, Arlington

University of Texas at El Paso, El Paso

University of Texas, Pan American, Edinburgh

Texas A&M University, College Station

Texas A&M University—Commerce

Texas A&M-Corpus Christi, Corpus Christi

Texas Christian University, Fort Worth

Texas Technological University, Lubbock

Texas Southern University, Houston

Texas Wesleyan University, Fort Worth

Trinity Valley Community College, Athens

Tyler Community College, Tyler

University of Houston, Houston

University of Houston, Victoria

Texas Woman's University, Denton

University of North Texas, Denton

UT Medical Branch, Galveston

West Texas A&M University, Canyon

Wiley College, Marshall

*References:*

Nichols, Rev. J. Marvin, *Texas Methodism: 81 Years*, Garland, News Book Print, 1898.

Evans, C. E., *The Story of Texas Schools*, Austin, Steck, 1955.

Flinn, Glenn, "The Wesley Foundation Work in Texas," in Olin Nail, *The History of Texas Methodism, 1900-1960*, Austin, 1961.

Vernon et al., *Methodist Excitement*.

Methodist Student Movement, Annual Reports, 1952-1953 through 1971-1972.

*Discipline* of the Methodist Church, 1952.

# CHAPTER 34

# RECOGNIZED HISTORIC SITES

Texas Methodists have found several ways to honor their heritage. Many have published histories of their local churches. Others maintain cases of artifacts to remind members of their connections to the members who have gone before them. One of the most popular forms of lifting up Methodist heritage is the erection of a plaque or other memorial. There are several categories of such recognition.

The General Commission on Archives and History of the United Methodist Church recognizes **Official Heritage Landmarks**. The *Book of Discipline* defines Heritage Landmark as "a building, location, or structure specifically related to significant events, developments, or personalities in the overall history of The United Methodist Church or its antecedents." General Conference action is necessary to designate a site as an Official Heritage Landmark. There are forty such Heritage Landmarks in the United States as of the 2004 General Conference. Two of those are in Texas. They are the Rutersville Cluster in Fayette County in the bounds of the Southwest Texas Conference and McMahan's Chapel in Sabine County in the Texas Conference. The General Commission on Archives and History also sponsors a program to recognize Historic Sites. A site may be so designated by annual conference action. The recognized Historic Sites in Texas include the following. Numbers refer to the order of registration with the General Commission on Archives and History.

| | | | |
|---|---|---|---|
| 1 | Oak Island Church, San Antonio, | 127 | McKenzie College, near Clarksville |
| 9 | Chauncey Richardson Grave, Rutersville | 142 | Art UM Church, Art |
| 30 | Fort Davis Church, Fort Davis | 143 | Castell UM Church, Castell |
| 92 | Travis Park UM Church, San Antonio | 144 | First UM Church, San Marcos |
| 106 | St John's UM Church, Richmond | 145 | Hilda UM Church, Hilda |
| 121 | Liberty Methodist Church, Liberty | 146 | New Fountain UM Church, New Fountain |
| 122 | Buda UM Church, Buda | 147 | Sabinal UM Church, Sabinal |
| 123 | Driftwood UM Church, Driftwood | 148 | Manchaca UM Church, Manchaca |
| 126 | Wesley UM Church, Austin | 149 | Simpson UM Church, Austin |

150 Floresville UM Church, Floresville

157 Willis UM Church, Willis

158 Liberty Hill UM Church, Liberty Hill

159 Pleasanton UM Church,Pleasanton

160 Monthalia UM Church, Cost

161 Dewville UM Church, Dewville

173 Burial and Monument Site of Alejo Hernandez, Old Bayview Cemetery, Corpus Christi

179 Ward Memorial UM Church, Austin

180 Bandera UM Church, Bandera

181 Chappell Hill UM Church, Chappell Hill

182 Sloan Memorial UM Church, Houston

191 Kyle UM Church, Kyle

192 First UM Church, Uvalde

193 First UM Church, San Saba

212 Dripping Springs UM Church, Dripping Springs

213 First UM Church, Jacksonville

215 Christine UM Church, Christine

216 First UM Church, San Augustine

222 First UM Church, Crockett

226 Travis Street UM Church, LaGrange

237 First UM Church, Caldwell

249 Marvin UM Church, Tyler

254 First UM Church, Huntsville

255 Martha's Chapel Cemetery, Walker County

256 First UM Church, Corpus Christi

257 First UM Church, Clarendon

277 Jackson Chapel UM Church, San Marcos

285 First UM Church, Goldthwaite

286 Lytle UM Church, Lytle

287 Leakey UM Church, Leakey

299 Thompsonville UM Church, Waelder

300 Waelder UM Church, Waelder

301 First UM Church, Gonzalez

305 Trinity UM Church, Houston

307 First UM Church, Georgetown

324 Coker UM Church, San Antonio

325 Eddy UM Church, Eddy

326 Bruceville UM Church, Bruceville

327 Mooreville UM Church, Mooreville

339 First UM Church, Waco, TX

343 The Reverend Samuel A. Williams, Gravesite, San Augustine

344 Carthage First UM Church Plant, Carthage

346 Perry First UM Church, Marlin

347 First UM Church, Alvarado

348 Bell's Chapel Cemetery and First Site of UMC, Rockette

352 Granbury First UM Church, Granbury

355 First UM Church, Hamilton

356 Acton UM Church, Acton

357 Moody-Leon UM Church, Moody

362 First UM Church, Arlington

363 First UM Church, Waxahachie

365 First UM Church, Ferris

366 Smithfield UM Church, North Richland Hills

367 Groesbeck First UM Church, Groesbeck

371 First UM Church, Valley Mills

378 First UM Church, Belton

381 First UM Church, Corsicana

382 Bosqueville UM Church, Bosqueville

383 White's Chapel UM Church, Southlake

388 First UM Church, Evant

390 Austin Avenue UM Church, Waco

391 Salado UM Church, Salado

392 First UM Church, Winters

394 Murray UM Church, Graham

395 Bethel UM Church, Waxahachie

397 St. Paul UM Church, San Antonio

403 Cahill UM Church, Alvarado

404 May UM Church, May

406 St. Andrews UM Church, Fort Worth

408 First UM Church, Blooming Grove

412 Stephenville First UM Church, Stephenville

413 Tenth Street UM Church, Taylor

414 Freyburg UM Church, Schulenburg

427 Grave of Rev. Hugh Martin Childress, Sr., Atoka Cemetery, west of Novice

428 Moody First UM Church, Moody

429 Blevins Cemetery, Eddy

Historic structures may be eligible for recognition by the **National Register of Historic Places**, a program of the National Park Service. Listing on the National Register is usually initiated by persons who wish to call attention to, and help preserve, a building whose architecture is worthy of note.

There are twenty-four Methodist sites in Texas currently listed on National Register. They are as follows:

Anderson Campground, Frankston

Alamo Methodist Church, San Antonio

Chappell Hill Methodist Church, Chappell Hill

Concord Methodist Church, Carthage

First Methodist Church, Cuero,

First Methodist Church, Georgetown

First Methodist Church, Marshall

First United Methodist Church, Paris

First Untied Methodist Church, Salado

First United Methodist Church, San Marcos

Grace Methodist Episcopal Church, Dallas

Marvin Methodist Episcopal Church, South, Tyler

Morning Chapel; Christian Methodist Episcopal Church, Fort Worth

Mt. Vernon African Methodist Episcopal Church, Palestine

Mt. Zion African Methodist Episcopal Church, Brenham

Mt. Zion United Methodist Church, Belton

Oak Lawn Methodist Episcopal Church South, Dallas

Old First Methodist Episcopal Church South, Wharton

Polk Street Methodist Church, Amarillo

St. James CME, Tyler

St. John's United Methodist Church, Stamford

St. John's Methodist Church, Georgetown

Webster Chapel United Methodist Church, Victoria

Wesley United Methodist Church, Austin

The most common form of historic recognition is a **Texas Historical Commission historic marker.** The THC is a state government agency which works with county historical commissions and other interested parties to recognize, preserve, and interpret historic places, events, and people in Texas. The historic markers program is an example of grassroots history at its best. The process of obtaining an historical marker is typically initiated at the local level when a person or group of persons wishes to erect a historic marker. An application is submitted first to the county's historical commission. That application must make a case for the subject's historical importance. It must also include a proposed text for the marker and documentation. Upon approval by the county historical commission, the application is forwarded to the THC. Staff historians then check the documentation and suggest revisions. After approval by the THC, the marker applicant pays the necessary fees for the casting of the metal marker. Most markers are unveiled with an appropriate ceremony which draws further attention to the historic site, person, or event.

# National Register of
## Historic Places

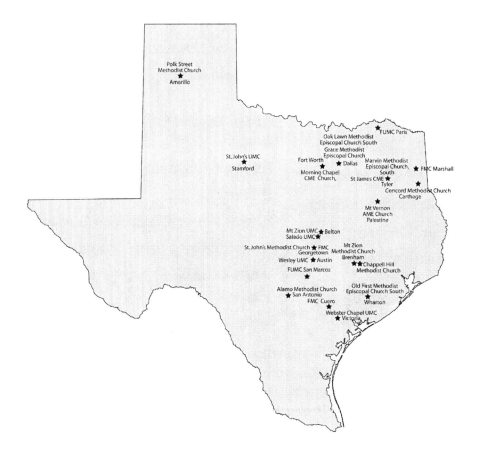

There are currently about 500 historical markers with some relationship to Texas Methodism. Some relate to the founding of particular church, some to educational institutions of the church, or to a particular Methodist preacher. New historical markers are being dedicated every year. The Texas Historical Commission website contains a searchable data base of National Register and Historical Marker texts. Visitors to the website at *www.thc.state.tx.us* can enter a key term and search the entire state or a selected county. Persons who wish to apply for historical marker designation for their own local church, cemetery, or other significant event or institution, can obtain the forms from this same website. Each county in Texas has a Historical Commission that helps local citizens secure historical markers in that county.

Still another form of recognition of historic Methodist sites is another THC program that recognizes **historic cemeteries.** Some of those cemeteries were associated with a particular Methodist church.

*References:*

www.nps.gov/nr/

atlas.thc.state.tx.us/shell-county.htm

# CHAPTER 35

# ARCHIVES, DEPOSITORIES, AND HISTORICAL SOCIETIES

The *Book of Discipline* calls for each United Methodist church to have a committee on archives and history. Thousands of dedicated Methodists work to preserve and interpret materials relating to their church's history. Each annual conference and jurisdiction has a Commission on Archives and History charged with the task of preserving the records of the conference and jurisdiction. The General Commission on Archives and History collects and preserves materials relating to the history of the United Methodist Church. Archives have been established at each of the connectional levels of the UMC.

The sophistication and usefulness of the archives have increased over time. There is evidence of the existence of a "conference trunk" containing the archives of the East Texas Conference as early as 1866. In 1884 Rev. J. W. Fields wrote to the *Texas Christian Advocate* that it was in that year that he relinquished custody of the trunk because he became a member of the newly-created Trinity Conference. (TCA 12/20/1884) The tradition of keeping Texas Conference historic documents in a trunk continued well into the 20th century. The actual trunk is preserved at the Conference Archives. Today the conference archives tend to be located at Methodist-related universities under the supervision of professional archivists. Even those university libraries which are not official depositories for conference archives, such as Southwestern University, have Texas Methodist collections.

Closely associated with the depositories have been several historical associations or societies whose purpose has been the preservation and publishing of Texas Methodist history. In the 1850s as the ranks of the pioneer preachers were thinned by death, *Advocate* editors made regular appeals for preachers to send memoirs for publication. Sometimes the publication of those memoirs spurred energetic debate over the events of early Texas Methodist history. John Wesley Kenney entered the fray by claiming that ". . . some of the writers on early Methodism in Texas had a good supply of Hasheesh, and wrote accordingly." (TCA, 2/16/1860)

Another flurry of interest in preserving Texas Methodist history occurred in the 1880s and 1890s. Deaths of Methodist giants of the Republic of Texas mounted, especially in the period from 1878 to 1882. Job Baker, David Ayres, Orceneth Fisher, Robert Alexander, J. W. P. McKenzie, and Joseph Sneed all died in that span. In 1886 interested parties created the **Methodist Historical Society**. Although the founders had high hopes for the organization, it failed. One participant in that society had been a missionary to the Republic. Homer Thrall was still alive and was passionate about Texas history in general and Methodist history in particular. He had already published the first comprehensive history of Texas Methodism (1872) and a state history (1876). Both works were informed by his participation in the events being described and his friendship with numerous historic figures in Texas history. Thrall died in 1894.

In that same era two younger men were rising to assume leadership in Texas Methodist historical studies. Claude C. Cody, professor of mathematics at Southwestern University had already published a biography of Francis Asbury Mood (1886). In 1891 a professional gambler named Elijah Shettles was converted and felt the call to preach. Cody and Shettles became the stalwarts of Texas Methodist history for the next generation. Their main expression was a revived **Texas Methodist Historical Association** founded in 1908. Its greatest accomplishment was the publication of the *Texas Methodist Historical Quarterly* (1909-1911). Although the *Quarterly* folded after only seven issues, its articles even today constitute an important resource for historians. Cody edited the *Quarterly* at Southwestern University. Shettles was assistant editor and collector of all things Methodist. He traveled widely and visited book stores wherever he went. Shetles also acted as a book and private collection buyer for Texas university libraries.

The TMHA of 1908 also failed, but there was a revival of interest in the middle 1930s. Texas Methodists celebrated a Centennial of Texas Methodism on September 4-6, 1934, by assembling in San Antonio for historical pageants, worship, and historical programs. Both the date and the location of the centennial celebration may appear odd. Readers of this *Atlas* will know that Methodist appointments were made to charges along the Red River almost twenty years before 1834. No Methodist activity can be found in San Antonio in 1834. The organizers of the 1934 Centennial Celebration did not ignore the earlier Texas work of William Stevenson, but chose to focus on the establishment of the religious society at McMahan's and the Caney Creek Camp Meeting as the events from which to date the centennial. The choice of San Antonio for the celebration is an indication of a central feature of Texas Methodist historical consciousness, i.e., that it has always transcended conference boundaries and embraced the whole state. San Antonio is the site of the Alamo which traditionally has functioned as Texas' most unifying sacred place. Two years later Texas Methodists again mixed church and secular history when all the MECS annual conferences met in Houston so they could take excursions to the San Jacinto Battlefield during its centennial celebrations of 1936.

# ARCHIVES & DEPOSITORIES

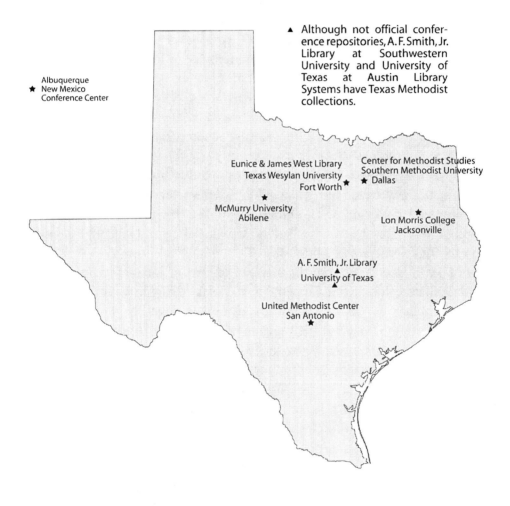

Albuquerque
★ New Mexico
Conference Center

▲ Although not official confer-
ence repositories, A. F. Smith, Jr.
Library at Southwestern
University and University of
Texas at Austin Library
Systems have Texas Methodist
collections.

Eunice & James West Library
Texas Wesylan University
Fort Worth ★

Center for Methodist Studies
Southern Methodist University
★ Dallas

★
McMurry University
Abilene

★
Lon Morris College
Jacksonville

A. F. Smith, Jr. Library
▲
University of Texas
▲

United Methodist Center
San Antonio
★

Another result of the 1934 Centennial was the publication of the *Texas Methodist Centennial Yearbook 1834-1934* edited by Olin Nail of the West Texas Conference. That volume is an odd collection of historic photographs, historical essays, and the *Journals* of the MECS conferences for 1934.

Nail was also the editor of the *History of Texas Methodism 1900-1960* published in 1961. Although that work claims to be written to extend Macum Phelan's two-volume history of Texas Methodism, it does not employ Phelan's narrative style. Instead Nail solicited thematic essays from different authors. Fortunately Nail was remarkably successful in obtaining essays from the persons most qualified to write them. Contributors included Glenn Flinn on the Wesley Foundations, Kenneth Copeland on Methodist Protestants, Alfredo and Clotilde Nanez on Spanish speaking Methodists, and I. B. Loud on African-American Methodists.

Nail's history was an outgrowth of the Texas Methodist Historical Commission which in turn had been set up by the Texas Methodist Planning Commission in November 1950. Bishops A. Frank Smith and W. C. Martin are given credit for suggesting that the new Historical Commission be formed and it be given the task of writing a history that would update Phelan.

Although the TMHC was able to publish the Nail work in 1961, it was very much a creature of the Texas Methodist Planning Commission rather than a membership society. In February 1975 an organization was formed at Bridwell Library that was designed to be a membership organization for persons interested in Texas Methodist history. That organization, the Texas United Methodist Historical Society, was initiated by Walter Vernon who was historian of the North Texas Conference. In 2005 the TUMHS began publishing *The Heritage Journal* edited by Robert Sledge at McMurry University.

The following is a list of official Methodist depositories containing resources relating to Texas Methodist history:

♦ General Commission on Archives and History, the United Methodist Church, P. O. Box 127, Madison, NJ 07940.

♦ Center for Methodist Studies at Bridwell Library, Southern Methodist University, P. O. Box 750476, Dallas, TX 75275-0476 is the depository for the South Central Jurisdiction, North Texas Conference, and the Rio Grande Conference.

♦ Texas Wesleyan University, Eunice & James L. West Library, 1201 Wesleyan Street, Fort Worth, TX 76105 is the depository for the Central Texas Conference.

♦ Archives New Mexico Conference, United Methodist Church, 2210 Silver Avenue, SE, Albuquerque, NM 87106 is the depository for the New Mexico Conference.

- Archives of Northwest Texas Conference, McMurry Station, Box 218, Abilene, TX 79697 is the depository for the Northwest Texas Conference.

- Southwest Texan Conference United Methodist Center, 16400 Huebner Road, San Antonio, TX 78248 is the depository for the Southwest Texas Conference.

- Lon Morris College, Jacksonville, TX 75766 provides facilities for the Texas Conference Archives.

*References:*

www.gcah.org

Nail, *History of Texas Methodism 1900-1960.* Austin, 1961.

CHAPTER 36

# HOMES AND HOSPITALS

Texas Methodism has been marked by the establishment and maintenance of institutions intended to care for others from the 1890s until the present. Methodists of the 1890's established an orphanage in Waco and a home in San Antonio for prostitutes wishing to reform their lives. Hospitals then followed in Houston, Dallas, Lubbock, Fort Worth, and the Valley. As more Texans lived longer lives, retirement homes all across the state became another service Methodists offered to Texans of all religious persuasions. The oldest institutions have all had to alter their ministries to accommodate demographic and social changes. Meeting the new challenges has been no easy task but has been accomplished because of both strong leadership and a firm base of support from ordinary Methodists from all the conferences in the state.

## The Methodist Children's Home

The origin of the Methodist Children's Home can be traced to the 1890 session of the Northwest Texas Conference, held in Abilene November 13-18. Some sources report that the presiding officer, Bishop Joseph Key, had gone to Abilene worried about a possible confrontation at the annual conference between the Holiness Movement advocates and their opponents. While discussing his anxieties with Waco pastor, Horace Bishop, the reverend suggested a project both sides could support—the establishment of a conference orphanage. A motion to that effect was passed, and Bishop Key appointed a committee to organize it. That committee named Rev. W. H. Vaughn as Business Manager. In that capacity Vaughn traveled through most of the conference in 1891 and 1892 soliciting pledges and other support for the orphanage. The *Texas Christian Advocate* for those same years contained numerous articles and letters urging Methodists to support such a venture. In one especially significant letter, Mrs. Kezia Payne DePelchin, for whom the DePelchin Faith Home in Houston was later named, used denominational rivalry to urge Methodists to establish a home. She mentioned a Baptist home (Buckner Orphans Home) in Dallas, a Catholic one in Galveston, the one she managed in Houston (Bayland), and the one in Corsicana run by the State of Texas. After listing those, DePelchin challenged the Methodists to add their effort to the list. Vaughn also investigated possible sites for the institution. Fort Worth, Oak Cliff (still in the Northwest Texas Conference in 1892), and Brownwood all proposed sites, but when Waco's offer was accepted in January 1894, the orphanage vision had already expanded. The other MECS annual conferences in Texas had been invited to take part, and at least three of them had representatives at the January 1894 meeting. The experience of so many failed schools had shown the wisdom of involving more than one annual conference in creating an institution. Waco's central location and excellent rail connections to the other annual conferences in Texas were distinct advantages in the siting. Waco had donated a ten-acre farm with a commodious two-story house so there was no construction delay. In October 1895 the Director reported that forty-three children were being cared for.

Although five MECS annual conferences in Texas (joined by the German Mission Conference in 1899) supported the Methodist Orphanage, it was also blessed with remarkable benefactors, Abe and Louisa Mulkey. The Mulkeys were perhaps the most renowned revivalist team in an era of revivals and camp meetings. One night during each revival he held, Abe Mulkey would make an appeal for the Orphanage. The collection that night would be directed to that cause. By 1901 he had raised $36,000 and the Board of Directors was confident enough of the venture's success to dedicate it on December 22, 1901. (In Methodist practice a building can be *consecrated* when it constructed and ready for use, but it can be *dedicated* only when it is debt-free.)

The orphanage expanded substantially in the first years of the 20th century. The campus was enlarged to twenty-eight acres, new buildings were constructed, and "inmate" population increased to about one hundred-fifty. The Home provided the necessities of food, clothing, and shelter, as well as spiritual guidance, medical care, education, and vocational training, especially on the 173-acre Bosque River bottom farm which the Home owned.

The Home weathered financial difficulties, epidemic disease, and maladminis- tration by inexperienced preachers. A typhoid epidemic in 1910 was a grim episode in its growth. The Home built goodwill all across the annual conferences. Grassroots support was vital, and receipts from the Christmas offering would continue to provide a significant proportion of the Home's budget. That support was cultivated through three methods that made the Methodist Home a truly statewide institution. The first was the *Sunshine Monthly*, inaugurated in November 1920 under the administration of W. F. Barnett. The magazine, which continues to the present as *Sunshine*, contained articles by the children, news of the Home, and public acknowledgement of the gifts sent to the Home. Eventually thousands of Texas Methodists who had never seen the campus felt a genuine love for the institution through the magazine. Another means of publicizing the Home was the musical tour. Children formed both choral and instru- mental groups and toured Methodist churches throughout Texas giving musical programs. The programs provided a means for children to give testimonies about how the Home had helped them and also provided a concrete link to the Home for many Methodists. The third method was a syndicated radio program that brought the Home's children into living rooms across the state. The signature song, *Let the Sun Shine In* was a perfect connection with the radio audience.

Hubert Johnson, who was manager from 1933 to 1966, oversaw major changes in the mission of the Home. Social and medical trends of the 20th century meant that there were fewer orphans. There was still a desperate need for custodial services for children because of divorce, desertion, mental illness, and child abuse, and the Home moved more in the direction of foster-home placement and family rehabilitation than its tradition role of providing care to orphans. Services expanded to include a Boy's Ranch which opened in 1973. The 2003 Annual Report of the Home reported assets of $263,000,000 and an annual budget of almost $17,000,000. In addition to the Waco Campus and Boy's Ranch near Axtell, the Methodist Children's Home offered foster care through offices in Albuquerque, Tyler, El Paso, Corpus Christi, Dallas, Houston, Lubbock, San Antonio, and Waco. In 2007 the Methodist Home opened the Sammy Baugh Cottage at Jayton.

*References*:

Ward, Patricia Dawson, *The Home: A History of the Methodist Home for Children in Waco, Texas*, Waco, Methodist Home Office of Development, 1980.

Vernon et al., *Methodist Excitement*.

www.methodistchildrenshome.org/index.html

*New Handbook of Texas*

McLean, John H. *Reminiscences*, Southern Methodist Publishing House, Dallas, 1918.

DePelchin, Mrs. K(ezia) letter to *Texas Christian Advocate, October 13, 1892.*

# Methodist Mission Home

Only a few years after the establishment of the Home in Waco, a dramatic conversion opened the way for creating another institution in San Antonio. In 1895 Mrs. M. L. Volino, proprietor of a brothel on San Saba Street in that city, experienced a religious conversion. She enlisted the aid of Methodists in San Antonio, especially members of Travis Park Methodist Church, to create a Rescue Home in the former brothel. She intended to provide a place of refuge for women who wished to turn away from prostitution. San Antonio Methodists raised $6,000 to pay a mortgage on the house on San Saba Street, members of the Woman's Parsonage and Home Mission Society of the West Texas Conference contributed offerings, and Mrs. Volino secured donations from area businesses. The Rescue Home came into existence. By 1909 there was a new name and a new function. The San Antonio Mission Home and Training School not only rescued women from prostitution, but also provided a home for unmarried pregnant women and their babies.

The Central Texas Conference began supporting the Home in 1918. By this date, the original purpose had given way to caring for unmarried mothers. When the Home received its charter from the State of Texas in 1925, both the West Texas Conference and the Central Texas Conference participated in the legal incorporation. In 1938 the Home moved to the former Baylor Hospital building on Ninth Street. The North Texas, Northwest Texas, and Texas Conferences agreed to assume co-responsibility for the Home along with the West Texas and Central Texas Conferences. In anticipation of that action the name of the Home was changed to the Texas Mission Home and Training School. The Rio Grande Conference trustees joined the board in 1956. The name was changed again in 1961 to Methodist Mission Home of Texas.

The Home provided maternity and adoption services and continued to expand, most notably in 1968 when it relocated to a twenty-five acre campus. Social trends of the 1960s and 1970s decreased the demand for maternity services. The legalization of abortion, greater acceptance of unwed motherhood, and more options for single parents combined to decrease the number of clients seeking Home services. The administration sought another ministry and found one in serving young people who were deaf. The first of the new clients entered the Home in 1974 and received training designed to increase their employment prospects and hence their independence. In 1998 the Home began serving young adults with other disabilities. Its Adoption Service division continued to provide adoption services.

*References:*

www.mfrs.org

Stockwell, Spencer L., *A History of the Methodist Mission Home of Texas*, 1966.

## Hospitals

Each of the five annual conferences wholly within the state of Texas embraced hospital ministries during the twentieth century. The Texas Conference became the first when, in 1924, it acquired a private hospital Dr. Oscar Norsworthy had started in 1908. The Methodist Hospital of Houston grew mainly because of generous philanthropists who provided the finances for world-class facilities and staff. Mr. and Mrs. Walter W. Fondren, Jesse H. Jones, William Clayton, Hugh Roy and Lillie Cullen, and Monroe D. Anderson were among the main benefactors. In 1951 Methodist Hospital relocated to the new Texas Medical Center where it became a teaching hospital for Baylor College of Medicine. The affiliation with Baylor brought Dr. Michael DeBakey to the Methodist Hospital. His innovations in cardiovascular surgery meant that Methodist Hospital would achieve international renown. The Methodist Hospital of Houston eventually developed into a complex of more than 1,500 beds, satellite hospitals in suburban Houston, a parking garage, and a hotel.

Ground was broken for the Dallas Methodist Hospital in 1923, and it began admitting patients in 1927. It was financed by local Methodists congregations and several fundraising campaigns. It has expanded since that beginning and now includes six facilities in Dallas County.

The Harris Methodist Fort Worth Hospital opened in 1930 under the leadership of Dr. Charles Harris. It, too, expanded so that it now consists of seven care-giving facilities in Fort Worth, Cleburne, Stephenville, Azle, and Bedford

The Depression and World War II put an end to hospital projects, but after the war Texas saw three more Methodist hospitals. The Northwest Texas Conference acquired an existing hospital in 1954. The Methodist Hospital of San Antonio received a charter in 1955, and the Knapp Memorial Methodist Hospital opened in Weslaco in 1962.

The San Antonio Methodist Hospital has since expanded to include fifteen facilities included in the Methodist Healthcare System.

Lubbock Methodist Hospital had its origins as the twenty-five bed Lubbock Sanitarium which opened in 1918. It became Lubbock General Hospital in 1941, Lubbock Memorial Hospital in 1945, and in 1954 was accepted by the Northwest Texas Annual Conference. In 1998 it merged with St. Mary of the Plains Hospital and became part of the Covenant Health System, a division of St. Joseph Health System. After its merger, it became the largest healthcare provider in the Lower Plains of Texas and Eastern New Mexico.

The lack of adequate healthcare facilities in the Valley prompted a cooperative effort between community and religion leaders to build a hospital. The McAllen District of the Southwest Annual Conference agreed to administer a hospital if the community could build it. Private foundations, local donors, and a federal government grant provided enough money to build such a building, and in 1962 the Knapp Memorial Methodist Hospital opened in Weslaco. In 1986 the relationship between the hospital and the church was amicably dissolved, and the hospital continues to serve as a not-for-profit institution.

*References:*

Sibley, Marilyn McAdams, *The Methodist Hospital of Houston: Serving the World,* Texas State Historical Association, Austin, 1989.

Allen, Louise and Carmichael, Enid, *The first 62 Years: As History of Methdodist Hosptial, Lubbock, Texas: 1918-1980,* Methodist Hospital Lubbock, Lubbock, 1980.

Vernon et al, *Methodist Excitement.*

Vernon, *Methodism Moves Across North Texas.*

Nail, ed. *Texas Methodist Centennial Yearbook.*

www.texashealth.org/hospitals (search on "history")

www.methodisthealthsystem.org

www.knappmed.org/about/history

www.sahealth.com

www.covenanthealth.org/view/AboutUs/history

# Homes And Hospitals

- ■ Children and Youth Residences
- • Methodist Mission Home
- ★ Hospitals
- ▲ Retirement Homes

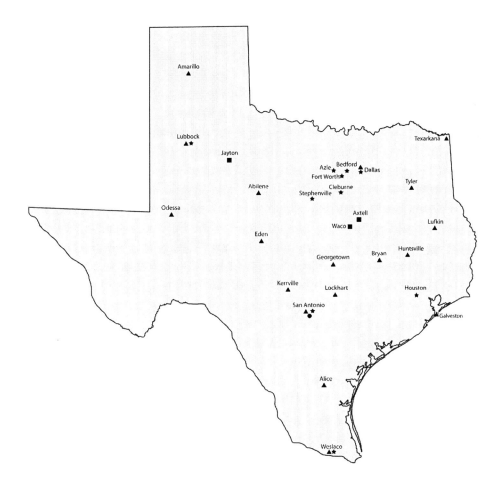

## Homes for Older Persons

In the closing decades of the 20th century Texas Methodists made retirement homes their most numerous social-service institution. In doing so, they were both continuing an old tradition and also responding to the "graying" of the population.

The earliest homes for older people consisted of individual dwellings for superannuated preachers. Methodist preachers fortunate enough to live until retirement age faced bleak prospects in the late 19th and early 20th centuries. Their salaries were seldom large enough so that they could put away a nest egg for retirement. A life of living in parsonages meant that they had not built up equity in a residence. Conference pensions did exist, but the amounts paid to conference claimants were meager. Some retired preachers lived with their adult children. Those without children sometimes depended upon the hospitality of preachers still serving churches. The senior author of this *Atlas* has childhood memories of retired Texas Conference preachers living with his family in the commodious parsonage at Brookshire. In many cities and small towns across Texas a sympathetic donor would give or will a house to the local church, the district, or the conference with the stipulation that a retired preacher could live there rent free. One layman, C. G. Woodson of Caldwell, provided several such houses for retired preachers. Although such actions were well intended and quite generous, they brought more problems than solutions. Questions about insurance, repairs, improvements, whether widows could continue staying in the house, which of the many deserving applicants should get the use of the house, were only a few of the vexing questions surrounding the issue of superannuate homes. The bylaws adopted by the Superannuate Homes Trustees of the newly organized Northwest Texas Conference at the 1910 Annual Conference hint at one of those difficulties. Rule 8 dealt with choosing among many deserving applicants it said, in part, ". . . giving preference to the most necessitous cases, and where the cases seem to be equally necessitous, then to the one who has served longest in the intinerant ministry." Rule 9, on the other hand, immediately carved out an exception to Rule 8 when it went on "When an individual or a community provides a Home and so desires, such individual or community may select the first occupant."

As the pension system improved and as more options for older persons appeared in society at large, Texas Methodists disencumbered themselves from the burden of a system guaranteed to result in conflict and ill will.

Texas Methodists turned to building group retirement homes. The result is that there now exist homes for older persons throughout the Texas annual conferences.

### New Mexico Conference
- Carlsbad, New Mexico–Landsun Homes

### Northwest Texas Conference
- Abilene, Texas is home of the *Sears Methodist Retirement System*. It currently has a wide variety of facilities in Abilene, Amarillo, Odessa,

Lubbock, Waco, and Tyler (under construction in 2007)
- King's Manor Methodist Home–Hereford, Texas

## North Texas Conference
- C. C. Young Memorial Home–Dallas, Texas
- Also in Dallas is Dickinson Place, a ministry of Highland Park UMC
- Wesley Village Retirement Community–Denison, Texas

## Central Texas Conference
- Courtyards at River Park–Fort Worth, but its connectional unit is the North Texas Conference
- Wesleyan Homes, Inc–Georgetown, Texas

## Texas Conference
- Clarewood House Retirement Community–Houston, Texas
- Holly Hall Retirement Community–Houston, Texas
- Methodist Retirement Communities of the Woodlands operates the following affiliated organizations:

  Cornerstone Retirement Community–Texarkana, Texas
  Crestview Retirement Community–Bryan, Texas
  Edgewater Retirement Community–Galveston, Texas
  Happy Harbor Methodist Home–La Porte, Texas
  PineCrest Retirement Community–Lufkin, Texas
  TownCreek Retirement Community–Huntsville, Texas

## Southwest Texas Conference
- Golden Age Home–Lockhart, Texas
- Morningside Ministries–San Antonio, Texas

*References*
sears-methodist.com/index.htm
*Journal, Northwest Texas Annual Conference, 1910.*
Vernon et al., *Excitement.*

CHAPTER 37

# THE AFRICAN METHODIST EPISCOPAL CHURCH

The end of the Civil War enabled the African Methodist Episcopal Church to send missionaries to Texas. The denomination traced its origins to Richard Allen, an African-American Methodist local preacher. In 1787 he led a group of African-Americans to withdraw from St. George's Methodist Episcopal Church in Philadelphia because they were segregated in the worship services. Other African-Americans soon followed their example so that within only a few years African-American churches existed in Pennsylvania, Maryland, New Jersey, New York, and Delaware. In 1816 sixteen delegates from churches in Baltimore, Maryland; Philadelphia, Pennsylvania; Wilmington, Delaware; Salem, New Jersey; and Attleboro, Pennsylvania, met in Philadelphia and organized the African Methodist Episcopal Church. They adopted the basic polity and doctrine of the Methodist Episcopal Church. Richard Allen was elected bishop.

During the Civil War AME missionaries quickly moved into areas of the South controlled by federal forces. The denomination sent preachers and teachers from New York south as early as 1863. On May 15, 1865, about a month after the surrender of the Confederate forces, Bishop Daniel Alexander Payne organized the South Carolina Conference. The following November the Louisiana Conference was founded. Its boundaries included Louisiana, Texas, Arkansas, and Mississippi. A Reverend Welch traveled to Texas organizing Texas churches in 1867. A notable example of those churches and a pioneer preacher is Chappell Hill AME Church founded by Rev. R. Haywood. Haywood had been born in North Carolina in 1819. After being removed to Alabama where he lived for two years, he came to Columbia in the Republic of Texas about 1840. A chance sidewalk meeting with Orceneth Fisher resulted in Haywood's conversion and exhorter's license. He exhorted for the next twenty-five years, and in 1866 Robert Alexander licensed him to preach. Alexander attended the 1866 MECS General Conference in New Orleans and while there visited with AME organizers.

# African Methodist Episcopal Churches
## 2007

Upon returning to Chappell Hill, Alexander suggested that Haywood affiliate with the AME Church. (The CME Church had not yet been organized.) The 1868 AME General Conference authorized a Texas Conference. Rev. Haywood became a stalwart of that conference, establishing churches in Chappell Hill, Bastrop, Austin, and San Antonio.

The Texas Conference authorized by the General Conference was organized at Galveston in 1868 with Rev. T. W. Stringer of Mississippi as the presiding officer. Fifteen appointments were made at that first conference. They included Galveston, Chappell Hill, Bryan, Austin, Columbia, San Antonio, Egypt, Nolan Chapel, Hempstead, Washington, Independence, Corpus Christi, Huntsville, LaGrange, and Henderson.

The AMEC expanded rapidly. In 1872 the Texas Conference voted to divide itself. The state was divided at the Brazos River into the Texas and West Texas Conferences. It was in that same year that the church founded Paul Quinn College in Austin. In 1877 that college moved to Waco where it received its charter in 1881. It remained in Waco until 1990 when it relocated to Dallas. In 1883 the AMEC established Bishop Ward Normal and Collegiate Institute for Negroes in Huntsville. That school had a brief existence.

Continued growth made possible the creation of a Central Texas Conference about 1880. The new conference's boundaries were defined by a line from Corpus Christi to Laredo to Eagle Pass, then back to San Antonio. From there the boundary turned north to Fort Worth. The districts in the new conference included Austin, Waco, and San Angelo. With a view to missionary activities, the conference also embraced, "the borders of the Republic of Mexico wherever there is an opportunity to preach or establish schools among the Mexicans."

Further division occurred in 1879 with the division of the Texas Conference along the International and Great Northern Railroad. (Modern readers can use U.S. Highway 79 as a reference.) into the Texas and the Northeast Texas Conferences.

Currently Texas constitutes District 10 of the AME Church. Its offices are in Dallas.

*References:*

Keeling, H. *T., History of African Methodism in Texas*, C. F. Blanks, Waco, 1885.

Wright, Richard R.,Jr., ed., *1816-1916: Centennial Encyclopedia of the African Methodist Church.*

Payne, Daniel A., *History of the African Methodist EpiscopalChurch*, A. M. E. Sunday School Union, Nashville, 1891.

Baldwin, John W., *An Early History of Walker County Texas*, M. A. thesis, Sam Houston State Teachers College, 1954.

U.S. Census Bureau, *Religious Census, 1906*, Government Printing Office, Washington, 1910.

CHAPTER 38

# COLORED METHODIST EPISCOPAL CHURCH (CME)

The events of Reconstruction resulted in the formation of a new branch of African-American Methodism, the Colored Methodist Episcopal Church (Renamed Christian Methodist Episcopal Church in 1954). That new denomination was sponsored by the MECS in an attempt to maintain influence over newly freed African-Americans, thousands of whom were joining the AME, AMEZ, and MEC denominations.

African-Americans constituted an important portion of Texas Methodism before the Civil War. Biracial worship services were very common. African-Americans were often relegated to galleries or other segregated portions of church buildings. Preachers were appointed to "Colored Mission" or "African Mission" in other parts of the South as early as 1829.

The appointments for 1858 for the East Texas Conference reveal appointments to Colored Missions in Harrison County, Red River County, Fannin County, and Smith County. The Marshall District reported 2,195 white members and 649 colored members. The Texas Conference that same year reported Colored Missions in Galveston, Houston, Oyster Creek, San Felipe, Columbus, Old Caney, Montgomery, Brazos County, Trinity County, Waco, Port Sullivan, Gonzales, and Clinton. In addition to the white preachers appointed to Colored Missions, there were numerous African-American exhorters. "Uncle Mark" who lived in Washington County achieved great fame because of his prowess as a preacher. When the man who held Uncle Mark announced that he was moving further west, Methodists in the area purchased Uncle Mark so he could remain in Washington County.

The historical literature on religious life and interaction of African-Americans and white southerners before 1865 is complex. Certainly African-Americans were able to introduce traditional African elements into Christianity. The motives of the masters included both cynical attempts to use religion as a means of social control, attempts to suppress religion, and sincere efforts to redeem lost sinners.

# Colored Methodist
# Episcopal Church

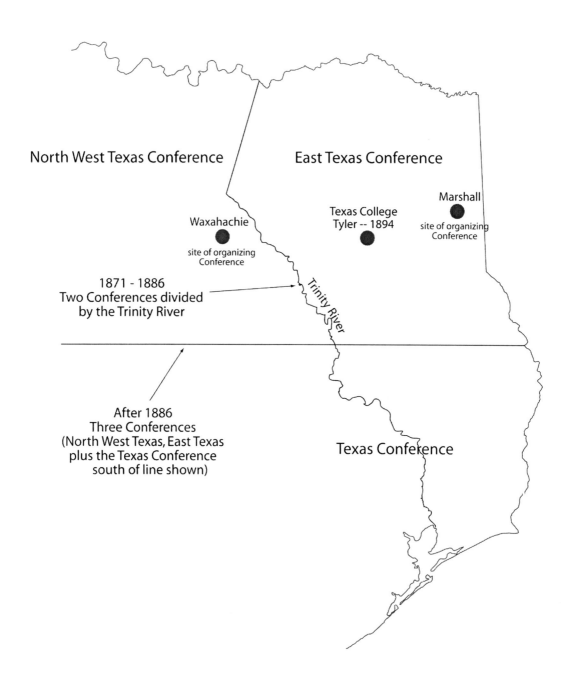

North West Texas Conference

East Texas Conference

Marshall

Texas College
Tyler -- 1894

site of organizing
Conference

Waxahachie

site of organizing
Conference

Trinity River

1871 - 1886
Two Conferences divided
by the Trinity River

After 1886
Three Conferences
(North West Texas, East Texas
plus the Texas Conference
south of line shown)

Texas Conference

In 1865 white Southern Methodists were shocked and dismayed as they observed African-Americans deserting the MECS for the MEC, AME, and AMEZ denominations. Bishop Joseph McTyeire estimated that the African-American membership of the MECS dropped from 124,000 to 78,742 immediately after the war. The MEC incurred the special hatred of white southerners. That denomination had ridden the coattails of the advancing Union Army which, for a time, helped it confiscate MECS church buildings for the MEC. The MEC did not help matters by injecting a high degree of triumphalism into many speeches and proclamations.

The MECS General Conference of 1866, meeting in New Orleans, appointed a committee "on the religious interests of colored people." That committee recommended that African-Americans in the MECS be organized into parallel and racially segregated churches and districts. When there were sufficient districts, they should be organized into annual conferences. When there were at least two annual conferences, those conferences should be organized into a new general conference. The committee recommendations were approved.

By May of 1870, five conferences had been organized under the name Colored Methodist Episcopal Church, South. They were the Memphis, Georgia, Kentucky, Alabama, and Mississippi Conferences. They met in Memphis, and called for the first general conference of the new denomination to be held the following December in Jackson, Tennessee. In the interim between May and December three more conferences organized, the Texas, Virginia, and South Carolina. A Texas delegate, the Rev. William Taylor, was therefore a member of the first general conference of the CME.

The General Conference at Jackson also elected two bishops. One of those, Bishop W. H. Miles came to Marshall, and on October 11, 1871, organized the East Texas Conference. He then went to Waxahachie and organized the North West Texas Conference. Those conferences were divided approximately by the Trinity River. The next General Conference (1874) authorized a third conference in Texas. That was finally accomplished around 1886 by the creation of the Texas Conference from the southern portions of the two older conferences. Texas is now home to five CME conferences, North West Texas, Dallas-Fort Worth, Texas, East Texas, and Central Texas. In 1894 a group of CME preachers organized Texas College in Tyler which has grown into a four year liberal arts institution specializing in teacher education. MECS conferences in Texas traditionally supported two other CME institutions, Paine College in Augusta, Georgia, and Lane College in Jackson, Tennessee.

*References:*

Jamison, Bishop M. F., *Autobiography and Work of Bishop M. F. Jamison*, Publishing House of the M.E. Church, South, Nashville, 1912.

Lane, Bishop Isaac, *Autobiography*, Nashville, Publishing House of the M.E. Church, South, 1916.

Hamilton, F. M., *A Plain Account of the Colored Methodist Episcopal Church in America, Being an Outline of Her History and Polity, Also, Her Prospective Work*, Nashville, Southern Methodist Publishing House, 1887.

Lakey, Othal Hawthorne, *The History of the CME Church, (Revised)* The CME Publishing House, Memphis, n.d.

CHAPTER 39

# AFRICAN METHODIST EPISCOPAL, ZION, CHURCH

The African Methodist Episcopal, Zion, Church began in New York City in the closing years of the 18th century. African-Americans, including James Varick, Abraham Thompson, and William Miller, suffered discrimination as they attempted to worship at John Street Methodist Episcopal Church.

They organized a congregation in 1796 where "they might have the opportunity to exercise their spiritual gifts among themselves" and found the organization necessary because of the "caste prejudice (which) forbade their taking the sacrament until the white members were all served." Other African-Americans in Philadelphia, Newark, Long Island, and New Haven organized similar churches in the years following. An association of those churches met in New York City on June 21, 1821, to form a denomination. Since the MEC had refused to ordain elders for them, that first annual conference was presided over by Rev. William Phoebus (MEC). Joshua Soule, also of the MEC, acted as secretary of the founding conference. James Varick, who had led the movement twenty-five years earlier, was recognized as the most influential leader of the conference.

The AMEZ Church expanded throughout the free states in the decades before the Civil War, and as early as 1863 sent missionaries into North Carolina, Florida, and Louisiana as federal forces made it possible for free African-Americans to travel in the South. The greatest successes occurred in the Carolinas. Missionary efforts in Texas lagged behind. A Texas Conference was organized at Stoneham (Grimes County) in November 1883. By that comparatively late date, African-American Texans had already experienced almost two decades of vigorous competition among CME, AME, and MEC organizers. The result was that the AMEZ was unable to build the Texas Conference into a strong conference. The second session of the Texas Conference as held at Dobbin (Montgomery County), and the third at Navasota (Grimes County). The Texas Conference did not hold sessions in 1886 or 1887, and in 1888 the only church

# AME Zion

reported in Texas was Stoneham with 13 members. By 1895 the AMEZ was able to report 47 churches in Texas. Hearne, Waco, and Calvert were the cities responsible for most of the growth in membership.

The denomination experienced continuing membership loss during the first half of the 20th century. Bishop James Clair Taylor, of the tenth Episcopal District, painted a somber picture in his 1952 report: ". . . [W]e have 6 organizations, no one of which has 50 members. . . we have two elders . . . our only fairly well established churches in this conference are at Calvert, Stoneham, Wellborn, and Dobbin."

The AMEZ Church reported 1,300,000 members in the United States in 2002. It also reported members in Ghana, Nigeria, the Ivory Coast, Liberia, Jamaica, and the Bahamas.

*References:*

*African Methodist Episcopal Zion Church, Official Journal, Thirty-fourth Quadrennial Session, General Conference May 7-21, 1952.*

Hood, J. W., *One Hundred Years of the AME Zion Church*, New York, 1895.

U.S. Census Bureau, *1906 Religious Census*, Government Printing Office, Washington, 1910.

www.theamezionchurch.org/history/html

*World Methodist Council, Handbook of Information 2002-2006*, Lake Junaluska, NC, 2002.

CHAPTER 40

# AME AND CME,
# REGIONAL SPECIALIZATION

There was considerable competition among the African Methodist Episcopal Church, the Colored Methodist Episcopal Church, and the Methodist Episcopal Church immediately following the Civil War. The African Methodist Episcopal Church, Zion, made some attempts to build churches for African-American Texans, but that denomination was unable to mobilize a sufficient number of missionaries to have a large impact in Texas. That denomination concentrated its missionary efforts in North and South Carolina.

Each of the other three denominations brought both strengths and liabilities to the competition. During the military phase of Reconstruction both the AME and MEC missionaries could count on protection and even direct assistance from the Freedmen's Bureau. In addition, the MEC effort in Texas was backed by northern philanthropy and the missionary apparatus of a vigorous denomination. AME missionaries had a very compelling message as they organized churches. They were able to claim complete African-American control over organization, ordination, and institutions. At least one aspect of emancipation, in their eyes, was being completely free to run one's churches.

Both the MEC and the AME criticized the CME as being too closely tied to the MECS and its pre-war support of slavery. Among the epithets used against the CME were "Rebel Church," "Democratic Church," and "Kitchen Church." Numerous incidents of conflict occurred between members of the three denominations. In 1872 the CME annual conference meeting in the MECS church at Marshall was interrupted by a party of women who "entered and ordered them out, calling them rebels, and sundry other hard names. The Bishop and his conference quietly retired and were soon tendered the occupancy of the Cumberland Presbyterian Church which they politely accepted." (*Texas Christian Advocate*, November 27, 1872). *Harper's New Monthly Magazine* (March, 1868) reported that the Freedman's Bureau captain in Brenham spent his Sundays attending to quarrels in Sunday Schools. On the other hand, the

# Most Predominant Denomination
# by County, 1916
# AME, CME, or MEC

African Methodist Episcopal
Colored Methodist Episcopal
Methodist Episcopal

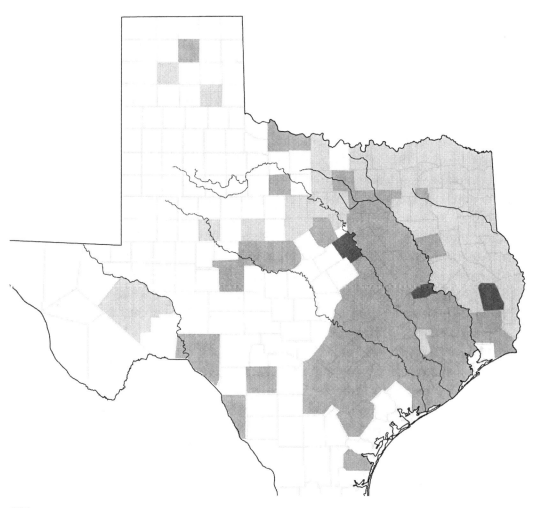

close ties between the MECS and the CME provided a channel for white southern philanthropy to African-American institutions. The Texas Annual Conference of the MECS regularly received fraternal visitors from the CME and took up a collection for that denomination well into the 1930s. The Disciplinary language "we recommend that financial support of the Colored (later Christian) Methodist Episcopal Church be continued by those jurisdictional divisions with which said church is historically related . . ." or something similar remained in the *Discipline* until the 1968 edition.

The competition between the MEC, AME, and CME churches often took the form of "church stealing" in which a missionary would try to persuade the members of a congregation to switch their denominational affiliation. Too often, of course, the result was ill will and property disputes. The major beneficiary of these conflicts seems to have been the Baptists. By becoming Baptists the local church could retain it autonomy and hope to bring the two parties in the dispute back together.

Eventually each of the African-American Methodist denominations (MEC, AME, AMEZ, CME) developed regional strongholds. In a manner analogous to the division of African and Asian mission fields by denominations, African-American Methodists agreed to divide the American South among the denominations. The CME was strongest east of the Trinity River in the same area as the East Texas and North Texas Conferences of the MECS. The AME Church was strongest west of the Trinity River. The CME became the majority African-American Methodist body in north Louisiana and rural Georgia as did the AME in south Louisiana. The AMEZ's stronghold was North Carolina. According to *The Census of Religious Bodies 1916*, 117 Texas counties had either CME or AME members. 43 of those counties had only AME and 22 counties had only CME members. In three counties (Tyler, Madison, and Bosque) the MEC was the largest African-American Methodist denomination. African-Americans in the MEC were more likely to be urban dwellers while AME and CME members were more likely to be rural. For example, in 1939 upon unification Houston alone had 13 African-American MEC churches. Even in counties in which there were both AME and CME churches, the disparity in membership was often huge as the following chart illustrates:

| COUNTY | AME | CME |
|---|---|---|
| Bowie | 38 | 1,098 |
| Cass | 12 | 1,055 |
| Ellis | 1,617 | 44 |
| Galveston | 677 | 68 |
| Gregg | 71 | 1,665 |
| Harrison | 60 | 1,024 |
| Limestone | 856 | 25 |
| McLennan | 1,202 | 51 |

*References:*

*Texas Christian Advocate*, November 27, 1872.

*Religious Bodies*, 1916, U.S. Department of Commerce, Washington, Bureau of the Census, 1916.

Jamison, Bishop M. F., *Autobiography and Work of Bishop M. F. Jamison*, Nashville, Publishing House of the M.E. Church, South, 1912.

Lane, Bishop Isaac, *Autobiography*, Nashville, Publishing House of the M.E. Church, South, 1916.

Hamilton, F. M., *A Plain Account of the Colored Methodist Episcopal Church in America, Being an Outline of Her History and Polity, Also, Her Prospective Work*, Nashville, Southern Methodist Publishing House, 1887.

Lakey, Othal Hawthorne, *The History of the CME Church*, (Revised), Memphis, The CME Publishing House, n.d.

Kealing, H.T., *History of African Methodism in Texas*, Waco, C.F. Blanks, Printer and Stationer, 1885.

Payne, Daniel A., *History of the African Methodist Episcopal Church*, Nashville, Publishing House of the A.M.E. Sunday School Union, 1891.

*Harper's Magazine*, March, 1868.

CHAPTER 41

# CONGREGATIONAL METHODIST CHURCH

The Congregational Methodist Church was founded in Monroe County, Georgia, at a meeting held on May 8, 1852. The twelve men who attended that meeting had become dissatisfied over the lack of lay representation in the conferences of the Methodist Episcopal Church, South. They sought an increased role for lay pastors in baptizing converts and receiving those converts into church membership. They also believed that title to church property should be held by the congregation and that the congregation should call preachers rather than having them appointed by a bishop. Another dissatisfaction with the MECS was the itinerant system. The extensive circuits with many preaching points served by circuit riders necessitated holding worship services whatever day of the week the circuit rider happened to arrive. Congregational Methodists wanted worship on Sunday. The preference for Sunday worship naturally made the Congregational Methodists more dependent upon lay preachers who did not itinerate. By August 1852 the new denomination had published its first *Discipline*.

The new denomination planted churches in Georgia, Alabama, and Mississippi. The Civil War interrupted church expansion, but as migrants from the southeastern states moved west, they took Congregational Methodism with them. In the 1880s there was serious consideration of merging with the Congregational Church, but the invitation to do so was declined. By 1901 there were ten annual conferences, including the Louisiana and Texas. The 1905 General Conference separated Texas and Louisiana into separate conferences.

The 1936 *Census of Religious Bodies* conducted by the U.S. Census Bureau provided the following statistics on Congregational Methodists in Texas:

|  | 1906 | 1916 | 1926 | 1936 |
|---|---|---|---|---|
| CHURCHES | 71 | 30 | 32 | 28 |
| MEMBERS | 2,759 | 1,896 | 1,755 | 1,424 |

Texas became increasingly important to Congregational Methodism in the first half of the 20th century. The 1936 Census of

209

# Congregational Methodist Church
## 2003

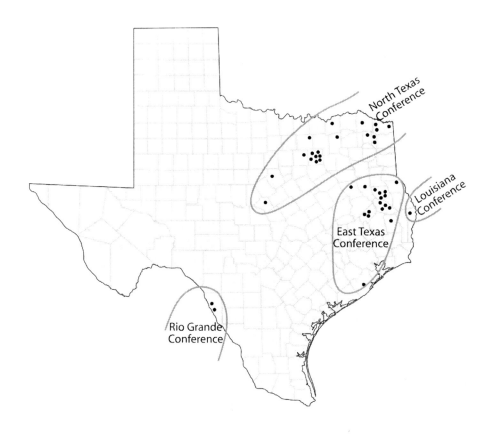

Religious Bodies reported that Texas now had more churches and more members than did the states of Georgia and Alabama where the denomination had begun. Most of those churches were in East Texas and North East Texas. In 1943 the denominational headquarters were established in Dallas. Those headquarters housed the publishing, administrative, and pastoral education work of the denomination. The administrative and publishing offices remained in Dallas until 1972 when the offices were relocated to Florence, Mississippi.

The Dallas headquarters also housed the Congregational Methodist Bible School from 1944 to 1953. In 1953 the Congregational Methodist Church moved its educational efforts to Tehuacana in Limestone County. In doing so, it changed its name first to Westminster College and Bible Institute and then to Westminster College. The relocation was prompted by the availability of college buildings. The facilities at Tehuacana had been used by the Presbyterian Church for Trinity University. When Trinity was relocated to Waxahachie in 1902, the Methodist Protestant Church moved its Westminster College from Collin County there. With church union in 1939, Westminster became part of the Methodist Church. The site was unoccupied from 1950 until September 1953 when it reopened under Congregational Methodist ownership. It remained there until 1972 when it, like the denominational headquarters, was relocated to Florence, Mississippi.

Congregational Methodist churches in Texas are members of four different annual conferences. The North Texas Annual Conference has 23 churches stretching across north Texas from Texarkana through the Dallas/Fort Worth Metroplex to Dublin and Comanche in the West. There is one Oklahoma church in the North Texas Annual Conference. The East Texas Annual Conference consists of 17 churches with the greatest concentration in Angelina and Nacogdoches Counties. Burkeville, Texas, is a part of the Louisiana Annual Conference. The Rio Grande Conference embraces ten churches in the Mexican state of Coahuila, but also includes two churches in Eagle Pass, Texas.

*References:*

U.S. Bureau of the Census, *Census of Religious Bodies, 1936.*

Fowler, Jr., Wilton, *A History of the Congregational Methodist Church, M. A. thesis, Stephen F. Austin State College, 1957.*

congregationalmethodist.net

CHAPTER 42

# THE WESLEYAN CHURCH, THE FREE METHODIST CHURCH

Defections from the MEC over slavery ran in two directions. Southern Methodists withdrew to form the MECS because the denomination was anti-slavery. Two northern groups withdrew because they perceived it to be pro-slavery. Those two denominations, the Wesleyan Church (previously known as the Wesleyan Methodist Connection and the Wesleyan Methodist Church) and the Free Methodist Church, eventually were able to plant churches in Texas.

### The Wesleyan Methodist Connection/Wesleyan Church

"The M. E. Church is not only a slave-holding but a *slavery-defending* church." So wrote the Rev. Orange Scott in his *The Grounds of Secession from the M. E. Church.* Scott and other MEC preachers including Laroy Sunderland, Jotham Horton, and Luther Lee were committed to the rising cause of abolitionism in the 1830s and 1840s. They thought that in doing so they were standing in the Wesleyan tradition. After all, John Wesley's writings agreed with them. The MEC began making accommodations to slavery soon after its creation. Francis Asbury petitioned George Washington to act against slavery, but Asbury also presided over the southern conferences because he knew that he was more acceptable on the slavery issue than was Bishop Coke.

Sectional tension between North and South in both civil and religious affairs increased in the 1830s. Many proponents of slavery shifted from an apologetic defense of slavery as a necessary evil to belligerent advocacy of slavery as a positive good sanctioned by the Bible. The tension increased as abolitionists were suppressed in their efforts to introduce anti-slavery resolutions at annual conferences, distribute abolitionist literature through church channels, and reaffirm the church's historic opposition to slavery at General Conference. As with the passage of the gag rule in the United States Senate which prohibited even debating the subject, abolitionist Methodists began to feel that the issue had gone beyond the issue of slavery. Slavery advocates were threatening the Constitution of the United State and the *Discipline* of the MEC.

MEC abolitionist sentiment, though nowhere in a majority, was relatively strong in Massachusetts, Ohio, Michigan, and New York. Preachers in all those states formed associations to promote their cause. Representatives from those associations met at Utica, New York, for two weeks beginning on May 31, 1843. Their strict adherence to democratic principles was reflected in the composition of the delegates. There were 30 travelling preachers, 40 local preachers and 80 lay delegates. They organized the **Wesleyan Methodist Connection.**

The new denomination combined fervent evangelism and social activism. The famous Women's Rights Convention of 1848 was held in the Seneca Falls Wesleyan Methodist Connection chapel. Many of its members participated in the Underground Railway, and in 1856 the denomination ordained a woman—exactly 100 years before the Methodist Church.

There have been two name changes, first to the Wesleyan Church of America and then to the Wesleyan Church in 1968 after a merger with the Pilgrim Holiness Church. The Wesleyan Church has approximately 5,000 churches in about 50 countries. It owns five colleges. The nearest one to Texas is in Bartlesville, Oklahoma. It is a member of the World Methodist Council. Denominational headquarters are in Indianapolis, Indiana.

The Wesleyan Church's anti-slavery origins delayed its establishment in Texas. Evangelization efforts in the recent past have resulted in an expansion in Texas including the founding of churches in New Braunfels (1990), Flower Mound (1993), and Plano (1985). The Wesleyan Church has also founded Spanish speaking churches in Dallas and San Antonio.

*References*:

Simpson, Matthew, ed., *Cyclopedia of Methodism*, Philadelphia, 1876.

World Methodist Council, *World Methodist Council Handbook of Information, 2002-2006*, Lake Junaluska, NC, 2002.

Scott, Orange, *The Grounds of Secession from the M. E. Church*, L. C. Matlack, Publisher, New York, 2nd ed., 1849.

www.wesleyan.org

www.dayspringchristian.org/history.htm

www.northcrest.org/northcrest

www.collincreekcommunity.org

## The Free Methodist Church

The Free Methodist Church also began in Western New York, at Pekin in 1860. It began as a reform movement within the Methodist Episcopal Church led by Rev. Benjamin Titus Roberts. The use of the word "Free" in the denominational name refers to its opposition to pew rent, slavery, and formalism in worship. Free Methodism spread across the Midwestern United States and the Pacific Coast. Its organization in Texas was delayed by its anti-slavery origins and its inability to recruit large numbers of missionary pastors to come to Texas.

The first Free Methodist preacher to be appointed to work in Texas was Rev. G. R. Harvey, a member of the Kansas and Missouri Conference. His name appears in the appointments for 1878 as being appointed to "the Texas District", which evidently comprised the entire state. The first church he organized was in Lawrence in Kaufman County. In 1879 Harvey supervised seven circuits. These circuits were concentrated in the Dallas area and included Terrell, Ennis, Dallas, Colby, and Johnson County.

Bishop B. T. Roberts organized The Texas and Louisiana Annual Conference on July 8, 1881, at a campground near Corsicana. Harvey transferred from the Kansas and Missouri Conference, and Philip Allen requested a transfer from the M.E.C. South. Those two preachers and two lay delegates constituted the conference. The Free Methodist Church had seated lay delegates at its conferences from its founding. The boundaries of the new conference were defined as the states of Texas and Louisiana. The Indian Territory was later added. The first appointments in the Texas and Louisiana Conference were to charges in Ennis, Corsicana, Waxahachie, Milford, Waco, Salado, Belton, Christmas Creek, Spring Hill, Fort Worth, Terrell, Longview, and three charges in Louisiana.

Free Methodism expanded rapidly in the next generation. The denomination benefited from the rise of the Holiness Movement and the faithful work of many lay pastors and evangelists, both men and women. Its prohibition of instrumental music during worship and its concentration in rural communities tended to keep the total conference membership down. The expansion of Free Methodism in the period 1880-1910 proceeded along several lines. First, the core area of the northern Blackland Prairie was strengthened by the founding of more churches and the establishment of Campbell Seminary in Campbell in 1909. Second, the church expanded along rail lines stretching westward from Dallas/Fort Worth. Louisiana was broken off from the conference, but New Mexico east of the 106th meridian was added. Churches were established in Amarillo, Wichita Falls, Abilene, and the southeastern corner of New Mexico. There was also expansion in two of the regions in which the MEC was expanding during the same period, East Texas lumber towns and new towns on the Coastal Plains. Migrants from the northern United States started churches in Zavalla, Jasper, Mount Enterprise, Alvin, Chocolate, Liverpool, Manvel, Sandy Point, and Sheridan in those regions.

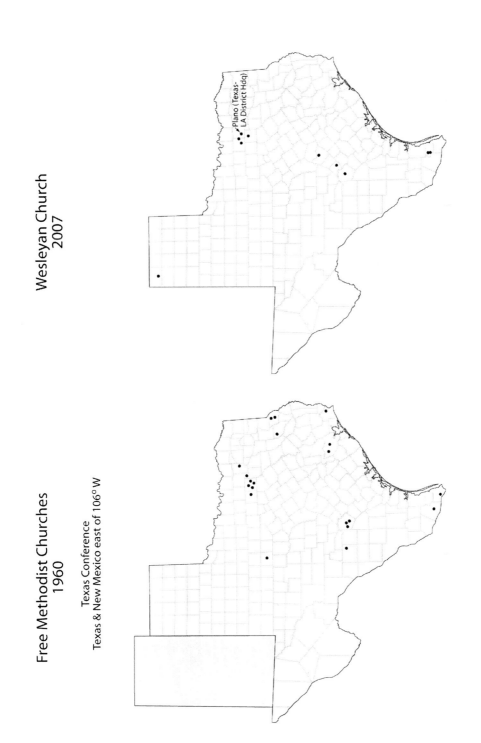

Wesleyan Church
2007

Plano (Texas-
LA District Hdq)

Free Methodist Churches
1960

Texas Conference
Texas & New Mexico east of 106° W

Growth was significant enough that in 1915 the Texas Annual Conference was divided. The East Texas Annual Conference was created and served the interests of Free Methodism until 1937 when the Texas Conference and East Texas Conference were reunited.

Declining membership led to reorganization. In 1997 the Texas Annual Conference became a mission conference (district) in the Pacific Northwest Conference. Vigorous evangelistic efforts led to the founding of churches serving Spanish speaking Free Methodists. That growth led to the reinstitution of the Texas Conference. The 2006 Free Methodist Church of North America Yearbook for 2006 reports 20 Free Methodist churches in Texas on December 31, 2005, with a total membership of 996 members. The denominational headquarters of the Free Methodist Church are in Indianapolis, Indiana.

## Free Methodist Institutions

When the Texas Annual Conference met at Lawrence, Kaufman County, in 1888, it authorized the establishment of a seminary to serve Free Methodist needs. They purchased a four-acre tract with two buildings, and opened a school in 1889. The seminary was in operation until 1892.

A more substantial educational effort began at the annual conference of 1909. That conference authorized a committee to begin plans for the establishment of a Free Methodist Seminary. The committee first chose a 75-acre tract on the interurban rail line about halfway between Dallas and Fort Worth. Just before they closed on the purchase of that tract, a site with three frame buildings on ten acres in Campbell became available. The committee decided to purchase the Campbell site, and opened a seminary in September 1910. The Campbell Free Methodist Seminary had a three-story main building and separate dormitories for men and women. The course of instruction was preparatory (high school level). Fire and financial difficulty preceded its relocation to McKinney in 1918 and its closing in 1922.

Free Methodists also established an encampment in Texas. In 1945 a committee was authorized to locate a suitable site. They found a site on Trinity Bay, approximately 40 miles east of Houston. Facilities sufficient to host annual conference were in place by July 1947. First a Sunday School, and then a church were organized at the camp ground. A church building was moved from Baytown onto the site, and annual conference continued to be held at Trinity Bay. The campground was sold in the 1970s.

*References:*

Anon. *The Texas Conference of the Free Methodist Church: Its Origins and Present Churches, published in observance of its 80th anniversary, 1881-1960,* n.d.

*Minutes of the Texas and Louisiana Conference of the Free Methodist Church.*

*Minutes of the Texas Conference of the Free Methodist Church.*

Hogue, Wilson T., *History of the Free Methodist Church of North America,* vol. 2, Chicago, The Free Methodist Publishing House, 1915.

*Free Methodist Church of North American Yearbook, 2006.*

M'Geary, John S., *The Free Methodist Church: A Brief Outline of its Origin and Development,* Chicago, W. B. Rose Publisher, 1917.

Jernigan, C. B., *Pioneer Days of the Holiness Movement in the Southwest,* Kansas City, Mo, Pentecostal Nazarene Publishing House, 1919.

Interview, Rev. Timothy Greenawalt by Wm. C. Hardt and John Wesley Hardt, Rockwall, Texas, Feb. 28, 2003.

CHAPTER 43

# CHURCH OF THE NAZARENE

Disputes over John Wesley's doctrine of sanctification embroiled Texas Methodists (and also members of other denominations) in their most significant theological controversy of the late 19th and early 20th centuries. The controversy was accompanied by ill will, bitterness, church trials, and expulsions, but it also resulted in the formation of a new Wesleyan organization, the Church of the Nazarene, which has provided a clear call to both personal and social holiness since its founding at Pilot Point, Texas, in 1908.

Sanctification had been part of Methodism since John Wesley's time. Some Methodists gave it special emphasis. For example, Phoebe Palmer, wife of a New York City physician, began holding the "Tuesday Meeting for the Promotion of Holiness" in 1838. In 1858 religious revivals in New York, Philadelphia, Chicago, and many other northern cities often featured calls to "entire sanctification." The organization of the Free Methodist Church in 1860 was related to that revivalism. As the Holiness Movement gained strength, it found both supporters and opponents in the established denominations. The dispute centered around whether John Wesley's "perfection" was a gradual process in which the Christian, after experiencing conversion, began a life working toward perfection or whether the perfection came as a distinct event in the form of another conversion experience known as a "second blessing." A clear statement of the doctrine was drawn up by the Holiness Association of Texas when that group wrote its constitution at Peniel in Hunt County.

> We believe in holiness, or entire sanctification, that it is a second definite work of grace in the heart whereby we are thoroughly cleansed of all sin, that only those who are justified and walking in the favor of God can receive this grace; that it is not absolute perfection. That belongs to God alone. It does not make man infallible—it is perfect love—the pure love of God filling a pure heart . . . .

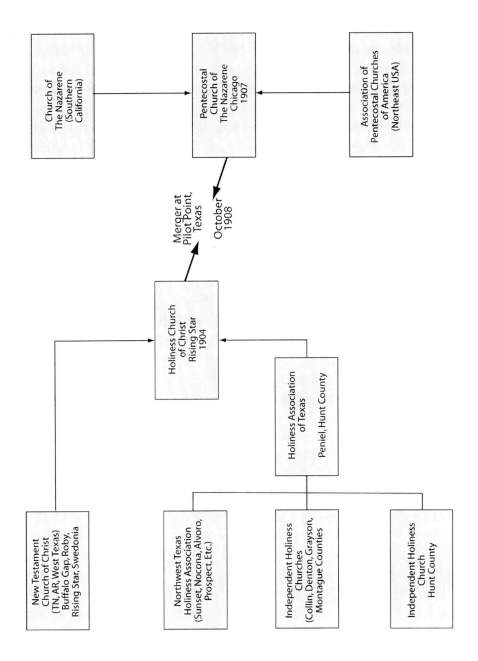

Church of The Nazarene (Southern California)

Pentecostal Church of The Nazarene Chicago 1907

Association of Pentecostal Churches of America (Northeast USA)

Merger at Pilot Point, Texas

October 1908

Holiness Church of Christ Rising Star 1904

Holiness Association of Texas

Peniel, Hunt County

New Testament Church of Christ (TN, AR, West Texas) Buffalo Gap, Roby, Rising Star, Swedonia

Northwest Texas Holiness Association (Sunset, Nocona, Alvoro, Prospect, Etc.)

Independent Holiness Churches (Collin, Denton, Grayson, Montague Counties)

Independent Holiness Church Hunt County

By the time this statement was made, holiness advocates had already been active in Texas for about a quarter century. The first organized holiness meeting that can be documented was at Calvert in February 1877. A revival team from Illinois conducted a revival there and also at Bremond, Marlin, Denton, Gainesville, Ennis, and possibly Dallas. The Calvert revival resulted in the conversion of the MECS preacher, R. H. H. Burnett, to the doctrine of entire sanctification. Holiness was so thoroughly linked with Methodism that when two Baptists received the second blessing at the Ennis revival, they were expelled from their church. The charge against them was that they were Methodists.

The next year another camp meeting was held by Rev. W. B. Colt, also of Illinois, at Rake Straw, twelve miles south of Corsicana. On October 10, 1878, at that camp meeting the Texas Holiness Association was formed. The THA was an interdenominational association embracing Southern Methodists, Methodist Protestants, Free Methodists, Cumberland Presbyterians, and Baptists. Its purpose was to organize annual camp meetings. The association conducted nine more revivals at Corsicana, Dallas, Bosqueville Springs (near Waco), Bremond, Meridian, Alvarado, and Scottsville (Harrison County). The success of these holiness revivals encouraged others at Waco, Greenville, Noonday (Harrison County), Hughes Springs, Bates, and Poetry. The last annual THA camp meeting that embraced the entire state organization was held in 1887, but smaller ones continued in the same spirit at several of the campgrounds that had been used by the state organization. The camp meetings conducted under Texas Holiness Association auspices undoubtedly paved the way for the establishing of holiness churches.

About this same time (1886) California revivalists Dennis Rogers and George Teel came to Collin County and were successful in establishing churches at Rock Hill, White's Chapel, Valdasta, and McKinney. By 1888, they had enlarged their efforts to Gainesville, and Uz and Evergreen in Montague County. Rogers began a newspaper, *True Holiness*, at McKinney and grouped the churches under the name of the Holiness Association.

A holiness presence in western Texas arrived in 1895 when Mrs. Mary Lee Harris moved to Buffalo Gap after the death of her husband, Rev. R. L. Harris who had been a missionary and revivalist with connections at various times to both the Free Methodist and MECS churches. After the MECS General Conference of 1894 passed a rule forbidding a revivalist from holding a revival without the approval of the MECS pastor appointed to the charge where the revival was being held, Harris left the MECS. He and Mrs. Harris, along with Mr. and Mrs. E. H. Sheeks and R. B. Mitchum, organized the New Testament Church of Christ in Milan, Tennessee. After her husband's death, Mrs. Harris traveled between Tennessee and Texas, establishing churches in Buffalo Gap, Swedonia, and Roby. The New Testament Church of Christ also maintained a gospel mission and training school. It started at Waco, moved to Buffalo Gap, and then to Hamlin. That school was a forerunner of Central Nazarene

# Holiness Concentration
## 1880s - 1910

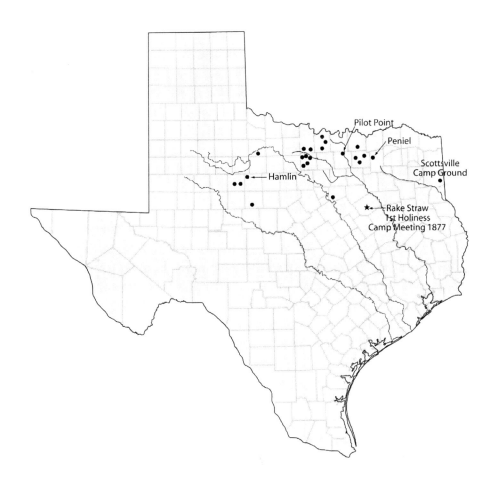

Pilot Point

Peniel

Scottsville
Camp Ground

Hamlin

Rake Straw
1st Holiness
Camp Meeting 1877

University in Bethany, Oklahoma. Both Mrs. Harris, after her remarriage, Rev. Mary Lee Cagle, and Mrs. Sheeks were preachers, a status they could not have in either the MEC or MECS.

Another holiness development in western Texas was the creation of a nine-point circuit by John T. Stanfield, an expelled Cumberland Presbyterian preacher. He created the Northwest Texas Holiness Association in 1899 to embrace those charges and several others (Sunset, Pella, Crafton, Chico, Duxbury, Forestburg, Nocona, Prospect, Alvord, Park Springs, New Port, Sandflat, and Evergreen).

By the first years of the 20th century at least 20 MECS preachers in Texas had been withdrawn or located voluntarily and were now preaching as holiness preachers, mainly as travelling revivalists, but a few as preachers of independent churches. Most notable were E. C. DeJernett and Bud Robinson. DeJernett, who had been secretary of the North Texas Annual Conference for three of its sessions, was serving the MECS church in Commerce in 1894. He requested location that year and bought acreage two miles north of Greenville. He created a holiness settlement, Peniel, complete with a college, orphanage, publishing house, and camp meeting on the site, partially financed by selling residential lots to holiness adherents. He was expelled from the MECS in 1898 for holding a revival in Atlanta, Texas, in defiance of the MECS preacher on that charge.

Bud Robinson had also recently been expelled from the MECS. Robinson, converted at a revival in Alvardo in 1880, had been licensed as an exhorter even though he was illiterate. Feeling the need for education, he enrolled in the Preparatory Department at Southwestern University as a thirty-one year old man. He was licensed to preach by the Georgetown Quarterly Conference. His holiness preaching ran afoul of the church authorities and was subjected to a church trial. The case against him was handled by the formidable J. H. McLean, Regent of Southwestern University. After his expulsion Robinson was a MEC preacher for ten years, and then became powerful Nazarene evangelist.

In 1898 DeJernett and C. B. Jernigan proposed to hold a convention of holiness preachers in Texas in conjunction with a revival Robinson was to hold in Terrell. They needed to meet to decide what to do with the converts their revivals were producing. Converts who were church members were often shunned by their former congregations. Converts who had not previously been members of a church needed a church to join. DeJernett and Jernigan were aware of the need to provide baptism, communion, marriage, and ordination to converts who desired them. The debate at Terrell produced three positions. Some wished to become Free Methodists. That denomination stood squarely in the holiness camp. Others wished to become MEC. That denomination was quite amenable to holiness preachers. A third faction wished to form a new denomination. There were difficulties with each position. Free Methodists did not allow instrumental music. Some of the holiness revivalists, especially those who conducted sidewalk preaching in the cities, felt that instrumental music was important to their effort. The MEC was closely associated with the Republican Party, and such association was seen as an obstacle in Texas. Another problem with MEC affiliation was the itinerant system. Joining the MEC meant that the preachers would be subject to a bishop's appointment. The prospect of a holiness preacher's assignment to a non-holiness congregation or vice versa was a real one. The preachers could not achieve consensus. They did agree to meet again at Peniel where a new holiness university was being built.

Rev. J. W. Lively, a former member of both the North Texas and East Texas Conferences of the MECS but now an MEC preacher, made an appeal for the holiness preachers assembled there at Peniel in 1899 to come home to the MEC.

> *Methodism is the mother of holiness. Come home and we will do as they used to do: give you a horse to ride, and a pair of old fashioned saddle bags, with a Bible on one side and a Methodist Hymnbook on the other; and put some money in your pockets, and send you out to preach holiness.*

Lively's offer was not too much of an exaggeration since the MEC Board of Church Extension did have resources to spend for just such purposes, but again the holiness preachers did not achieve consensus.

Still other meetings at a Holiness Camp Ground and Peniel eventually resulted in the formation of the Holiness Association of Texas. It was still not a denomination, but an association of preachers who had been ordained by several denominations.

As these developments were occurring, C. B. Jernigan had begun organizing churches centered on Van Alstyne. He called them Independent Holiness Churches. His efforts flourished in Denton, Grayson and Collin Counties. Pilot Point, in Denton County, became a focus of holiness activities with an orphanage, rescue home, school, and publishing efforts. The center of holiness activities in North Texas thus shifted from Peniel to Pilot Point. In 1904 he merged those churches with the New Testament Church of Christ Churches at Rising Star into the Holiness Church of Christ.

Texas was not the only site for holiness organizing. Phineas Bresee, pastor of the First Methodist Church of Los Angeles, California (MEC), received the second blessing in 1884. For the next decade he preached sanctification as preacher, presiding elder, and revivalist. A desire to evangelize the poor in Los Angeles led to a break with the "Mother Church" and the formation of the Church of the Nazarene in 1895. By 1905 there were twenty-six more Churches of the Nazarene, mostly in Southern California, but others in Seattle, Oakland, Boise, Salt Lake City, Omaha, and other cities.

There were also holiness churches springing up in eastern cities. Rural Methodists in New England and New York tended to be amenable to the doctrine of holiness, but friction occurred in the cities. Recent converts who had received the second blessing

# Church of the Nazarene
## 2002

were often not welcome in Methodist churches in northeastern cities that had become bastions of conservatism and worldliness. Many of the converts associated themselves with city missions. Several of those missions eventually organized themselves into the Association of Pentecostal Churches.

The West Coast Church of the Nazarene and the East Coast Association of Pentecostal Churches met in Chicago in 1907 to merge. The new body adopted the name the Pentecostal Church of the Nazarene.

Texans representing the Holiness Church of Christ attended the general assembly in Chicago in 1907 which created the Pentecostal Church of the Nazarene as observers. They were much more than observers. They were honored guests and active participants in the discussions. The idea that they would also join the fold was so prevalent that when the new denomination's boards were chosen, vacancies were left so that Holiness Church of Christ representatives would have seats upon merger. The Texans invited the general assembly to meet for its second session in Texas. The invitation was accepted, and on October 8, 1908, the Independent Holiness Church merged with the Pentecostal Church of the Nazarene at Pilot Point. In 1919 the name of the denomination was changed to the Church of the Nazarene.

The Pilot Point union of 1908, rather than the Chicago merger of 1907, is seen as the origin of the Church of the Nazarene. It was in 1908 that the denomination became a truly national church. The Texas contribution was considerable. Both the California and Northeastern branches were overwhelmingly urban. After Pilot Point, the Pentecostal Church of the Nazarene embraced both rural and urban churches.

The Church of the Nazarene grew vigorously. By 1936 and the publication of the *Census of Religious Bodies,* Nazarenes reported 136,227 members in 2,197 churches. Texas figures were 8,646 members in 152 churches. The church supported missionary endeavors and established churches in Scotland, South Africa, and Peru, among other locations. Nazarene churches in the United States were most plentiful in the great American heartland of the Midwest and Great Plains. Denominational headquarters in Kansas City, Missouri, are well situated to serve those churches. There are more than 300 Nazarene Churches in Texas. The Church of the Nazarene is a member of the World Methodist Council.

*References:*

Jernigan, Charles B., *Pioneer Holiness Days in the Southwest,* Pentecostal Nazarene Publishing House, Kansas City, MO, 1919.

Robinson, Reuban A. (Bud), *My Life's Story* Wesleyan Heritage Library, Wesleyan, Heritage, Publications, 1997,1998.

Smith, Timothy L. *Called Unto Holiness,* Nazarene Publishing House, Kansas City, Mo, 1962.

U.S. Commerce Department, Bureau of the Census, *Statistics of Religious Bodies,* Government Printing Office, Washington, D.C.,1936.

*Journal of the East Texas Conference of the MECS, 1889.*

*Journal of the North Texas Conference of the NTC, 1889.*

*World Methodist Council, Handbook of Information: 2002-2006,* World Methodist Council, Lake Junaluska, NC, 2002.

CHAPTER 44

# EVANGELICAL METHODIST, SOUTHERN METHODIST, AND SOUTHERN CONGREGATIONAL METHODIST CHURCHES

Twentieth century disputes between liberals and conservatives in Methodism played out in several arenas. Those disputes became especially heated in the 1920s. Methodist schools saw battles over the teaching of evolution and biblical criticism. Progressive activists relished their victories in the prohibition of alcoholic beverages and women's suffrage, but for the most part did not carry their fervor into new causes. Some activists turned their attention to disarmament and world peace as the horror of World War I became more widely known, and both the MEC and MECS renewed efforts at alleviating rural poverty in Appalachia. General Conferences of the 1920s made increasing concessions to worldliness such as softening denominational prohibitions against attending circuses and theaters. Card playing, dancing, and participating in secular pursuits on the Sabbath also became more acceptable.

Some conservative Methodists, especially in the South, looked upon such changes as taking the church too far away from its Wesleyan origins. The Union of the MECS, MEC, and MP Churches in 1939 was the last straw for at least some conservative Southern Methodists. Their response was to form new denominations, the Southern Methodist Church and the Evangelical Methodist Church. Some members of the Congregational Methodist Church became unhappy with a series of revisions of the *Discipline* (1957, 1972, and 1978). A major impact of those revisions was the elimination of the District Conference. The result was the formation of the Southern Congregational Methodist Church which adopted the 1919 edition of the *Discipline*.

# Denominations founded after 1939

| Denomination | Texas Locations | Origins | Notes | In their own words . . . |
|---|---|---|---|---|
| Evangelical MC | Abilene, Copperas Cove, Duncanville, Haltom City Killeen, Mansfield Odessa, Seagoville, Slaton, Sweetwater, Wilson<br><br>Mid States Conference headquarters in Fort Worth. | May 1946 meeting in Memphis leads to Nov. 1946 organization in Kansas City. | J.H. Hamblen, former pastor at First Methodist Abilene, becomes first general supt.<br><br>Headquarters are in Indianapolis. | With a firm conviction that the gulf that separates conservative and liberal thought in the church is an ever-widening chasm which can never be healed, the Evangelical Methodist Church came into being to preserve the distinctive doctrines of primitive Methodism, founded upon the inspiration and authenticity of the Bible and upon the Articles of Religion as set forth by John Wesley. |
| Southern MC | Lindale, Mesquite | Committee of Laity opposed to 1939 Union assembled in Columbia, South Carolina in 1940 to continue traditions of the MECS. | Texas is part of the South-Western Conference, composed of Louisiana, Arkansas and Texas.<br><br>Headquarters are in Orangeburg, SC. | The Southern Methodist Church is a doctrinally conservative, Bible-believing denomination seeking to preserve and proclaim historic Methodism.<br><br>The roots of the church lie in the Methodist Episcopal Church South. Though the church polity no longer reflects the episcopal roots of the mother church, the rich doctrinal heritage of Methodism has been preserved. |
| Southern Congregational MC | Columbus, Pasadena, Gainesville | Founded January 12, 1985, by members of the Congregational Methodist Church who felt congregational authority was being eroded. | The SCM Church contains the three Texas churches plus 26 others in Mississippi, Alabama, Georgia, and Tennessee.<br><br>Headquarters are in Alma, GA. | The Southern Congregational Methodist Church was organized because the people wanted to:<br>• Continue their heritage of proclaiming the fundamental Bible Doctrines set forth by John Wesley and preached and taught in the Methodist tradition for more than two centuries.<br>• Keep the original legislative form of government developed by the founding fathers of the Congregational Methodist Church, with Church, District, Annual, and General Conferences.<br>• Preserve the Congregational form of government subject to the local congregation.<br><br>The organizational meeting adopted the Tenth Edition of the Constitution and Government of the Congregational Methodist Church. |

# Evangelical Methodist Church
# Southern Methodist Church
# Southern Congregational Methodist Church
# 2007

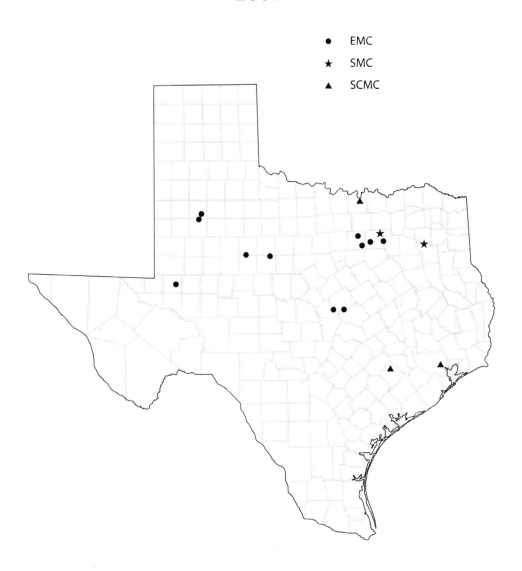

| | |
|---|---|
| ● | EMC |
| ★ | SMC |
| ▲ | SCMC |

*References*

www.emchurch.org

www.southernmethodistchurch.org

www.scmchurch.com

*Discipline of the Southern Congregational Methodist Church,* 2nd ed., 2001

# CONCLUSION

Although the UM conferences in Texas are part of the South Central Jurisdiction, the jurisdiction carries with it little emotional attachment or sense of identity. Most Texas Methodists would consider the jurisdiction a device by which to elect bishops and little more. Texas Methodists find their identity at the state rather than jurisdictional level. When they feel the need to form multi-conference organizations, they are most likely to form state organizations.

Multi-conference participation in historical societies, observance of the two centennials in 1934 and 1936, schools, an orphanage, and Wesley Foundations have been noted in previous chapters. Another significant stream of statewide Methodism has been the work of two other closely related bodies, the Texas Methodist Planning Commission and the Texas Methodist Foundation.

The TMPC has its origins in meetings among delegates from various Texas conferences to the 1948 General Conference in Boston. They agreed to return to their respective annual conferences and present resolutions calling for the creation of a Methodist Planning Commission. In October 1948 representatives from the conferences met at the Methodist Home in Waco where they were encouraged in the work by Bishops A. Frank Smith and W. C. Martin. The next year was devoted to writing a constitution and by-laws which were adopted on November 8, 1949.

The Planning Commission conducted a number of initiatives during the 1950s. Those included pulpit exchanges between preachers of different conferences, preaching missions to Spanish speaking churches in the Rio Grande Valley, commissioning the writing of a new history of Texas Methodism, bringing officers of the various Methodist schools together in the Texas College Association, and conducting simultaneous evangelism campaigns in the conferences.

The greatest impact of the Planning Commission was the reactivation of the Texas Methodist Foundation which had been created in the late 1930s and allowed to wither. The Texas Methodist Foundation re-opened in Austin on June 15, 1960, with Monroe Vivion of the Texas Conference as the executive director. Its purpose was "to support the benevolent, charitable, educational, and missionary undertakings of the Methodist church in Texas." The Foundation accomplished that purpose by supplying financial services to churches, institutions, and individuals. It made loans to churches at favorable interest rates and, as a non-profit, could offer competitive rates to churches wishing to deposit their funds. The Texas Methodist Foundation was so successful that several annual conferences also created Foundations.

# INDEX OF CONFERENCES

# ALPHABETICAL INDEX

All place names refer to Texas locations except where noted.

## C

Evangelical Methodist Church 13, 227

Evangelical United Brethren 11, 13, 90-91, 102, 104

Evergreen 220, 222

# F

Fagan, Harold 115

Fairfield Female Institute 146

Fannin County 53, 149, 199

Fields, J. W. 43, 182

Fisher, Orceneth 36, 168, 183, 196

Fleming, Archie 116

Florence, Mississippi 153, 211

Follansbee, James 145

Fondren, Mr. and Mrs. Walter Wr. 191

Fontaine, Edward 31

Forestburg 222

Fort Towson 18

Fort Worth 6, 53, 56-57, 61, 64, 67, 73, 78, 80-81, 84, 99, 101, 120-126, 128, 132, 135-136, 138, 141, 147, 155-156, 160, 162, 170-171, 176, 178-179, 185, 187-188, 191, 195, 198, 201, 211, 214, 216

Fort Worth University 151

Fowler Academy 145

Fowler, Littleton 18, 26-28, 31, 33, 35, 41, 43, 51, 143

Franklin District High School 148

Franklin, M. B. 148

Fredericksburg College 97, 148

Free Methodist Church 6-7, 11, 212, 214, 216-218

Free Methodist Seminary 153, 216

Freedmen's Bureau 205

Friend, L. S. 43

# G

Gaines Ferry 19, 26, 28, 36

Gainesville 220, 228

Galveston 30, 31, 34-35, 37-38, 43, 56-57, 92-93, 99, 101-102, 104, 124, 135-136, 139, 141-142, 145, 154, 158, 169-171, 176, 187, 195, 198-199, 207

Galveston County 145

Galveston Medical College 145

Galveston Wesley House 135

Garcia, Doroteo 86

Gay, Joe 115

General Commission on Archives and History 50, 177, 182, 185

Georgetown 20, 68, 81, 99, 118, 122, 141-142, 147, 154-157, 160, 162-163, 174, 178-179, 195, 222

German Mission Conference (MECS) 96-97, 162, 171, 188

Gilmer Female Institute 145

Goldberg, Charles 92

Golden Age Home 195

Goliad 5, 24, 28, 45-6, 93, 143, 145, 158

Gomer, J. M. 104

Gonzales 44, 48, 199

Graham, James 148-149

Granbury Institute (High School) 148

Grayson County 147

Greenville 75, 115, 150, 155, 220

Gregg County 50

# T

#  Y

#  Z

How to order more copies of
# HISTORICAL ATLAS OF TEXAS METHODISM
## BY WM. C. HARDT AND JOHN WESLEY HARDT

CALL: 1-800-747-0738
FAX: 1-888-252-3022
Email: orders@hannibalbooks.com
Write: Hannibal Books
P.O. Box 461592
Garland, Texas 75046
Visit: www.hannibalbooks.com

Number of copies of *Historical Atlas of Texas Methodist*                    :\_\_\_\_

Multiply total number of copies: \_\_\_\_ by $34.95 =

Total cost of books: $_____

Add $5 for postage and handling for the first book plus $1 for each additional book in the order.

Shipping total: $_____

Texas residents add 8.25% sales tax: $_____

Total order: $_____

Number on enclosed check _____

Credit card # _____ Exp. date_____
  (Visa, MasterCard, Discover, American Express accepted)

Name _____

Address _____

City, State, Zip _____

Phone _____

Email _____

Printed in the United States
104925LV00003B/27-114/P